Communications in Computer and Information Science   1859

Rationale

The CCIS series is devoted to the publication of proceedings of computer science conferences. Its aim is to efficiently disseminate original research results in informatics in printed and electronic form. While the focus is on publication of peer-reviewed full papers presenting mature work, inclusion of reviewed short papers reporting on work in progress is welcome, too. Besides globally relevant meetings with internationally representative program committees guaranteeing a strict peer-reviewing and paper selection process, conferences run by societies or of high regional or national relevance are also considered for publication.

Topics

The topical scope of CCIS spans the entire spectrum of informatics ranging from foundational topics in the theory of computing to information and communications science and technology and a broad variety of interdisciplinary application fields.

Information for Volume Editors and Authors

Publication in CCIS is free of charge. No royalties are paid, however, we offer registered conference participants temporary free access to the online version of the conference proceedings on SpringerLink (http://link.springer.com) by means of an http referrer from the conference website and/or a number of complimentary printed copies, as specified in the official acceptance email of the event.

CCIS proceedings can be published in time for distribution at conferences or as post-proceedings, and delivered in the form of printed books and/or electronically as USBs and/or e-content licenses for accessing proceedings at SpringerLink. Furthermore, CCIS proceedings are included in the CCIS electronic book series hosted in the SpringerLink digital library at http://link.springer.com/bookseries/7899. Conferences publishing in CCIS are allowed to use Online Conference Service (OCS) for managing the whole proceedings lifecycle (from submission and reviewing to preparing for publication) free of charge.

Publication process

The language of publication is exclusively English. Authors publishing in CCIS have to sign the Springer CCIS copyright transfer form, however, they are free to use their material published in CCIS for substantially changed, more elaborate subsequent publications elsewhere. For the preparation of the camera-ready papers/files, authors have to strictly adhere to the Springer CCIS Authors' Instructions and are strongly encouraged to use the CCIS LaTeX style files or templates.

Abstracting/Indexing

CCIS is abstracted/indexed in DBLP, Google Scholar, EI-Compendex, Mathematical Reviews, SCImago, Scopus. CCIS volumes are also submitted for the inclusion in ISI Proceedings.

How to start

To start the evaluation of your proposal for inclusion in the CCIS series, please send an e-mail to ccis@springer.com.

Hans-Georg Fill · Marten van Sinderen ·
Leszek A. Maciaszek
Editors

Software Technologies

17th International Conference, ICSOFT 2022
Lisbon, Portugal, July 11–13, 2022
Revised Selected Papers

 Springer

Editors
Hans-Georg Fill
University of Fribourg
Fribourg, Switzerland

Marten van Sinderen
University of Twente
Enschede, The Netherlands

Leszek A. Maciaszek
Wrocław University of Economics Institute
of Business Informatics
Wrocław, Poland

Macquarie University
Sydney, Australia

ISSN 1865-0929   ISSN 1865-0937 (electronic)
Communications in Computer and Information Science
ISBN 978-3-031-37230-8   ISBN 978-3-031-37231-5 (eBook)
https://doi.org/10.1007/978-3-031-37231-5

This Springer imprint is published by the registered company Springer Nature Switzerland AG
The registered company address is: Gewerbestrasse 11, 6330 Cham, Switzerland

Preface

The present book includes extended and revised versions of a set of selected papers from the 17th International Conference on Software Technologies (ICSOFT 2022), held in Lisbon, Portugal, from 11–13 July 2022.

ICSOFT 2022 received 102 paper submissions from 33 countries, of which 10% were included in this book.

The papers were selected by the event chairs and their selection is based on a number of criteria that include the classifications and comments provided by the program committee members, the session chairs' assessment and also the program chairs' global view of all papers included in the technical program. The authors of selected papers were then invited to submit a revised and extended version of their papers having at least 30% innovative material.

The purpose of the International Conference on Software Technologies is to bring together researchers, engineers and practitioners interested in software technologies. The conference areas are "Software Engineering and Systems Development", "Software Systems and Applications" and "Foundational and Trigger Technologies".

The papers selected to be included in this book contribute to the understanding of relevant trends of current research on Software Technologies, including: Data Mining and Data Analysis, Empirical Software Engineering, Cybersecurity Technologies, Application Software, Decision Support Systems, Open-Source Development, Quality Management, Software Engineering Tools, Testing and Testability and Data-Driven Software Engineering.

We would like to thank all the authors for their contributions and also the reviewers who have helped to ensure the quality of this publication.

July 2022

Hans-Georg Fill
Marten van Sinderen
Leszek A. Maciaszek

Organization

Conference Chair

Leszek A. Maciaszek   Wrocław University of Economics Institute of
Business Informatics, Poland and Macquarie
University, Australia

Program Co-chairs

Hans-Georg Fill   University of Fribourg, Switzerland
Marten van Sinderen   University of Twente, The Netherlands

Program Committee

Wasif Afzal	MDH, Sweden
Paulo Alencar	University of Waterloo, Canada
Vincent Aranega	University of Lille, France
Marco Autili	University of L'Aquila, Italy
Davide Basile	ISTI CNR Pisa, Italy
Jorge Bernardino	Polytechnic of Coimbra - ISEC, Portugal
Marco Bernardo	University of Urbino, Italy
Dominique Blouin	Télécom Paris, France
Dominik Bork	TU Wien, Austria
Thomas Buchmann	Deggendorf Institute of Technology, Germany
Fergal Caffery	Dundalk Institute of Technology, Ireland
Alejandro Calderón	University of Cádiz, Spain
Ana Castillo	Universidad de Alcalá, Spain
Anis Charfi	Carnegie Mellon University, Qatar
Steven Costiou	Inria, France
Estrela Cruz	Instituto Politécnico de Viana do Castelo, Portugal
Lidia López Cuesta	Universitat Politècnica de Catalunya, Spain
João Cunha	Polytechnic of Coimbra, Coimbra Institute of Engineering, Portugal
Sergiu Dascalu	University of Nevada, Reno, USA
Cléver Ricardo de Farias	University of São Paulo, Brazil
Serge Demeyer	University of Antwerp, Belgium

Steven Demurjian	University of Connecticut, USA
Amleto Di Salle	University of L'Aquila, Italy
Gencer Erdogan	SINTEF, Norway
Morgan Ericsson	Linnaeus University, Sweden
Letha Etzkorn	University of Alabama in Huntsville, USA
Eduardo Fernandez	Florida Atlantic University, USA
Amit Ganatra	Charotar University of Science and Technology, India
Vinicius Garcia	Federal University of Pernambuco, Brazil
Felix Garcia Clemente	University of Murcia, Spain
Paola Giannini	University of Piemonte Orientale, Italy
Jose Gonzalez	University of Seville, Spain
Christiane Gresse von Wangenheim	Federal University of Santa Catarina, Brazil
Hatim Hafiddi	INPT, Morocco
Jean Hauck	Universidade Federal de Santa Catarina, Brazil
Mercedes Hidalgo-Herrero	Universidad Complutense de Madrid, Spain
Andreas Hinderks	UX7Consulting, Germany
Ralph Hoch	TU Wien, Austria
Andreas Holzinger	Medical University Graz, Austria
Jang-Eui Hong	Chungbuk National University, South Korea
Miloslav Hub	University of Pardubice, Czech Republic
Thomas Hupperich	University of Münster, Germany
Zbigniew Huzar	Wroclaw University of Science and Technology, Poland
Judit Jasz	University of Szeged, Hungary
Bharat Jayaraman	State University of New York at Buffalo, USA
Florian Johannsen	University of Applied Sciences Schmalkalden, Germany
Francisco José Domínguez Mayo	University of Seville, Spain
Hermann Kaindl	TU Wien, Austria
Herbert Kuchen	University of Münster, Germany
Rob Kusters	Open Universiteit Nederland, The Netherlands
Youness Laghouaouta	INPT, Morocco
Giuseppe Lami	Consiglio Nazionale delle Ricerche, Italy
Gary Leavens	University of Central Florida, USA
Pierre Leone	University of Geneva, Switzerland
Letitia Li	BAE Systems, USA
Horst Lichter	RWTH Aachen University, Germany
David Lorenz	Open University, Israel
Daniel Lucrédio	Federal University of São Carlos, Brazil
Ivan Lukovic	University of Belgrade, Serbia

Chung-Horng Lung	Carleton University, Canada
Stephane Maag	Télécom SudParis, France
Tomi Männistö	University of Helsinki, Finland
Manuel Mazzara	Innopolis University, Russian Federation
Andreas Meier	Zurich University of Applied Sciences, Switzerland
Antoni Mesquida Calafat	Universitat de les Illes Balears, Spain
Gergely Mezei	Budapest University of Technology and Economics, Hungary
Antao Moura	Federal Universisty of Campina Grande, Brazil
Takako Nakatani	Open University of Japan, Japan
Elena Navarro	University of Castilla-La Mancha, Spain
Paolo Nesi	University of Florence, Italy
Jennifer Pérez	Universidad Politécnica de Madrid, Spain
Dana Petcu	West University of Timisoara, Romania
Dietmar Pfahl	University of Tartu, Estonia
Giuseppe Polese	Università Degli Studi di Salerno, Italy
Mohammad Mehdi Pourhashem Kallehbasti	University of Science and Technology of Mazandaran, Iran
Stefano Quer	Politecnico di Torino, Italy
Werner Retschitzegger	Johannes Kepler University, Austria
Filippo Ricca	University of Genoa, Italy
Andres Rodriguez	UNLP, Argentina
Colette Rolland	Université de Paris1 Panthèon-Sorbonne, France
António Rosado da Cruz	Instituto Politécnico de Viana do Castelo, Portugal
Gustavo Rossi	Lifia, Argentina
Gwen Salaün	Grenoble INP, Inria, France
Johannes Sametinger	Johannes Kepler University Linz, Austria
Nickolas Sapidis	University of Western Macedonia, Greece
Peter Schneider-Kamp	University of Southern Denmark, Denmark
Istvan Siket	Hungarian Academy of Science, Hungary
Harvey Siy	University of Nebraska at Omaha, USA
Kari Smolander	Aalto University, Finland
Ketil Stolen	SINTEF, Norway
Hiroki Suguri	Miyagi University, Japan
Rosa Sukamto	Universitas Pendidikan Indonesia, Indonesia
Yonglei Tao	Grand Valley State University, USA
Francesco Tiezzi	University of Camerino, Italy
Claudine Toffolon	Université du Mans, France
Porfirio Tramontana	University Federico II of Naples, Italy
Tullio Vardanega	University of Padua, Italy
Roberto Verdecchia	Vrije Universiteit Amsterdam, The Netherlands

Tony Wasserman   Carnegie Mellon University Silicon Valley, USA
Dietmar Winkler   Vienna University of Technology, Austria
Dinghao Wu   Penn State University, USA
Jinhui Yao   Xerox Research, USA
Murat Yilmaz   Gazi University, Turkey

Additional Reviewers

Ana Alves   Polytechnic of Coimbra, Coimbra Institute of
                                    Engineering, Portugal
Victor Lorena   Universidade Federal de Pernambuco, Brazil
Jonathan Neugebauer   University of Münster, Germany
Laura Troost   University of Münster, Germany
Hendrik Winkelmann   University of Münster, Germany

Invited Speakers

Witold Pedrycz   University of Alberta, Canada
Peter Fettke   German Research Center for Artificial
                                    Intelligence (DFKI) and Saarland University,
                                    Germany
Moshe Y. Vardi   Rice University, USA

Contents

Tool Assisted Empirical Approach to Reusability Models Assessment

Andreea Cristina Lung, Simona Motogna$^{(\boxtimes)}$ ⓘ, and Vladiela Petraşcu ⓘ

Department of Computer Science, Babes-Bolyai University, M.Kogalniceanu Street, Cluj-Napoca, Romania
{simona.motogna,vladiela.petrascu}@ubbcluj.ro

Abstract. In software development, reuse became an important aspect in increasing productivity and performance and in reducing costs. The extend to which software can be reused have been captured by several reusability assessment models proposed in literature. In this chapter we propose an empirical analysis of three reusability models with the scope of long term evaluation of reusability in open source software. We successfully reproduced the models and applied them to several versions of large Java open source projects. We investigate the long term evolution of reusability, its relation to metrics and other quality factors. Results show a significant difference in the reusability models, but reflect a clear influence of complexity, cohesion, coupling, size and documentation.

Keywords: Software quality · Reusability · Empirical study

1 Introduction

Nowadays, in the times of *ubiquitous computing*, the main challenge that must be faced by software engineers is the development (within time and budget) of reliable systems, despite their complexity and under the reality of continuous change. One way to address this challenge is by systematic software reuse, that has been shown to increase both productivity and quality of the final product. Therefore, reuse has become a goal reached by many organizations or individual developers in order to speed up their development times and boost performance of their teams.

Literature defines *reuse* as the use of existing artifacts or knowledge to create new software [12], and *reusability* as the extent to which a program can be reused in other applications [23] or, more generally, the degree to which an asset can be used in more than one system, or in building other assets [18]. While reuse has established itself as an activity that brings many savings to software development, reusability assessment aims to identify the assets that will facilitate those savings [33].

Two common scenarios that highlight the need for reusability evaluation can be described as: (i) *External reuse*: when a project requires the use of a third party component and the development team might need to choose from different options. Aspects such as adaptation costs, updating and trusting the reusable component in the project must be considered. (ii) *Internal reuse*: many software companies develop their own repository of reusable components. These may be used in several similar projects, thus

ⓒ The Author(s), under exclusive license to Springer Nature Switzerland AG 2023
H.-G. Fill et al. (Eds.): ICSOFT 2022, CCIS 1859, pp. 1–20, 2023.
https://doi.org/10.1007/978-3-031-37231-5_1

reducing development costs. Reusability evaluation of these components might lead to defining coding rules that will improve their reuse and maintenance.

Evaluating software reusability, however, is a difficult task. Reusability being a high level quality factor, there is no direct means to compute it. Literature has identified several quality attributes/factors influencing it and several metrics used to quantify those attributes. Moreover, it is hard to establish the exact relation among these attributes and the amount of their contribution (weight) to the final reusability score. To make things even more cumbersome, some of these factors influence or depend on each other, so that the associated metrics' sets overlap. As a consequence, to date, there is no general consensus on how to compute reusability of a component. Various reusability assessment approaches have been proposed and empirically validated in the literature, for different types of software assets, relying on different factors, with different weights and different underlying computational models.

Our aim with the current study is to replicate and evaluate some of these approaches, by tracking reusability and related quality factors over several versions of a number of open-source projects (longitudinal evaluation), with the purpose of comparing them and analysing the long-term evolution of reusability at project level in relation to the evolution of the other quality factors considered. We accomplish this with the aid of an in-house tool developed to support our analysis. We motivate our goals by the following:

- *Reusability Approaches' Evaluation and Comparison*: As mentioned above, the assessment approaches proposed in the literature have been empirically validated on a limited number of projects/components. Most of the papers describing them include guidelines for reaserchers and practitioners, encouraging them to further test the respective models on new datasets, so as to either raise the level of assurance with respect to the validity of their estimations or to help improving the model.
- *The choice of Open-source Projects*: Open-source code sharing platforms include libraries, frameworks and other assets easy to be reused. Finding the right component to integrate in a software system, on one hand, and preserving the reuse potential of developed code, on the other hand, might be challenging tasks. As a result, measuring the reusability level becomes an important aspect of such software systems.
- *Longitudinal Evaluation*: The fact that we study reusability in the context of software evolution, namely by investigating several versions of the software systems, is a core contribution of our aproach. Especially for software systems that are specifically created for reuse purposes, keeping a track record of how reusability evolves across the development of the project can become a very tedious, but significant task, as any moment of low consideration towards software quality could lead to a decrease in the reusability level, hence decreasing the re-use potential of the library or framework altogether and affecting how people who use it interact with it or driving away new potential users of that library. For this reason, factors affecting reusability should also be tracked during development.
- *Tool Support*: A recent survey on existing reusability estimation approaches [26] has emphasized limited tool support available for computing reusability and associated metrics. We aim a contribution towards covering this gap, by means of the

implemented tool. This could be further extended, so as to accomodate other estimation models, in addition to the currently existing ones.

This present chapter follows our previous work [22] by extending it in regards to: accompany evolution of reusability of a project with the distribution of reusability at class level; extending the analysis of constituents factors of reusability and by adding the exploration of quality factors that influence reusability. Even more, we present details about the artefact that we implemented and was used as an essential supporting tool in the whole study. The rest of the paper is organized as follows. Section 2 describes the candidate reusability models considered in our study and summarizes related work on the topic. Section 3 introduces our exploratory case study, by detailing the research questions stated and providing details on the criteria used for selecting reusability models and target applications. Implemented tool support in described in Sect. 4, while obtained results are analysed in detail in Sect. 5. We cover threats to validity in Sect. 6 and conclude in Sect. 7, by overviewing our contribution and sketching future research goals.

2 Preliminaries

2.1 Reusability Models

Several approaches aimed at estimating software reusability have been proposed in the literature, at different granularity levels (e.g. class, component or project), based on various quality factors and employing different computation techniques. Following a systematic literature review, we have selected seven such approaches as potential candidates to be included in our study, namely those described in [5, 8, 30, 32, 39, 42, 43]. The set has been further refined based on the selection criteria described in Sect. 3, the selected models being the ones from [8, 32, 43]. These are detailed in the respective papers and summarized by us in [22]. Below, we describe the four remaining ones and motivate the exclusion for each case.

The authors of [30] proposed a reusability estimation model depending exclusively on three metrics from the CK (Chidamber and Kemerer [11]) metric suite, namely DIT (Depth of Inheritance Tree), RFC (Response For a Class) and WMC (Weighted Methods per Class). While investigating the effect of internal structural characteristics of software on its reusability, they used the NASA thresholds [36] corresponding to the those metrics. Empirical studies and a weighted combination of polynomials based on the above-mentioned metrics were used in order to derive an estimator.

The purpose of the empirical study was to confirm three hypotheses the authors make, with respect to the influence of internal design factors on reusability. Namely, based on domain knowledge and previously reported research results from literature, they state that: (1) A high DIT value for a class leads to higher reusability of that class; (2) A high WMC for a class implies its lower reusability and (3) lower and higher values of RFC are associated with low reusability of the classes in question. In this purpose, two medium complexity java projects are investigated, each including a considerable number of reusable classes (between a third and a half of the total number of classes).

Information on whether a class is reusable or not is gathered from human experts. At first, based on the available design models, the values of the three metrics are derived for each class from within each project (DIT and WMC values are derived from static class diagrams, while RFC values are obtained based on sequence diagrams). Then, a binning strategy is applied for each metric, taking the NASA threshold values for that metric as reference. The ration between the number of reusable classes distributed in a bin and the total number of classes per it gives the percentage influence of that particular bean on reusability. Graphical representations of the relation among bin values and associated percentage values for each metric are used in order to validate the previously stated hypotheses.

Using the data from the empirical study and regression utilities in MATLAB, an equation corresponding to each metric is proposed. These equations are listed below (α, γ and ψ correspond to DIT, RFC and WMC values, respectively, while α_r, γ_r and ψ_r denote their percentage influence on reusability).

$$\alpha_r = 7.8\alpha^{1.4}$$

$$\gamma_r = -0.006\gamma^2 + 1.23\gamma + 11.1$$

$$\psi_r = 0.001\psi^3 - 0.16\psi^2 + 7\psi - 2.7$$

Each equation captures the functional relation between the respective metric and its percentage influence on reusability, fitting in the associated data distribution from the empirical study. The final reusability index for a project is obtained by integrating the multifunctional equations above, by the formula:

$$RI = f(DIT, RFC, WMC) = 0.33 \left(\frac{1}{n}\right) \sum_{k=1}^{n} \alpha_{rk} + 0.27 \left(\frac{1}{n}\right) \sum_{k=1}^{n} \gamma_{rk} + 0.40 \left(\frac{1}{n}\right) \sum_{k=1}^{n} \psi_{rk},$$

where n is the number of classes in the project, and $\alpha_{rk}, \gamma_{rk}, \psi_{rk}$ are computed as indicated above, for each class index k. The three weights corresponding to metrics (0.33, 0.27 and 0.4, respectively) have been arrived at using a Goal-Question-Metric paradigm, with support from domain experts so as to judge the contribution of each metric to the final reusability score.

Evaluation and validation has been performed using two commercial Java projects, the RI values provided by the model being close to the ones available from industry data (the latter ones being arrived at using a manual inspection approach). It is assumed that the differences are due to the influence of the remaining metrics from the CK suite on reusability.

However, despite the clear RI computation formula, the fact that the estimation only relies on three metrics, together with its exclusive focus on low-level structural attributes and the manual approach used for the reference/ground-truth reusability values have been considered exclusion criteria with respect to our current study.

In [5], a new reusability measure is proposed, called REI (REusability Index), aggregating metrics corresponding to both low/high-level structural attributes and external quality factors. The authors motivate the necessity of their approach by the fact that existing reusability models suffer from at least one of the following drawbacks: either (1) they only deal with individual attributes/factors affecting reusability, without integrating their corresponding metrics into a whole or (2) they focus exclusively on structural characteristics of software, ignoring external quality factors that impact its reusability.

The starting point for deriving the new index has been represented by the reusability model proposed in [17], that identifies eight factors to be considered: incurred reuse, maintainability, adaptability, external quality, documentation, availability, complexity and price. For each factor, except price, one or several metrics have been chosen, leading to a total of twelve metrics involved. The values of these metrics have been tracked for fifteen Maven projects, together with a reuse indicator for each project, taken as the ground truth value - the number of associated Maven downloads (given the fact that each download corresponds to an actual reuse of the respective project). Using this data and Backwards Linear Regression, REI has been derived as a function of seven variables: NDEP (Number of DEPendencies - incurred reuse), DOC (quality of DOCumentation), OP_BUGS (number of OPen BUGS - external quality), NCOMP (Number of COMPonents - availability), LCOM/ WMC/ NOC (Lack of Cohesion in Methods/ Weighted Methods per Class/ Number Of Classes - complexity).

$$REI = Constant + \sum_{i=0}^{i<num\_metrics} B(i) * metric(i)$$

The concrete values of the coefficients can be found in [5]. According to those values, NCOMP and DOC seem to have the strongest positive influence on reusability, while NOC and NDEP have the greatest negative impact.

The authors have validated their approach by means of an empirical case study, using a workbench of fifteen open source projects extracted from the Maven Repository, both libraries and frameworks (different from those used in order to derive the index). The goal was to contrast REI with two other reusability quantifiers proposed in the literature (one of them being QMOOD_R [8]), according to the metric validation criteria defined by the [2] standard, namely: correlation, consistency, predictability, discriminative power and reliability. The ground truth value has been taken again as the number of Maven downloads corresponding to an asset (the dependent variable). The study has shown that REI is the best reusability assessor from the three (the next being QMOOD_R), outperforming the other two in all criteria and showing signinficant improvements in terms of prediction accuracy and classification efficiency.

Even though this approach is sound, thoroughly described in [5] and validated, the fact that one of the metrics involved in the computation of REI, and whose value was shown to highly affect the estimation - DOC - cannot be automatically computed, but depends on human judgement applied on the available project documentation, has been an exclusion criterion with respect to our work.

Various quality attributes that influence reusability have been identified in the literature, together with associated metrics, however a clear relation among them and their precise contribution to reusability is hard to establish using conventional model-based approaches. Starting from this reality, the authors of [39] propose a reusability assessment model for object-oriented software components based on a neuro-fuzzy inference system. Such a hybrid system is a mixture of a fuzzy inference system and a neural network, the later being used for tuning the parameters of the model, so as to minimize the estimation error. The metrics used by the proposed model belong to the well-known CK metric suite, namely WMC, DIT, NOC, CBO and LCOM.

The input data to the neuro-fuzzy inference engine are the (tuned) values of the above metrics corresponding to a software component, and the output is a crisp value indicating its reusability. Tuning is necessary, so as to squish the input values into the [0, 1] interval. Then, according to the general model of a neuro-fuzzy system, the first neuron layer fuzzifies the input values, using membership functions. In order to define membership functions, three linguistic variables (LOW, MEDIUM and HIGH) have been associated to each of the five metrics used, while reusability has been assigned six such variables (PERFECT, HIGH, MEDIUM, LOW, VERY LOW and NIL). The following two neuron layers deliver the weights corresponding to the rules that will be fired and their normalized values, respectively. Finally, the last two layers perform defuzzification, by computing the reusability scores associated to the weights (using the input values and the rules base) and then summing them up into a final crisp reusability value. A Sugeno-type fuzzy inference model is used, so output membership functions used to defuzzify can only be linear or constant.

Training has been performed using the dataset provided in [39] (around 50 entries), for 1000 iterations. The purpose was to tune/adjust the membership function parameters, so as to minimize the difference between delivered and expected output. Before training, the initial rules section was done using the ID3 tree decision generation algorithm. For training, a hybrid method has been used, consisting of back-propagation form of the steepest descent method for parameters of the input membership functions and least squares estimation for parameters of the output membership functions. The error was reduced by each iteration and stabilized at a value near 0.042.

Validation of the proposed approach has been done by testing the system on a 14-entries dataset. The delivered reusability scores were close to the expected ones, the average error registered being around 0.039.

For the purpose of our study, the optimizations and tuning needed for the input metric values (which are not completely described in [39]), together with the need to define and train the model from scratch (since the final shape of the membership functions is not detailed by the paper) on a dataset for which the source of the associated reusability scores provided (expected values) has not been mentioned, have all constituted exclusion criteria.

The paper [42] also advocates the use of soft computing techniques (fuzzy systems, neural networks and genetic algorithms) to determine a relation among the various factors affecting reusability. The authors approach reusability in the context of component-based software development and propose two assessment models (implemented in MATLAB), based on fuzzy logic and neural networks, respectively. They take into account five factors, namely Modularity (MD), Interface Complexity (IC), Maintainability (MN), Flexibility (FL), Adaptability (AD), and start from the intuitive assumption that, for better reusability, IC should be less, MD, MN and FL should be more and AD should be as high as possible.

For the fuzzy logic model, they consider three linguistic variables associated to each input factor (Less, Modder and More) and five such variables for reusability (Least, Less, Modder, More and Most). As mentioned in the paper, input values for the five factors have been assumed using tools (not explicitely named). For the fuzzification step, they have used three of the available membership functions in MATLAB, namely triangular, trapezoidal and gaussian. Then a rule base has been fired, containing all 3^5 rules. Experiments have been reported, using different combinations of input values and membership functions.

As for the neural network approach, a network with two hidden layers has been used and it has been trained with the dataset generated by the fuzzy approach. The training has been done using the Feed Forward Back Propagation algorithm (using the MATLAB *Trainml* function), which is considered the fastest backpropagation algorithm available in MATLAB. Following the training, simulations have been performed, by selecting different input values.

The authors also report having compared the proposed models by means of a sensitivity analysis showing that the neural network model is more stable than the fuzzy approach. However, that analysis was not made explicit in [42].

Due to the absence of details concerning both the tools used to assess the values of the input factors and the 243-items rule base used by the inference engine (domain experts' knowledge being needed in order to propose such rules), and also to the incompleteness of validation information in the paper, the approach presented in [42] has not been included in our study.

2.2 Related Work

Following the introduction of the *reusable component* concept by McIllroy back in 1968 [24] and of *reusability* within the first quality model proposed by McCall in 1977 [23], the two have been active areas of research and practice. Concerning reusability, apart from the approaches aimed at proposing new estimation models - based on existing metrics quantifying its constituent factors (such as those presented in the previous subsection), a significant body of research has been devoted to either improving/extending the metrics' base - so as to fit particular types of reusable assets, or simply surveying the available literature - so as to either provide a general overview of the affecting factors and corresponding metrics or to evaluate and contrast some of the existing assessment approaches.

Belonging to the first category is the paper [41], in which the authors provide a critical evaluation of CK metrics and suggest improvements that are further mentioned in [39]. In case of DIT, for instance, the effect of multiple inheritance is discussed, while in case of NOC, the necessity of a recursive definition is argued and such a proposal is made.

In [13], the goal is to be able to rank Java components extracted from Internet by a search engine, based on their reusability. The latter is defined by adaptability, that is by the effort needed to integrate the asset in a new system. In this purpose, the authors propose new coupling and cohesion metrics for such components, each reflecting both the functional complexity of the component and the transitive nature of the attribute itself. Each of the proposed metrics has been validated against four existing ones, delivering better results in terms of reusability assessment and ranking.

In [35], a very recent paper on the topic, the authors are concerned with metrics used to quantify the reusability of software components, as employed by the CBSD paradigm. They motivate their work by the fact that, even though various metrics or metric suites exist in the literature (such as CK, MOOD, McCabe, Halstead, QMOOD) they are not really applicable to component-based development, since they do not target component interfaces. Or, in CBSD, reusability is to be understood in terms of composability of such intefaces. As such, they study quality factors associated to software components and propose a component reusability metric suite specifically targeted at JavaBeans. The proposed metrics have been validated both experimentally and against Briand's framework.

In [33] - paper belonging to the survey category, the author summarizes various existing reusability estimation approaches and associated metrics, based on a taxonomy distinguishing between empirical and qualitative ones. While empirical approaches use objective, quantifiable software attributes as a basis for reusability metrics, qualitative ones rely on offering guidelines and assigning reusability estimators to components, based on compliance to those guidelines. The paper emphasizes the fact that, despite the considerable amount of approaches proposed in the literature - 11 empirical and 3 qualitative ones being considered in the study - work remains to be done in the area of introducing domain attributes and contextual information (along with internal attributes) as a basis for reusability metrics.

In [27], the goal is to conduct a systematic literature survey in order to discover relevant reusability metrics for software components. A total of 39 papers have been investigated and summarized, leading to the identification of 36 quality factors influencing reusability and 37 reusability metrics (12 for black box components and 25 for white/glass box components).

Recently, the authors of [26] have performed an extensive literature survey, aimed at identifying software reusability factors, existing metrics used to quantify them, as well as available tool support to compute these metrics. To address the research goals, they have searched through five databases (IEEE Xplore, ACM DL, SpringerLink, ScienceDirect and Google Scholar), and investigated a total of 175 papers. They have identified a number of 44 factors that impact reusability, in either a positive or negative way. With respect to metrics, they conclude that most of them deal with class-level reusability and report them using five categories, namely coupling, cohesion, complexity, inheritance ans size. Available tool support for computing these metrics is considered as limited; this and the lack of a quantifiable measure for reusability are considered among the main issues that need to be addressed by research and practice.

Other survey studies that attempt to review existing approaches to measuring software reusability, such as [1, 3] or [40], also provide a high level view and comparison of those models, without evaluating and contrasting them in a practical/experimental manner.

Unlike the case of general surveys or reusability assessment proposals, the literature on the particular topic of long-term reusability behavior and evolution tracking - where our contribution resides, seems to be quite sparse.

In [8], the authors perform a study of several versions of two large commercial frameworks, in order to validate their model for estimating individual software quality factors like reusability. However, they do not employ any kind of ground truth value or reference point to compare their results against and they do not contrast their approach to similar ones in the literature. They only base their assumption that the model performs well on the expectation that a general trend in the evolution of reusability, either positive or negative, should be visible among versions.

In [4], the authors extend their previous research in the field, by performing an evolutionary study of reusability in two open-source projects, Jasmin and pBeans, over 6, respectively 10 versions of the projects. The analysis is made at package level, the aim being twofold: to prove the applicability of their proposed reusability model, on the one side, and to study the changes in reusability between versions, together with the factors that triggered them, on the other. However, similar to the previous case, comparison of their proposal to related ones in the literature is missing; moreover, no kind of empirical value or expert opinion is used, so as to validate the accuracy of their results.

The paper [14] is a reusability evolution study in terms of a number of different factors that affect it, namely coupling/cohesion, class growth, complexity, fan-in and fan-out metrics. The study coveres 10 versions of the Easy-Mock open-source project. The authors state several hypotheses with respect to the evolution of the considered attributes and their overall effect on sofware quality. However, the study is mostly focused on the individual quality attributes and how they generally impact reusability and does not provide a concrete reusability measurement model.

3 Exploratory Case Study

3.1 Research Questions

The study was designed and performed as an exploratory case study according to existing recommended practices [20, 37, 38] and established empirical research methodology guideline [34]. We followed a Goal-Question-Metric methodology [9], and defined our main objective as *"empirical exploration of reusability computational models with the purpose of assessing them and understand their constituent and dependant factors in the context of open source Java projects"*. This main objective is further operationalized in the following research questions:

RQ1: What is the distribution of reusability within the projects? Given the size of applications, some packages or classes may be easier to be used than others. On one hand, this is strongly related to the implemented functionality of that package or class, but on the other hand, it might also be the result of ignoring reusability purpose when developing it. For this reason, we aim to analyze the distribution of reusability at the class level in each project.

RQ2: Which are the constituents factors of reusability? Each reusability model under investigation uses different factors in its computation. We are interested in inspecting which is the contribution of each constituent factor to the computed reusability score.

RQ3: Which are the factors influencing reusability? We take an insight on the impact of some quality factors considered important by practitioners on reusability. Namely, we explore the relation between reusability and maintainability, complexity, respectively documentation.

These three research questions are used also as criteria to assess the selected reusability computational models. We intend to see how each model is behaving considering these three perspective.

3.2 Case Study Preparation

We took into consideration selection of computational models and selection of applications to be included in our investigation.

Selection of Reusability Estimation Models: Considering the reusability computational models presented in Sect. 2.1, we define some inclusion criteria for models to be considered in our study:

- replicability of computational formula and calculation instructions - such that implementing the model in our tool would be possible;
- reliability: the model should have been tested on a significant number of projects in order to prove its validity;
- availability of constituent metrics: the metrics used in formula are either easy to be implemented or computed by trustworthy tools.

Selection of Applications: We briefly present the three Java projects selected for this exploratory case study. The inclusion criteria consisted of:

- open source software: in order to respond to the need of investigating the source code and also to have available devemopment history;
- mature projects both in terms of size, complexity and development period;
- wide adoption: it should be used on a large scale, for a significant period of time.

JUnit4 [19] a unit testing framework for Java, was considered in 2013 the most included external library within the Java projects hosted on GitHub [44]. It consists of 47,402 lines of code, 1,505 classes and used by 1.8 million users and 28 versions (from which we used 23 in our study, meaningful for reusability assessment).

Atmosphere [7] is an event-driven framework for building asynchronous web applications that supports WebSockets, Server Sent Events (SSE), Long-Polling, HTTP Streaming and JSONP, with a development period of 14 years. In terms of size, Atmosphere counts 61,841 Lines of code, 899 classed and 219 versions (30 were included in our study).

Mockito [28] is mocking framework for Java applications that enables developers to write clean and readable Java Unit tests. Voted by StackOverflow as the best mocking framework for Java (according to their website [28]), it is the largest projects that we considered: 90,926 lines of code, 1,970 classes and 605 versions investigated (from which we investigated 45).

The steps we followed are: (i) implement the three selected models, (ii) apply them on a set of versions corresponding to the selected applications, namely 23 versions of JUnit (out of 28), 45 versions of Mockito (out of 605) and 30 versions of Atmosphere (out of 219); followed by (iii) analysis of the similarities and differences between results.

4   Tool Support for Reusability Monitoring

One of the main objective of this approach was to provide an easy to use tool that can assist practitioners in monitoring and improving the reusability attribute of their projects. The tool was also designed with the purpose of supporting case studies research, as the one described in this paper. Lastly, we wanted it to be extendable, such that other models could be easily added to the tool.

The main features of the tools include:

– provide analytics for a selected project, for all available versions;
– allow selection of models and metrics to be tracked;
– view the data as a series of charts and interact with it in different ways, delivering a dynamic user interaction with selected attributes to be tracked.

The tool is a web single-page application that renders a series of graphs and other data visualisation elements in a portrait-style layout. The charts are interactive in nature. They can be scaled, zoomed in/out, they supports multiple types of selections and hover interactions and they can also be downloaded as .png files. Another useful feature is that one can toggle on and off the displayed traces on a chart, depending if they want to view only specific traces of the dataset plotted, or all of them. When toggling traces on/off the chart re-scales itself to the most optimal size to accomodate the new selection of data points plotted. Dash framework, which was used as the UI base technology, enables for a very fine-grained customization of the hover interactions, labels and the general layout of the charts as well. Some key features of the application can be observed in Fig. 1. All the figures used in Sect. 5 have been generated with the tool.

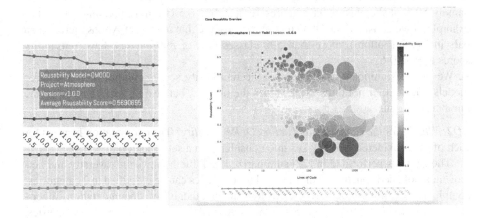

Fig. 1. Tool screenshots: hover interaction (left), class reusability overview chart (right).

The most important tools/technologies used in the implementation include: SourceMeter (for computing metrics), Plotly (charting library), Dash (UI framework), Gensim (NLP topic modelling library) and srcML (source code to XML parser).

5   Results and Discussions

This section contains our results analyzed according to the research questions defined in Sect. 3.1.

RQ1: What is the distribution of reusability within the projects?
The tool allowed us detailed investigations, to look at one moment (one version) and understand how reusability scores are distributed at the level of classes and also, to analyze how reusability evolve during release version history. The evolution of reusability in application history was explored in detail in [22], with the conclusion that variations tend to appear in earlier versions, and the later versions of the applications become somewhat constant in terms of reusability scores.

Then we analyze how, given a certain version of an application, the reusability score is associated to classes. We have chosen randomly several versions from each application and represented the value of reusability scores corresponding to the three models in relation with the number of classes. The results can be observed in Figs. 2.

As a general trend, we notice the output values by the same reusability model tend to take up a certain interval of values, with very small variations for each project, and from one version to the other. Even though the number of values in each of these bins (unit intervals) changes often from one version to another, the general intervals for the distributions tend to stay constant. For PDS, we can recognize a common Gaussian-like form of the general distribution (pink bars in Fig. 2, however for the other two models (Taibi purple bars, respectively QMOOD green bars), the shape is hard to predict, since it is not always uniform in nature.

This allowed us to draw two relevant **key points**:

A. Given the nature of selected applications, the reusability scores have good values, namely 50% of the classes have scores greater than 0.5 (from a maximum of 1). For example, if we consider QMOOD model, we observe that in case of Atmosphere, green bars in Fig. 2 (bottom), more than 500 classes (out of 899 classes) have reusability scores around 0.6.
B. We notice significant differences in the reusability scores computed by the three models. These refer not only to the values themselves, but also in the relation with the number of classes.

RQ2: Which Are the Constituents Factors Of Reusability? The computation formula for each of the considered model takes into consideration a set of factors.

The analysis performed in [22] summarized in Table 1 shows the diversity and heterogeneity of used constituent metrics. All used metrics can be classified in 7 categories: complexity, coupling/modularity, cohesion, understandability, documentation, inheritance, respectively size/messaging. PDS uses 20 metrics, namely 3 complexity metrics, 5 coupling metrics, 1 for cohesion, 5 for documentation, 2 for inheritance and 5 corresponding to size (no metric for understandability). Taibi model uses 7 metrics: one for each of the following categories: complexity, coupling, cohesion, inheritance and size, respectively two metrics corresponding to understandability, the only model taking into consideration this category. QMOOD uses only 4 metrics, related to coupling, cohesion and size (2 metrics). This diversity explains why the corresponding reusability scores behave differently.

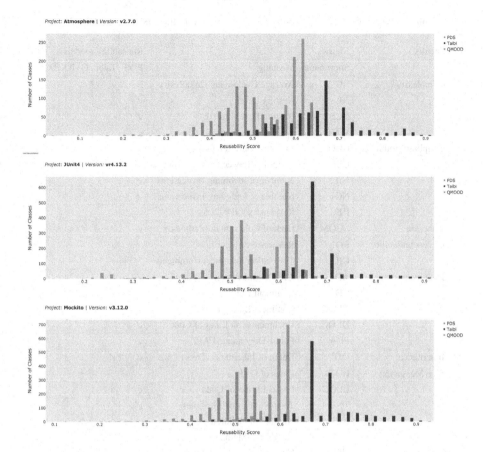

Fig. 2. Reusability per number of classes: in Atmosphere, version 2.7.0 (top), JUnit4, version 4.13.2 (middle) and Mockito, version 3.12.0 (bottom).

Another perspective that we investigated when looking at the constituent factors, was to explore the importance of each factor in the computational formula. Which of the considered factors is better correlated with the computed reusability score? The tool is also useful in showcasing the impact that each of the quality attributes tracked in a model has on the computation of the final reusability score reported by that model. We can select pairs of the form *(Reusability, Constituent Quality Attribute)* and study the types of relationships between the plotted curves (positive/negative ones). In this way, we can identify patterns in the evolution of the final score obtained that might be the result of one of the attributes influencing it in a certain direction, namely:

i) In case of *PDS* model, complexity has the strongest correlation with reusability, as studied in [22] and depicted in Fig. 3, especially for Mockito and JUnit4, while for Atmosphere the correlation is weaker.

ii) In case of *Taibi* model, all three analyzed projects exhibit a strong direct correlation during their lifespan between modularity and reusability score, as shown in Fig. 4.

Table 1. Overview of quality factors and metrics used in the analyzed models [22].

Factors	Metrics		Reusability models		
	Short name	Meaning	PDS	Taibi	QMOOD
Complexity	ACC	Average Cyclomatic Complexity		✓	
	NL	Nesting Level	✓		
	NLE	Nesting Level Else-If	✓		
	WMC	Weighted Methods per Class	✓		
Coupling/Modularity	CBO	Coupling Between Objects	✓	✓	✓
	CBOI	Coupling Between Objects Inverse	✓		
	NII	Number of Incoming Invocations	✓		
	NOI	Number of Outgoing Invocations	✓		
	RFC	Response set For Class	✓		
Cohesion	LCOM5	Lack of Cohesion in Methods 5	✓	✓	✓
Understandability	ROI	Relevance of Identifiers		✓	
	CIC	Correlation Identifiers Comments		✓	
Documentation	AD	API Documentation	✓		
	CD	Comment Density	✓		
	CLOC	Comment Lines of Code	✓		
	DLOC	Documentation Lines of Code	✓		
	PDA	Public Documented API	✓		
Inheritance	DIT	Depth of Inheritance Tree	✓	✓	
Size/Messaging	LOC	Lines of Code	✓		
	LLOC	Logical Lines of Code	✓		
	TNA	Total Number of Attributes	✓		
	NOC	Number of Children			✓
	NM	Number of Methods		✓	
	NPM	Number of Public Methods			✓
	NG	Number of Getters	✓		
	TNOS	Total Number of Statements	✓		

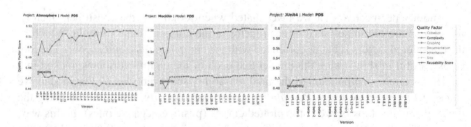

Fig. 3. Complexity impact on Reusability for PDS model [22].

iii) Considering *QMOOD* model, there are two factors that have a signficant impact on reusability: cohesion manifesting a strong correlation for Atmosphere and Mockito, and a good correlation in case of JUnit4 (see Fig. 5 (top)), respectively messaging (quantified in the model as the Number of Public Methods) which exposes a negative influence on reusability (see Fig. 5 (bottom)).

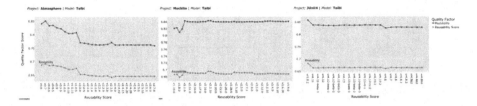

Fig. 4. Modularity impact on Reusability for Taibi model (extended from [22]).

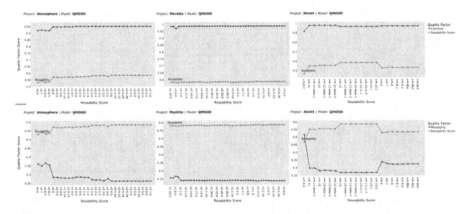

Fig. 5. QMOOD model: Cohesion impact on reusability (top), respectively messaging impact (bottom) (extended from [22]).

In conclusion, the **key points** regarding constituents factors can be summarized in:

A. Similar results from literature have been confirmed by our case studies, re-iterating the impact of complexity, cohesion, coupling, size, inheritance and documentation have on reusability.

B. We notice significant differences in the three reusability models, considering the importance of their constituents factors. As stated before, this is mainly due to the different factors used in the computation formula.

RQ3: Which are the factors influencing reusability? It is not the scope of this study to determine all factors and metrics that can have a positive or negative impact on reusability. We investigate three aspects, because they are measured and tracked in all software projects by practitioners, but also their interdependency with reusability have been reported by research studies, namely maintainability [16,21], complexity [6,25,31,33], respectively documentation [10,33].

The values we used for the external factors are quantified by the Sourcemeter metrics of ACC *(Average Cyclomatic Complexity)*, CD *(Comment Density)* for Documentation and MI *(Maintainability Index* - the original version) for maintainability. Running the tool with selected factors and models, as shown in Fig. 6, we managed to draw some observations.

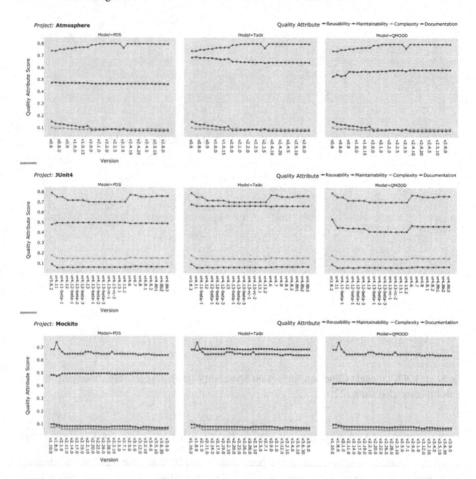

Fig. 6. External factors influences for all three models in Atmosphere (top), JUnit4 (middle) and Mockito (bottom).

Complexity and **Documentation** seem to display a common constant pattern of their average values over time for all 3 projects. *Complexity* seems to be affecting reusability more in the case of PDS (see also Fig. 3, while for Taibi, the documentation part has a stronger influence. This result is justified, as PDS is dependent on various metrics relating to the complexity of code, while Taibi's calculation model includes Understandability as a quality metric, which inherently ties in to the quality of internal documentation. QMOOD also displays a more significant connection to *complexity* and seems to have little correlation to documentation.

The most prominent correlation to **maintainability** is displayed by the QMOOD model, which succeeds in tracking maintainability evolution trends for 2 out of the 3 projects analyzed. The relationship seems to be a strong one and is backed up by the design of the model itself, which uses a number of overlapping metrics for both reusability and maintainability, so a good estimation of maintainability should also translate into a good estimation of reusability. The other two models do not indicate a good correlation, which might be interpreted as an indicator for the depreciation of Maintainability Index, as reported in [15,22,29].

The **keypoints** related to external factors are:

A. The three case studies considered confirmed the influence of documentation, complexity and maintainability on reusability, but in different weights.
B. The metrics considered in the computational formula and their weight are also responsible for the differences the models present when analysing the dependencies with external factors.

6 Threats to Validity

As this study can be considered as an empirical research, we need to address validity threats. The design and the unfolding of the study had been closely following existing good practices in the domain [34,38]: stating the objective, refining it in research questions, design the case study, and then collect, process and analyze the data. We address internal, external and construct threats to our approach.

Internal threats related to the factors that might influence the results obtained in the study, are related to the reusability computational models, respectively to the results obtained from the considered projects. The highest risk is represented by the implementation of the models, and this was one of the exclusion criterion in our study. Even so, in some cases (such as Design Size in QMOOD, Relevance of Identifiers and Correlation Identifiers Comments in Taibi model), the model definition was not sufficient. We tried to overcome this situation by supplementary references of the above metrics. We also tried, whenever possible, to use existing tools, with a trustworthy usage history. The threats related to data were addressed by manually examining the source code to explain the variation in metrics.

External threats related to the generalization of the results, were addressed in the process of selecting the applications, as described in Sect. 3.2. One important factor to address these threats was to consider open source projects, that expose the source code and the development history. We also tried to address the small number of projects included in the case study, by considering a large number of versions for each project, which gave a good perspective for the evolution of the reusability during a significant number of versions.

Construct threats were addressed by trying to follow as close as possible the description of the models, such that our implementation should resemble their definition and to use metrics tools whenever possible.

Finally, the last threat might come from incompleteness of the study, as not all available versions of the sample projects were included into the study. As our focus was on long term evolution of the reusability, we attached a higher priority to examine the entire development period, rather than on considering all versions of them.

7 Conclusions and Future Work

Irrespective of the particular type (in-house vs. external) or scale it is used on (class vs. component vs. project level), reuse is an inherent part of today's software development.

In order for it to deliver its promises of increased system quality and productivity, the reusability score of components being reused should be as high as possible.

Reusability, however, is hard to quantify, due to the large number of quality attributes and metrics affecting it and in the absence of a clear relation among them. Despite the number of estimation approaches proposed in the literature, much work remains to be done with respect to their validation, as well as in the area of investigating the impact of various quality factors on reusability.

Our current study contributes to the the body of research on the topic by providing a tool-based comparison of three reusability estimation approaches, which we use in order to track reusability indexes coresponding to three open-source Java projects, over several versions of these projects. In addition, we also investigate the long-term influence on reusability of its constituent quality attributes, as well as the dependency among reusability and a related quality factor, namely maintainability.

The main conclusion of our empirical study is that there still are important steps to be made in defining reusability evaluation, since there exists significant differences in values reported by different tools. No reusability evaluation model is universally accepted. The results are also useful for the practitioners, since the tool can offer effective information about resusability scores and their evolution for real life projects. Depending on own priority, a certain model can be selected and reusability scores and their modification throughout project lifespan can be monitored.

As future research goals, we set the following:

- Extending our tool, by including other reusability assessment approaches, as well as estimation models based on soft computing techniques, that have been proven to deliver promising results.
- Extending the project workbench used for analysis, so as to increase the confidence in the accuracy of the results delivered.
- Enhancing the set of quality factors whose evolution we track along with reusability, so as to provide a clearer view of their relation and dependency and hopefully bring a contribution towards refinement of existing assessment models.

References

1. Younoussi, S., Roudies, O.: All about software reusability: a systematic literature review. J. Theor. Appl. Inf. Technol. **76**, 64–75 (2015)
2. IEEE standard for a software quality metrics methodology. IEEE Std., pp. 1061–1998 (1998). https://doi.org/10.1109/IEEESTD.1998.243394
3. Ahmar, I., Abualkishik, A., Yusof, M.: Taxonomy, definition, approaches, benefits, reusability levels, factors and adaption of software reusability: a review of the research literature. J. Appl. Sci. **14** (2014). https://doi.org/10.3923/jas.2014.2396.2421
4. Amin, F.E., Mahmood, A.K., Oxley, A.: An evolutionary study of reusability in open source software (2012). https://doi.org/10.1109/ICCISci.2012.6297166
5. Ampatzoglou, A., Bibi, S., Chatzigeorgiou, A., Avgeriou, P., Stamelos, I.: Reusability index: a measure for assessing software assets reusability. In: Capilla, R., Gallina, B., Cetina, C. (eds.) ICSR 2018. LNCS, vol. 10826, pp. 43–58. Springer, Cham (2018). https://doi.org/10.1007/978-3-319-90421-4_3

6. Anguswamy, R., Frakes, W.B.: A study of reusability, complexity, and reuse design princi-ples. In: Proceedings of the 2012 ACM-IEEE International Symposium on Empirical Soft-ware Engineering and Measurement, pp. 161–164 (2012). https://doi.org/10.1145/2372251. 2372280

7. Atmosphere (2021). https://github.com/Atmosphere/atmosphere. Accessed 01 Mar 2022

8. Bansiya, J., Davis, C.: A hierarchical model for object-oriented design quality assessment. IEEE Trans. Softw. Eng. **28**(1), 4–17 (2002). https://doi.org/10.1109/32.979986

9. Basili, V., Caldiera, G., Rombach, H.D.: The goal question metric approach. In: Encyclope-dia of Software Engineering (1994)

10. Boxall, M., Araban, S.: Interface metrics for reusability analysis of components. In: 2004 Australian Software Engineering Conference. Proceedings, pp. 40–51 (2004). https://doi. org/10.1109/ASWEC.2004.1290456

11. Chidamber, S.R., Kemerer, C.F.: A metrics suite for object-oriented design. IEEE Trans. Soft Ware Eng. **20**(6), 476–493 (1994)

12. Frakes, W., Terry, C.: Software reuse: metrics and models. ACM Comput. Surv. **28**, 415–435 (1996). https://doi.org/10.1145/234528.234531

13. Gui, G., Scott, P.D.: Measuring software component reusability by coupling and cohesion metrics. J. Comput. **4**, 797–805 (2009)

14. Gupta, N.K., Rohil, M.K.: Software quality measurement for reusability. In: International Conference on Software Engineering and Mobile Application Modelling and Development (ICSEMA 2012), pp. 1–6 (2012). https://doi.org/10.1049/ic.2012.0157

15. Heitlager, I., Kuipers, T., Visser, J.: A practical model for measuring maintainability. In: Quality of Information and Communications Technology, 6th International Conference on the Quality of Information and Communications Technology, QUATIC 2007, Lisbon, Portugal, September 12–14, 2007, Proceedings, pp. 30–39 (2007). https://doi.org/10.1109/ QUATIC.2007.8

16. Henry, S., Lattanzi, M.: Measurement of software maintainability and reusability in the object oriented paradigm. https://hdl.handle.net/10919/19813 (1994)

17. Hristov, D.V., Hummel, O., Huq, M., Janjic, W.: Structuring software reusability metrics for component-based software development. In: ICSEA 2012 (2012)

18. ISO/IEC 25010: Systems and software engineering (2011). https://www.iso.org Accessed 2015

19. JUnit4 (2021). https://junit.org/junit4/. Accessed 01 Mar 2022

20. Kitchenham, B., Pickard, L., Pfleeger, S.L.: Case studies for method and tool evaluation. IEEE Softw. **12**(4), 52–62 (1995). https://doi.org/10.1109/52.391832

21. Lee, Y., Chang, K.H.: Reusability and maintainability metrics for object-oriented software, pp. 88–94. Association for Computing Machinery (2000). https://doi.org/10.1145/1127716. 1127737

22. Lung., A., Motogna., S., Petraşcu., V.: Empirical evaluation of reusability models. In: Pro-ceedings of the 17th International Conference on Software Technologies - ICSOFT, pp. 265–275. INSTICC, SciTePress (2022). https://doi.org/10.5220/0011143100003266

23. McCall, J., Richards, P., Walters, G.: Factors in software quality. Nat Tech. Information Ser-vice 1, (1977)

24. McIlroy, M.D.: Mass-produced software components. In: Proceedings of the NATO Confer-ence on Software Engineering, Garmisch, Germany (1968)

25. Mehboob, B., Chong, C.Y., Lee, S., Lim, J.: Reusability affecting factors and software met-rics for reusability: a systematic literature review. Softw.: Pract. Exper. **51** (2021). https:// doi.org/10.1002/spe.2961

26. Mehboob, B., Chong, C.Y., Lee, S.P., Lim, J.M.Y.: Reusability affecting factors and software metrics for reusability: a systematic literature review. Softw.: Pract. Exper. **51**(6), 1416–

1458 (2021). https://doi.org/10.1002/spe.2961, https://onlinelibrary.wiley.com/doi/abs/10.1002/spe.2961

27. Mijač, M., Stapic, Z.: Reusability metrics of software components: survey (2015). https://doi.org/10.13140/RG.2.1.3611.4642

28. Mockito (2021). https://site.mockito.org/. Accessed 01 Mar 2022

29. Molnar, A.-J., Motogna, S.: A study of maintainability in evolving open-source software. In: Ali, R., Kaindl, H., Maciaszek, L.A. (eds.) ENASE 2020. CCIS, vol. 1375, pp. 261–282. Springer, Cham (2021). https://doi.org/10.1007/978-3-030-70006-5_11

30. Nair, T.G., Selvarani, R.: Estimation of software reusability: an engineering approach. SIGSOFT Softw. Eng. Notes **35**(1), 1–6 (2010). https://doi.org/10.1145/1668862.1668868

31. Padhy, N., Singh, R., Satapathy, S.C.: Software reusability metrics estimation: algorithms, models and optimization techniques. Comput. Electr. Eng. **69**, 653–668 (2018). https://doi.org/10.1016/j.compeleceng.2017.11.022, https://www.sciencedirect.com/science/article/pii/S0045790617323327

32. Papamichail, M.D., Diamantopoulos, T., Symeonidis, A.L.: Measuring the reusability of software components using static analysis metrics and reuse rate information. J. Syst. Softw. **158**, 110423 (2019). https://doi.org/10.1016/j.jss.2019.110423, https://www.sciencedirect.com/science/article/pii/S0164121219301979

33. Poulin, J.S.: Measuring software reusability. In: Proceedings of the Third International Conference on Software Reuse: Advances in Software Reusability, pp. 126–138. Society Press (1994)

34. Ralph, Paul (ed.): ACM Sigsoft Empirical Standards for Software Engineering Research, version 0.2.0 (2021). https://github.com/acmsigsoft/EmpiricalStandards

35. Rathee, A., Chhabra, J.K.: Metrics for reusability of java language components. J. King Saud Univ. Comput. Inf. Sci. **34**(8), 5533–5551 (2022). https://doi.org/10.1016/j.jksuci.2022.05.010, https://www.sciencedirect.com/science/article/pii/S1319157822001598

36. Rosenberg, L.H., Hyatt, L.E.: Software quality metrics for object-oriented system environments (1995)

37. Runeson, P., Höst, M.: Guidelines for conducting and reporting case study research in software engineering. Empirical Softw. Eng. **14**, 131–164 (2008)

38. Runeson, P., Host, M., Rainer, A., Regnell, B.: Case Study Research in Software Engineering: Guidelines and Examples, 1st edn. Wiley Publishing (2012)

39. Sandhu, P., Singh, H.: A reusability evaluation model for oo-based software components. World Acad. Sci. Eng. Technol. Int. J. Comput. Electric. Autom. Control Inf. Eng. **2**, 912–917 (2008)

40. Sandhu, P., Aashima, Kakkar, P., Sharma, S.: A survey on software reusability, pp. 769–773 (2010). https://doi.org/10.1109/ICMET.2010.5598467

41. Sandhu, P., Singh, H.: A critical suggestive evaluation of CK metric, p. 16 (2005)

42. Singh, C., Pratap, A., Singhal, A.: Estimation of software reusability for component based system using soft computing techniques. In: 2014 5th International Conference - Confluence The Next Generation Information Technology Summit (Confluence), pp. 788–794 (2014). https://doi.org/10.1109/CONFLUENCE.2014.6949307

43. Taibi, F.: Empirical analysis of the reusability of object-oriented program code in open-source software. Int. J. Comput. Inf. Eng. **8**(1), 118–124 (2014). https://publications.waset.org/vol/85

44. Weiss, T.: We analyzed 30,000 github projects - here are the top 100 libraries in java, js and ruby (2013). https://www.overops.com/blog/we-analyzed-30000-github-projects-here-are-the-top-100-libraries-in-java-js-and-ruby/. Accessed 27 Aug 2022

Microservices Deployment on a Multi-platform Ecosystem: A Contract-Based Approach

Zakaria Maamar[1]([⊠]) [iD], Noura Faci[2,3] [iD], and Joyce El Haddad[3] [iD]

[1] University of Doha for Science and Technology, Doha, Qatar
zakaria.maamar@udst.edu.qa
[2] Univ Lyon, UCBL, CNRS, INSA Lyon, LIRIS, UMR5205, 69622 Villeurbanne, France
noura.faci@univ-lyon1.fr
[3] Université Paris-Dauphine, Université PSL, CNRS, LAMSADE, 75016 Paris, France
joyce.elhaddad@dauphine.fr

Abstract. To address the limitations of running monolithic applications, many organizations opt for microservices as a technology of choice that would make these applications agile. In addition to microservices, organizations are tapping into other technologies like cloud and edge to ensure computational, communication, and storage resource provisioning to their applications. To confirm this provisioning, this paper presents a contract-based approach for deploying microservices on top of a multi-platform ecosystem consisting of cloud, edge, and IoT devices. The approach integrates different contracts that capture the orchestration and choreography interactions during the deployment of microservices on different platforms. Technologies like Kubernetes and Amazon Web Services implementing a case study are used to demonstrate this deployment's technical doability.

Keywords: Cloud · Contract · Deployment · Edge · IoT · Microservice

1 Introduction

Despite the ongoing progress of Information and Communication Technologies (ICT), a good number of organizations still run monolithic applications for multiple reasons such as complexity to breakdown into small and manageable units, complexity to capture cross-cutting functional flows, and complexity to re-engineer existing practices. To mitigate this multi-facet complexity, design principles like Service-Oriented Architecture (SOA) [8] and technologies like Commercial-Off-The-Shelf (COTS) [19] are recommended to organizations with focus on the technology of microservices in this paper. According to Butzin et al. [6], the term microservice was coined in 2014 constituting an architectural style for the development of applications as a suite of small services, having each a separate but collaborative execution and communication process. Netflix is among the successful adopters of microservices. In a post by NGINX[1], Netflix shares its experience of transitioning *"from a traditional development model*

---

[1] www.nginx.com/blog/microservices-at-netflix-architectural-best-practices.

© The Author(s), under exclusive license to Springer Nature Switzerland AG 2023
H.-G. Fill et al. (Eds.): ICSOFT 2022, CCIS 1859, pp. 21–41, 2023.
https://doi.org/10.1007/978-3-031-37231-5_2

with 100 engineers producing a monolithic DVD-rental application to a microservices architecture with many small teams responsible for the end-to-end development of hundreds of microservices that work together to stream digital entertainment to millions of Netflix customers every day".

To maintain a competitiveness advantage besides opting for microservices, organizations can also count on other ICT like the Internet-of-Things (IoT). IoT is about making things such as sensors and actuators act upon the cyber-physical surrounding so that contextualized, smart services are provisioned to users and organizations. IoT is a perfect illustration of Weiser's definition of ubiquitous computing when he states in 1999 that *"the most profound technologies are those that disappear. They weave themselves into the fabric of everyday life until they are indistinguishable from it"* [28]. A recent trend promotes the blend of IoT with microservices, which raises many research questions and opens up many research opportunities (e.g., [2,6], and [25]).

Another recent trend in today's ICT landscape is IoT integration into cloud and edge computing (e.g., [11] and [15]). The massive amount of data about things needs to be captured adequately, communicated immediately, processed rapidly, analyzed smartly, shared cautiously, and protected efficiently. Data could be goods' freshness in a transit facility, inpatients' vitals in ICU, and air-pollution levels in cities. First, cloud has been the model of choice to expose resources (traditionally software, platform, and infrastructure) as services shifting the burden of managing resources internally to cloud providers in-return of fees. Second, edge addresses the inability of cloud to satisfy some non-functional requirements (e.g., data freshness and data protection) that some application domains (e.g., medical and financial) impose. Data transfer from things to (usually distant) clouds could take time because of high latency, be subject to interceptions, alterations, and misuses when transferred over open networks, and depend on network availability and reliability[2]. Contrarily, edge is to deploy computational, communication, and/or storage resources "next" (or nearby) to where data is collected minimizing its transfer and avoiding its exposure to unnecessary risks.

This chapter differs from what we presented in [17] by examining the conceptual and technical deployment of microservices on an ecosystem of multi-platforms consisting of cloud, edge, and IoT devices (*aka* things). This deployment is enforced through contracts while considering the following elements in this ecosystem: forms of interactions being vertical *versus* horizontal, types of things being static *versus* mobile, and properties of resources (compute, store, and communicate) that things, edges, and clouds would require to host microservices. Our contributions are, but not limited to, analysis of microservices deployment on top of cloud, edge, and things; design and development of a contract-based approach to host microservices based on resources that cloud, edge, and things use/consume, and technical demonstration of the hosting approach backed with different experiments. The rest of this chapter is organized as follows. Section 2 presents the concepts of microservices, IoT, cloud, edge, and contract. Section 3 details the contract-based approach for deploying microservices from a conceptual perspective. Implementation details of the deployment approach are given in Sect. 5. Section 6 concludes the chapter and identifies future work.

---

[2] Puliafito et al. report that *"the average round trip time between an Amazon Cloud server in Virginia (U.S.A.) and a device in the U.S. Pacific Coast is 66 ms; it is equal to 125 ms if the end device is in Italy; and reaches 302 ms when the device is in Beijing"* [22].

2 Background

This section consists of 4 parts that present in brief micorservices, IoT, cloud and edge, and contracts, respectively.

Microservices in Brief. Despite the limited consensus on the definition of microservices, the ICT community agrees on 2 characteristics [12]: *high cohesion* in the sense that a microservice's activities correspond to a single business operation, and *loose coupling* in the sense that microservices are quickly deployable and easily replaceable. From a communication perspective, a microservice adopts 2 models, request-response and publish-subscribe, to interact amidst their loosely-coupled nature. And, from a deployment perspective, the cloud infrastructure would be the option of choice, should potential microservice-based applications prioritize high availability and high performance at an affordable cost. A cloud infrastructure provides elastic load-balancing when requests are assigned to several instances of a microservice. In addition, the infrastructure supports automatic auto-scaling depending on the current number of a microservice's instances. From an overall perspective, designers should select a deployment option (either virtual machines or containers) for their microservices as well as decide on where these microservices should run on a single or multiple platforms.

Internet of Things in Brief. The abundant literature about IoT (e.g., [1], [4, 10], and [29]) does not help come up with a unique definition. We discuss some references as follows. First, Barnaghi and Sheth provide an overview of IoT requirements and challenges [4]. On the one hand, requirements include quality, latency, trust, availability, reliability, and continuity that should impact efficient access and use of IoT data and services. On the other hand, challenges result from today's IoT ecosystems that feature billions of dynamic things that make existing search, discovery, and access techniques and solutions inappropriate for IoT data and services. Second, Abdmeziem et al. discuss IoT characteristics and enabling technologies [1]. Characteristics include distribution, interoperability, scalability, resource scarcity, and security. And, enabling technologies include sensing, communication, and actuating. These technologies are mapped onto a three-layer IoT architecture that are referred to as perception, network, and application, respectively. Finally, Qin et al. [23] define IoT from a data perspective as *"In the context of the Internet, addressable and interconnected things, instead of humans, act as the main data producers, as well as the main data consumers. Computers will be able to learn and gain information and knowledge to solve real world problems directly with the data fed from things. As an ultimate goal, computers enabled by the Internet of Things technologies will be able to sense and react to the real world for humans".*

Cloud and Edge in Brief. Despite the popularity of both cloud and edge, De Donno et al. note the continued confusion in their definitions [9]. On the one hand, cloud is known for its *aaS operation model that adopts pay-per-use pricing and supports on-demand hardware and software resources. However, despite the popularity of cloud, it does not, unfortunately, suit all applications where low latency needs to be enforced and high transferred-data security needs to be achieved. On the other hand, edge (some refer to it as fog) was first introduced by Satyanarayanan et al. in 2009 [24] and generalized by Cisco Systems in 2014 [5] as a new ICT operation model that would make computational, storage, and communicating resources "close" to where data is captured and/or located. Edge would process data closer to its source, so that network traffic is reduced and both quality-of-service and quality-of-experience are improved [27]. The extension from cloud to edge is not trivial due to their subtle similarities and differences. Their suitability for certain applications is an open debate [20]. Despite the separate niches that cloud and edge target, many works like [9] and [14] acknowledge that they complement each other.

Contracts in Brief. The adoption of contracts is commonly reported in the ICT literature as per the survey paper [18]. Existing works adopt them for multiple purposes like monitoring, regulation, and security. In [3], contracts are established between customers (either persons or software) and things' providers. Both providers and customers engage in contract negotiation to specify terms related to purchasing and/or selling data. Contracts could refer to data rights (e.g., derivation and reproduction), and purchasing policy (e.g., contract termination and refund). In [13], contracts involving local transportation services' providers, regional authority, and passengers refer to QoS expectations. Changes in contracts' conditions to improve the perceived and delivered QoS have been quick and facilitated based on collected data. In [21], Pan et al. develop a credit-based resource management system to control how much edge resources are made available for IoT devices with respect to predefined policies that consider priority, application types, and past behaviors. To enforce these policies, smart contracts regulate IoT devices' behaviors in a non-deniable and automated manner.

In this chapter, we enforce the deployment of microservices thanks to contracts. To the best of our knowledge, little exists when it comes to identifying contracts in the context of microservices, things, and edge/cloud and, defining contracts' types and lifecycles. To address this lack of studies, we adopt in the next sections contracts to achieve this enforcement.

3   Microservices Deployment

This section consists of 4 parts. The first part presents the foundations of the approach for deploying microservices. The second part discusses how the approach is put into action. The third part formalizes the deployment in terms of parameters and operations.

3.1   Setting-Up the Foundations

The approach to deploy microservices takes into account 3 aspects: types of things, forms of interactions, and properties of resources.

Types of Things. In our ecosystem, static and mobile things exist in compliance with the work of Ghosh et al. who adopt the terms of mobile nodes like smartphones and PDAs and fixed access-points [11]. A mobile thing could temporarily become static for reasons like running out of resources before resuming the roaming and suspending the roaming until some conditions are met. By having static and mobile things, different opportunities and restrictions are related to each type during the interactions with the environment and resource consumption.

- A static thing is assigned to a physical location and cannot move due to its size, security concerns, and safety regulations, for example. In terms of opportunities, a static thing could rely on stable communication channels, could continuously be monitored and fed with resources, and could constitute a reliable platform for critical operations. In terms of restrictions, a static thing could have limited interaction circles waiting to be discovered by others, and could "easily" be subject to attacks.
- A mobile thing is fitted with necessary wireless communication means that would make it reachable. In terms of opportunities, a mobile thing could discover new resources and run into new peers while roaming, and could be close to resources and/or other peers reducing dependence on reliable communication channels. In terms of restrictions, a mobile thing could be dependent on on-board resources making its roaming limited, could have limited computational, communication, and storage capabilities, and could be excluded from supporting critical operations.

Forms of Interactions. In our ecosystem, horizontal and vertical interactions occur between homogeneous and heterogeneous peers, respectively. A peer is either a thing, an edge, or a cloud. First, horizontal interactions are useful when forming alliances of peers that would handle complex users' demands as well as offloading demands from one peer to another. And, vertical interactions are a mix of bottom-up from things to edges then clouds conveying data, and top-down from clouds to edges then things conveying commands.

Properties of Resources. The objective of discussing resources in our ecosystem is to shed light on the impact of their availabilities on deploying microservices on things, edges, and/or clouds. Some resources are limited like storage while others are (temporarily) non-shareable like data. Building upon work on resource management [16], we consider 5 consumption properties for resources, unlimited (ul), shareable (s), limited (l), limited-but-renewable (lr), and non-shareable (ns). Unless stated a resource is by default unlimited and/or shareable.

- Limited means that the consumption of a resource is restricted to a particular capacity and/or period of time.
- Limited-but-renewable means that the consumption of a resource continues to happen since the (initial) agreed-upon capacity has been increased and/or the (initial) agreed-upon period of time has been extended.
- Non-shareable means that the concurrent consumption of a resource must be coordinated (e.g., one at a time).

3.2 Actioning the Deployment

To action the deployment of microservices for execution, specific actions need to be taken to ensure the readiness of the platforms that will host these microservices. This readiness depends on resource availabilities, ongoing loads, and locations of platforms.

In compliance with the loosely-coupled nature of microservices, we assume hereafter that the microservices of a business IoT application respond to events that peers generate after completing their execution. Therefore, it is neither expected that all microservices will be deployed nor there will be a specific control logic that dictates the deployment order of microservices. Finally, those microservices responding to same events will form clusters.

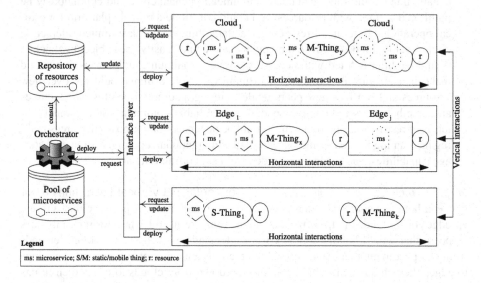

Fig. 1. Illustration of choreOrchest in action [17].

A "straightforward" approach to deploy a microservices-based business application would be associated with either an orchestration model or a choreography model. The former relies on a centralized component, orchestrator, that would decide on where microservices would be deployed. Contrarily, the latter relies on peer-to-peer interactions to let communicating platforms decide on where microservices would be deployed. To cater for the needs of our cloud, edge, and IoT ecosystem, we mix choreography and orchestration models into what we refer to as choreOrchest. The success of this mix would depend on knowing when to switch from orchestration to choreography and *vice-versa*, and has been adopted by others. For instance, in [26], Valderas et al. note that although choreography should prevail because of the decentralized nature of microservices, the composition's flow logic is distributed over many microservices and implicitly defined by the interactions between these microservices preventing the development of a complete picture of the composition progress. To address this lack of complete picture, Valderas et al. suggest orchestration that would be built upon a single model allowing to coordinate, in a centralized way, the interactions of microservices.

Figure 1 illustrates how we action choreOrchest. An orchestrator[3] running on top of the pool of microservices is responsible for selecting those that will be deployed on the available platforms like clouds, edges, static things, and/or mobile things. The

---

[3] Many orchestrators could exist but this aspect is not considered.

orchestrator is aware of the platforms' resource availabilities along with the microservices' needs of resources. These availabilities are reported in the repository of resources that all platforms regularly update. Once the orchestrator consults the repository of resources and decides on which platforms the microservices will be deployed, it requests the interface layer to deploy and track them until completion.

Worth mentioning in Fig. 1 the vertical and horizontal interactions that would allow choreOrchest to create a "synergy" between all the platforms. This synergy assumes that each platform maintains a vicinity list containing those peers that would be willing to support this platform in hosting some microservices in return of a fee. We associated this willingness with o oading that could happen "before" and "during" the deployment of microservices. "Before" means that a nearby platform (regardless of its current load) will support another platform handle the deployment of some microservices. "During" means that a resource assigned to a platform becomes unavailable preventing the deployment of microservices. This requires assigning these microservices to other platforms. For instance, a limited-but-renewable resource impacts a microservice's execution when the renewal is no longer possible. Details about offloading (p_j) function are given in Sect. 3.3.

3.3 Formalizing the Deployment

Table 1 presents the parameters that formalize the problem and solution of deploying microservices on top of cloud, edge, and thing platforms. While some of these parameters like budget and execution-time overlap with those presented in [7] such as operational-cost, compute-resource-utilisation, service-availability, response-time, and latency, the rest like hosting-income, resource-property, and platform-vicinity provide unique features to our approach.

We formalize the strategy to deploy microservices as a tuple

$$< \mathcal{B}, \{ms_i, et_{ms_i}, re_{ms_i}\}, \{?p_{ms_i}^{o \oplus p_k}, ?hi(p_{ms_i}^{o \oplus p_k}), ?re(p_{ms_i}^{o \oplus p_k}), ?rp(re(p_{ms_i}^{o \oplus p_k}))\} > \tag{1}$$

where

1. "?" refers to dynamic elements obtained at run time.
2. The input elements are
   - $\mathcal{B}$: budget to cover all the expenses associated with deploying and executing the multi-microservices of a business application.
   - $\{ms_i\}$: set of microservices that need to be deployed and executed regardless of their order in the business application.
   - re_{ms_i}: resource that a microservice consumes during deployment and execution.
   - et_{ms_i}: time that the deployment/execution of a microservice lasts over a platform.
3. The output elements are
   - $\{p_{ms_i}^{o \oplus p_k}\}$: multi-set of platforms upon which the microservices will be deployed then executed. Platforms are either selected by the orchestrator (o) or recommended by some peer (p_k).

Table 1. List of parameters.

Parameter	Acronym	Description
Budget	$\mathcal{B}$	budget for completing the deployment and execution of a multi-microservices business application.
Platform	p	platform upon which a microservice will be hosted for deployment and execution.
Microservice	ms	microservice of a multi-microservices business application.
Hosting income	hi	income that a platform secures when hosting a microservice for deployment and execution; the highest income is assigned in a descending order to cloud, edge, static thing, then mobile thing.
Resource	re	resource that a microservice consumes during hosting and execution; a resource is linked to a platform and has a property.
Resource property	rp	property of a resource that is either unlimited, shareable, limited, limited-but-renewable, or non-shareable.
Execution time	et	time that a microservice takes to deploy and execute on a platform; the maximum time is assigned in a descending order to mobile thing, static thing, edge, then cloud.
Platform vicinity	pv	dynamic list of peers that are reachable from a hosting platform according to a predefined radius/distance allowing to offload a microservice from the platform to one of these peers; at any time the list could be empty.
Platform load	pl	current load of hosting concurrent microservices on a platform.

hi and et are inversely proportional
hc and et are inversely proportional

- $rp(re(p_{ms_i}^{o \oplus p_k}))$: property of a resource that a platform considers for allowing the deployment and execution of the microservice at least once (failure could happen) based on the execution times of this microservice and other microservices running on this platform.
4. Finally, the facilitating elements are
   - $\{pl_{p_j}\}$: current hosting load of a platform that could trigger offloading some microservices to peers in the vicinity based on a certain threshold. Offloading would impact the hosting income of the platform to compensate these peers.
   - $\{pv_{p_j}\}$: list of platforms that are in a platform's vicinity and willing to offer support before and after executing a microservice.

In the input elements above, a platform uses re and et parameters to decide on either accepting or refusing to host a microservice. The strategy to deploy and execute a set of microservices ($\{ms_i\}$) is summarized with the following actions:

1. The orchestrator consults $\mathcal{R}_{re}$ that is the repository of resources offered by the platforms $\{re_{p_j}^1, re_{p_j}^2, ...\}$ where $p_j \in \mathcal{F}og \cup \mathcal{C}loud \cup \mathcal{F}\text{-}Thing \cup \mathcal{M}\text{-}Thing$. A platform is free to publish or not its resources along with their properties and costs. It is worth noticing that a limited resource would be less expensive if it were limited&renewable.
2. The orchestrator consults $\mathcal{P}_{ms}$ that is the pool of microservices in order to check the execution times ($\{et_{ms_i}\}$) and needs of resources ($\{re_{ms_i}\}$) of $\{ms_i\}$.

3. The orchestrator proceeds with matching the microservices to relevant platforms (based on their resources and these resources' properties) taking into account 2 objective functions:
   - The business application would like to secure the deployment and execution of all $\{ms_i\}$ while meeting $\mathcal{B}$.
   - Each platform would like to maximize its income (*Total-Income*).

$$Total\text{-}Income(p_j) = \sum_{k=1}^{M} x_{p_j}^k * hi(re_{p_j}^k, rp(re_{p_j}^k)) \tag{2}$$

where
   - M represents the total number of resources that p_j makes available.
   - $x_{p_j}^k \in \{0, 1\}$ corresponds to a matching result that the orchestrator provides. In other words, $x_{p_j}^k$ is equal to 1 if $re_{p_j}^k$ is selected to support deploying and executing ms_i, otherwise $x_{p_j}^k$ is equal to 0.

In conjunction with the actions above, we formalize microservices-platforms matching as follows:

1. Form n clusters where each cluster hosts some $\{ms_i\}$ that are dependent on each other through events as per Sect. 3.2. The number of microservices in a cluster is restricted to a threshold to avoid "crowded" clusters. It is expected that microservices in clusters would be strongly coupled thanks to events while clusters would be loosely coupled to the extent that some would not be connected to any cluster.
2. Rank the clusters based on their numbers of microservices in decreasing order in a list (L). This order should reduce the time when processing the smallest clusters.
3. Determine the candidate set of platforms (P_{C_1}) for the first cluster (C_1) in L by minimizing the total hosting income for the microservices in C_1 with respect to the budget. Each platform $p_j \in P_{C_1}$ calls offloading(p_j) as follows:
   (a) Evaluate the offloading trade-off between "the income to host and execute a microservice" and "the fees to pay to other peers in p_j's vicinity list VC(p_j), should the peers accept to host and execute the microservice".
   (b) **If** this trade-off is below a certain offloading threshold, p_j selects the peer in VC(p_j) that has the lowest fee and adds this peer to P_{C_1}.
   (c) **Else** p_j hosts and executes the microservice.
4. For the next clusters ($C_{i,i>1}$) in L, proceed as follows:
   (a) Consider the platforms ($P_{C_{i-1}}$) assigned to the previous cluster (C_{i-1}) as potential platforms for hosting the microservices in C_i.
   (b) Using $P_{C_{i-1}}$, build a set of all platforms that would accept to host microservices in C_i ($P_{C_{i-1}}^{accept} \subseteq P_{C_{i-1}}$). For each platform $p_j \in P_{C_{i-1}}^{accept}$, calls offloading ($p_j$).
   (c) **If** ((there are still microservices in C_i without platforms) or ($|P_{C_{i-1}}^{accept}| <$ a certain value)) and (that the number of times (nb) calling for the vicinity list of platforms in $P_{C_{i-1}}^{accept}$ is less than a limit value), proceed as follows:
      i. Establish a vicinity list for each platform $\in P_{C_{i-1}}^{accept}$; the outcome is VC($P_{C_{i-1}}^{accept}$) and increment nb by one.
      ii. Go to Step 4.b using VC($P_{C_{i-1}}^{accept}$) as input instead of $P_{C_{i-1}}$.
   (d) **Else** proceed as in Step 3 using C_i as input instead of C_1.
   (e) Go to Step 4.a and proceed with the next cluster C_{i+1}.

Input: $\{p_j\}, \{ms_i\}, B$
Output: $\{p_{ms_i}^{o \oplus p_k}\}$
begin

    Form&Rank $\{C_l\}$ from $\{ms_i\}$ Build $P_{C_1} \mid min(Total\text{-}Income(p_j \in C_1)) \le B$
    forall the $p_j \in P_{C_1}$ **do**
        p_j.Offloading(Δ_j) **if** $\Delta_j \le \sigma$ **then**
            $P_{C_1} \leftarrow P_{C_1} \cup \{p_k\}_{k \in VC(p_j)}$
        end
        else
            $P_{C_1} \leftarrow P_{C_1} \cup \{p_j\}$
        end
    end
    forall the $C_{l,l>1}$ **do**
        Build $P_{C_l} = Accept(C_l, P_{C_{l-1}})$ **forall the** $p_j \in P_{C_l}$ **do**
            p_j.Offloading(Δ_j)
        end
        if $(\exists ms_i) \vee ((|P_{C_l}| < \omega) \wedge (nb < \epsilon))$ **then**
            forall the $p_j \in P_{C_l}$ **do**
                Build $VC(p_j)$
            end
            nb++
            forall the $p_k \in VC_{P_{C_l}}$ **do**
                p_k.Offloading(Δ_j)
            end
        end
        else
            forall the $p_j \in P_{C_l}$ **do**
                p_j.Offloading(Δ_j)
                if $\Delta_j \le \sigma$ **then**
                    $P_{C_l} \leftarrow P_{C_l} \cup \{p_k\}_{k \in VC(p_j)}$
                end
                else
                    $P_{C_l} \leftarrow P_{C_l} \cup \{p_j\}$
                end
            end
        end
    end
    return $\{P_{C_l}\}_{l=1,...} = \{p_{ms_i}^{o \oplus p_k}\}$
end

Algorithm 1. chore$\mathcal{O}$rchest strategy.

4 Contracts to Regulate Microservices Deployment

To regulate microservices deployment in terms of who did what, when, and where, contracts are used [17]. In this section, we present types of contracts and then, interactions between contracts.

4.1 Types of Contracts

Figure 2 illustrates the 3 types of contracts that we deem necessary for managing microservices deployment and execution over thing, edge, and cloud platforms. These contracts are discovery, deployment, and collaboration. The figure also illustrates how the contracts impact each other. Indeed, the value of a QoS non-functional property in a contract is changed because of a counterpart property in another contract. In the following, each contract is defined along with its QoS non-functional properties.

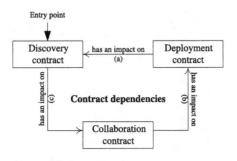

Fig. 2. Types of contracts [17].

Discovery contract is established between microservices, a third party (e.g., broker), and potential hosting platforms. The following QoS non-functional properties could populate a discovery contract (Fig. 3 as example):

- Discovery time that the third party would need to connect microservices to platforms.
- Discovery quality that microservices and platforms would each expect from the third party. Because of microservices' and platforms' separate expectations, we specialize discovery quality into dQuality$_{ms}$ for the microservices that target a certain hosting level like reliability by the platforms and dQuality$_{pl}$ for the platforms that target a certain execution time of the hosted microservices. Since discovery quality is assessed after the hosting of microservices over platforms occurs effectively, the deployment contract's QoS non-functional properties (discussed next) will impact the discovery contract as per Fig. 2 (a). Any deviation from a discovery contract's agreed-upon clause like drop in execution time due to a poor hosting level should be communicated the third party that could consider this deviation when recommending potential platforms to microservices in the future.

Deployment contract is established between microservices and confirmed platforms upon the third party's recommendations as stated in the discovery contract description. The following QoS non-functional properties could populate a deployment contract (Fig. 4 as example):

- Deployment time that a platform would need to have a microservice ready for execution, should the microservice require a particular set-up.
- Execution time that a platform would need to have a microservice executed.

```
"name" : "DiscoveryContract",
"id": 1,
"partners" : [
    {"FirstParty" : "Broker"}, {"SecondParty" : "Microservice ms"},
    {"ThirdParty": "Platform p"}
],
"terms" : [
    {
        "qosMetric": "DiscoveryTime",
        "constraint" : "less than",
        "value" : 20,
        "unit " : "minute"
    },
    {
        "qosMetric": "dQuality_ms",
        "constraint" : "more than",
        "value" : 20,
        "unit " : null
    },
    {
        "qosMetric": "dQuality_pl",
        "constraint" : "less than",
        "value" : 180,
        "unit " : "second"
    }
]
```

Fig. 3. Example of a JSON instantiated discovery contract [17].

```
"name" : "DeploymentContract",
"id": 2,
"partners" : [
    {"FirstParty" : "Platform p"}, {"SecondParty" : "Microservice ms"}],
"terms" : [
    { "qosMetric": "DeploymentTime",
        "constraint" : "less than", "value" : 3, "unit " : "minute"
    },
    { "qosMetric": "ExecutionTime",
        "constraint" : "less than", "value" : 24, "unit " : "minute"
    },
    { "qosMetric": "HostingLevel",
        "constraint" : "more than", "value" : 90, "unit " : null
    },
    { "qosMetric": "DelegationQuality",
        "terms" : [
            { "ThirdParty" : "Platform p2",
                "depTimeImpact" : "positif", "depTimeImpactValue" : 1, "depTimeImpactUnit " : "minute",
                "execTimeImpact" : "negatif", "execTimeImpactValue" : 2, "execTimeImpactUnit " : "minute"
            },
            { "ThirdParty" : "Platform p3",
                "depTimeImpact" : "negatif", "depTimeImpactValue" : 5, "depTimeImpactUnit " : "minute",
                "execTimeImpact" : "positif", "execTimeImpactValue" : 3, "execTimeImpactUnit " : "minute"
            }
        ]
    },
    { "qosMetric": "eQualityms",
        "value" : null
    },
    { "qosMetric": "eQualitypl",
        "value" : null
    }
]
```

Fig. 4. Example of a JSON instantiated deployment contract [17].

– Hosting level that a microservice would require without degrading its performance
  nor the performance of the platform. A platform's hosting level could be related to
  its capacity of performing without failures nor interruptions over a period of time,
  and would depend on its technical capabilities.

- **Delegation quality** that a platform would use to make a microservice aware of the (positive/negative) offloading impact on this microservice's deployment time and execution time. Like with the discovery contract's discovery-quality property, we specialize delegation quality into $eQuality_{ms}$ for the microservices that end-up executed on different platforms and $eQuality_{pl}$ for the platforms that receive microservices for hosting upon the requests of other platforms. Since delegation quality is assessed after the offloading of microservices occurs effectively, the collaboration contract's QoS non-functional properties will impact the deployment contract as per Fig. 2 (b). Any deviation from a deployment contract's agreed-upon clause like increase/decrease in an offloaded microservice's hosting level due to a better/worse platform should be communicated to this microservice's owner so, that, he decides in the future on accepting/rejecting offloading demands.

Collaboration contract is established between either homogeneous peers like things-things, edges-edges, and clouds-clouds or heterogeneous peers like things-edges, things-clouds, and edges-clouds. The following QoS non-functional properties could populate a collaboration contract (Fig. 5 as example):

- **Offloading time** that a platform would need to transfer a microservice to another platform for deployment and execution.
- **Offloading quality** that a microservice would use to report its experience of being deployed and executed on a different platform from the one that is reported in the discovery contract. This experience refers to deployment-time and execution-time properties that should be benchmarked to the same properties in the deployment contract. Along with this experience, offloading quality is shared with the third party involved in the discovery so, that, future recommendations of platforms to host microservices could be adjusted, whether the quality turns out positive or negative. This means that a collaboration contract's QoS non-functional properties will impact the discovery contract as per Fig. 2 (c).
- **Collaboration quality** that a platform would use to decide in the future on offloading microservices to other platforms. Collaboration quality should be benchmarked to the deployment contract's delegation-quality property as per Fig. 2 (b). Like with both the discovery contract's discovery-quality property and the deployment contract's delegation-quality property, we specialize collaboration quality into $cRecommendingQuality_{pl}$ for the platform recommending a peer and $cRecommendedQuality_{pl}$ for the platform that is recommended by a peer and is dependent on the deployment contract's $eQuality_{ms}$.

4.2 Interactions Between Contracts

In Fig. 2, interactions (a), (b), and (c) capture the impacts that some contracts could have on each other. Indeed, the deployment contract impacts the discovery contract and the collaboration contract impacts both the discovery contract and the deployment contract. By impact, we mean the completion of a contract at run-time leads into results that would be integrated into the preparation of another contract or updating an existing one.

```
"name" : "CollaborationContract",
"id": 3,
"partners" : [
    {"FirstParty" : "Platform p1"}, {"SecondParty" : "Platform p2"},
    {"ThirdParty" : "Microservice ms"}
],
"terms" : [
    {
        "qosMetric": "offloadingTime",
        "constraint" : "less than",
        "value" : 5,
        "unit " : "minute"
    },
    {
        "qosMetric": "offloadingQuality",
        "value" : null
    },
    {
        "qosMetric": "cRecommendingQualitypl",
        "value" : "high"
    },
    {
        "qosMetric": "cRecommendedQualitypl",
        "value" : "high"
    }
]
```

Fig. 5. Example of a JSON instantiated collaboration-contract [17].

1. **from:** Deployment Contract **to:** Discovery Contract. On the one hand, the satisfaction level (abstracting deploying-time and execution-time properties) of a microservice towards a platform upon which it has been deployed (i.e., $dQuality_{ms}$) needs to be reported to the third party so, that, future discovery cases that could involve this platform could be handled differently. On the other hand, the satisfaction level (abstracting hosting-level property) of a platform towards the microservices it has received for hosting (i.e., $dQuality_{pl}$) needs to be reported to the third party so, that, future discovery cases that could involve these microservices would be handled differently. Thanks to details reported to the third party, this one does not rely on what microservices and platforms announce in terms of technical requirements and capabilities, respectively. But, the third party also relies on what happens at run-time when completing deployment contracts.

2. **from:** Collaboration Contract **to:** Deployment Contract.] On the one hand, the satisfaction level (abstracting $eQuality_{ms}$ property) of a microservice towards a new platform, that is different from the initial platform reported in the discovery contract, should be reported to this initial platform so, that, future delegation cases that could involve this new platform would be handled differently. On the other hand, the satisfaction level (abstracting $eQuality_{pl}$ property) of a platform towards the microservices it has received for hosting upon the request of the initial platform reported in the discovery contract should be reported to this initial platform so, that, future delegation cases that could involve these microservices could be handled differently. Thanks to details reported to the initial platform, this one does not rely on what microservices and other platforms announce in terms of technical requirements and capabilities, respectively. But, the initial platform also relies on what happens at run-time when implementing collaboration contracts.

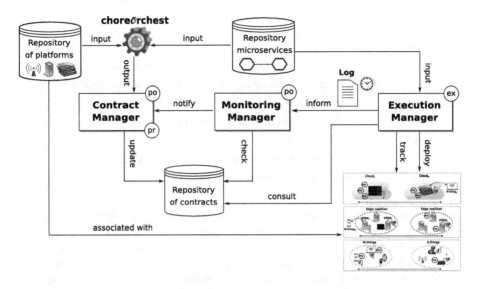

Fig. 6. Architecture of the contract-based system for microservices deployment [17].

3. **from:** Collaboration Contract **to:** Discovery Contract. The satisfaction level (abstracting offloading-quality property) of a microservice towards a new platform, that is different from the one identified during the discovery, needs to be reported to the third party so, that, future discovery cases that could involve the first platform that recommends this new platform would be handled differently.

5 Implementation

This section discusses the technical aspects of choreOrchest using a set of microservices related to farming. Along with this discussion, the role of contracts in tracking the progress of microservices deployment is presented in this section as well.

5.1 System Architecture

Figure 6 is the architecture of the system that consists of 3 repositories (platforms, microservices, and contracts), 4 components (choreOrchest, contract, monitoring, and execution managers), and one *log* file. In this figure, pr, ex, and po stand for pre-execution, execution and post-execution stages, respectively, and arrowed lines correspond to interactions between all the repositories, choreOrchest, the managers, and the *log*.

During the pre-execution stage, choreOrchest determines the deployment strategy based on first, the microservices' technical requirements and platforms' technical capabilities and second, these platforms' ongoing/changing loads (Sect. 3.3). Based on choreOrchest's outcomes, the contract manager prepares all types of contracts (discovery, deployment, and collaboration). Still in the pre-execution stage, different

Table 2. List of microservices.

Microservice	Description
ms_1	Track changes in temperature during the day, month, and year
ms_2	Measure air pressure for predicting specific weather changes
ms_3	Measure air humidity when requested
ms_4	Detect potential fire and flood hazards
ms_5	Cover open burning
ms_6	Select appropriate tarps according to sensitive crops
ms_7	Adjust water use smartly for crop irrigation

values are assigned to the QoS non-functional properties according to their roles in finalizing the contracts. For instance, Discovery time, dQuality$_{ms}$, dQuality$_{pl}$, and Deployment time are assigned random values according to a specific range, e.g., [5, 10], while eQuality$_{ms}$, eQuality$_{pl}$, and Offloading quality are assigned $null$, and cRecommendingQuality$_{pl}$ and cRecommendedQuality$_{pl}$ are assigned $high$. To address the cold-start concern, we assumed that, at initialization time, all platforms trust each other confirming the high level of collaboration between them. During the execution stage, the execution manager consults the repository of contracts to deploy the microservices (using deployment contracts) and then, proceeds with tracking their execution and potentially offloading some to other platforms (using collaboration contracts). This manager also measures the effective values of relevant QoS non-functional properties like Discovery time, Deployment time, and Execution time. These values are stored in the log that the monitoring manager uses during the post-execution stage for benchmarking against the corresponding values in the deployment contracts. Should there be any discrepancy according to some thresholds, the monitoring manager would notify the contract manager that would flag a contract as either violated (i.e., late identification of platforms) or failed (i.e., late confirmation of delegation request). Otherwise, the contract manager flags the contract as successful.

5.2 Deploying the Microservices

While chore$\mathcal{O}$rchest makes decisions about where to deploy microservices, the execution manager implements these decisions. Both have been developed using Java-based Spring Boot framework. Regarding the microservices, each was endowed with its own REST endpoint interface and containerized as a Docker image deployed on Kubernetes that runs on AWS. Finally, Kafka was used as an event streaming platform to allow microservices publish, subscribe, store, and process events.

For experimentation purposes, our scenario about farming included 7 microservices as per Table 2. This number has been doubled to have a good sample of microservices to deploy over the different run-time platforms including 2 clouds, 1 edge, and 1 thing featured with 4 GB, 2 GB, and 1 GB of RAM, respectively. Table 3 illustrates the event-based communication between these microservices.

During the experimentation, the microservices are submitted to the execution manager that deploys them on the available platforms based on the strategy implementation

Table 3. Event-based communication between the microservices.

Microservice	Subscribed events	Issued events
ms_1	Every day at 8am or Receipt of farmer request	Sudden drop in temperature (e_1)
ms_2	e_1	Low-pressure (e_2)
	e_3	Announcement of storm (e_5)
ms_3	e_2	Instability in humidity variation (e_3) or Chance of high rain (e_4)
ms_4	e_4	Open burning for crop management and for trash/debris removal (e_6)
	e_5	Cleared soil (e_7) or no risk (e_8)
ms_5	e_6	Alarm raised (e_9)
ms_6	e_7	Human-assistance needed (e_{10})
ms_7	e_8	Sprinklers blocked (e_{11})

Table 4. Performance measures.

Microservice	choreOrchest host choice time (ms)			Total microservice deployment time (ms)			Host type
	Max	Min	Avg	Max	Min	Avg	
ms_1	2929	2243	2611	25228	23939	24504	Thing
ms_2	5633	4217	4831	29063	26894	27894	Edge
ms_3	4768	4081	4387	21986	15989	18070	Edge
ms_4	5067	4121	4518	22164	16406	18446	Edge
ms_5	4865	4088	4430	22352	16060	18141	Edge
ms_6	4782	4107	4435	22415	16337	18034	Edge
ms_7	4930	4080	4453	22697	16177	18123	Edge
ms_8	7705	6796	7243	31112	29022	29995	Cloud
ms_9	7161	6653	6928	20611	19514	19997	Cloud
ms_{10}	7162	6709	6913	20255	19542	19907	Cloud
ms_{11}	7170	6680	6894	20879	19483	19992	Cloud
ms_{12}	7383	6684	6920	20476	19538	20012	Cloud
ms_{13}	7247	6409	6882	20647	19598	20043	Cloud
ms_{14}	7448	6823	7053	21354	19931	20751	Cloud

defined by choreOrchest. For each microservice, 3 deployment runs were performed at 3 different times of the day totaling 9 deployment runs. To assess the system's performance, we measured choreOrchest's host choice time and the total microservice deployment time per run. Table 4 contains the maximum, minimum, and average values per microservice.

5.3 Materializing the Contracts

To regulate microservices deployment over platforms using contracts, we conducted a series of experiments to compute the average execution time of the monitoring and contract managers. Due to the limited availability of real datasets that could satisfy our technical needs and requirements, we resorted to creating 2 datasets ($d1$ and $d2$) during the pre-execution stage and using our existing dataset ($d3$) that was obtained from Table 4. Table 5 reports details about each dataset in terms of number of microservices, number of platforms, and QoS values whether real or generated.

Table 5. Details about the datasets of the experiments [17].

dataset	# of microservices	# of platforms	real QoS values	generated QoS values
$d1$	1050	30	–	discovery time, deployment time, execution time, hosting level, offloading time
$d2$	20	510	–	discovery time, deployment time, execution time, hosting level, offloading time
$d3$	15	30	deployment time, offloading time	discovery time, execution time, hosting level

Table 6. Impact of number of microservices on the monitoring and contract managers [17].

# of microservices	average execution time in ms
50	709,1
150	2587,3
250	5567,0
350	7837,3
450	11344,7
550	16044,2
650	20823,4
750	27248,6
850	34761,7
950	42227,3
1050	49351,0

The first series of experiments were applied to $d1$ evaluating the impact of incrementing by 100 the number of microservices from 50 to 1050 on the average execution time of both managers. Each experiment was executed 10 times. Table 6 shows that the average execution time increases exponentially with the number of microservices. However, even with a large number of microservices, the achieved performance remains acceptable. In the second series of experiments that were applied to $d2$, we evaluated the impact of incrementing by 50 the number of platforms from 50 to 500 on the average execution time of both managers. As expected, the average execution time increases exponentially with the number of platforms as per Table 7. However, even with a large number of platforms, we still achieve an acceptable performance.

To conclude the series of experiments, we conducted two more. The first one was applied to *d2* with exactly 30 platforms resulting into an average execution time of 187,4 ms for both managers. Finally, the second one was applied to *d3* checking the validity of the previous experiment's results. The average execution time of both managers is 184,4 ms which is in line with these results.

Table 7. Impact of number of platforms on the monitoring and contract managers [17].

# of platforms	average execution time in ms
50	479,7
100	2087
150	4998
200	10116,6
250	15316,4
300	22947,9
350	31323,8
400	39518,9
450	55676,8
500	69392,2

6   Conclusion

In this chapter, we presented a contract-based approach for the deployment of microservices in an ecosystem of edge, cloud, and IoT platforms. On the one hand, the approach through chore𝒪rchest mixes orchestration and choreography to make on-the-fly deployment decisions based on types of things, properties of resources, and forms of interactions. Prior to validating chore𝒪rchest using a microservice-based application for farming, the chapter adopted contracts to enforce the deployment of microservices. On the one hand, contracts included discovery, deployment, and collaboration illustrating the multi-facet complexity of managing microservices. To demonstrate the technical doability of the contract-based approach, a system's architecture was first, designed identifying the necessary repositories, chore𝒪rchest, and managers, all implemented in Java. The system supported different experiments examining for instance, the impact of increasing the number of microservices on the performance of the system's managers.

In term of future work, we would like to address the 2 following questions related to monitoring and enforcement: how to assess the performance of contracts and how to proceed with their renewals without impacting ongoing contracts are some monitoring-related; and how to build trust among all the stakeholders for long-term collaboration.

Acknowledgements. The authors would like to thank Fadwa Yahya, Mohammad Askar, Vanilson Arruda Burégio, and Edvan Soares for their contributions to the work reported in this chapter.

References

1. Abdmeziem, M.R., Tandjaoui, D., Romdhani, I.: Architecting the internet of things: state of the art. In: Koubaa, A., Shakshuki, E. (eds.) Robots and Sensor Clouds. SSDC, vol. 36, pp. 55–75. Springer, Cham (2016). https://doi.org/10.1007/978-3-319-22168-7_3
2. Ali, S., Jarwar, M., Chong, I.: Design methodology of microservices to support predictive analytics for IoT applications. Sensors 18(12), 4226 (2018)
3. Balint, F., Truong, H.: On supporting contract-aware IoT dataspace services. In: IEEE International Conference on Mobile Cloud Computing, Services, and Engineering. San Francisco, USA (2017)
4. Barnaghi, P., Sheth, A.: On searching the internet of things: requirements and challenges. IEEE Intell. Syst. 31(6), 71–75 (2016)
5. Bonomi, F., Milito, R., Natarajan, P., Zhu, J.: Fog computing: a platform for internet of things and analytics. In: Bessis, N., Dobre, C. (eds.) Big Data and Internet of Things: A Roadmap for Smart Environments. SCI, vol. 546, pp. 169–186. Springer, Cham (2014). https://doi.org/10.1007/978-3-319-05029-4_7
6. Butzin, B., Golatowski, F., Timmermann, D.: Microservices approach for the internet of things. In: Proceedings of the 21st IEEE International Conference on Emerging Technologies and Factory Automation (ETFA'2016). Berlin, Germany (2016)
7. Štefanič, P., Rana, O., Stankovski, V.: Budget and performance-efficient application deployment along edge-fog-cloud ecosystem. In: Proceedings of the 11th International Workshop on Science Gateways (IWSG'2019). Ljubljana, Slovenia (2019)
8. Chung, J., Chao, K.: A view on service-oriented architecture. Serv. Oriented Comput. Appl. 1(2), 93–95 (2007). https://doi.org/10.1007/s11761-007-0011-2
9. De Donno, M., Tange, K., Dragoni, N.: Foundations and evolution of modern computing paradigms: Cloud, IoT, Edge, and Fog. IEEE Access 7, 150936–150948 (2019)
10. DZone: the internet of things, application, protocols, and best practices (2017). https://dzone.com/guides/iot-applications-protocols-and-best-practices
11. Ghosh, A., Khalid, O., Bin Rais, R., Rehman, A., Malik, S., Ali Khan, I.: Data offloading in IoT Environments: modeling, analysis, and verification. EURASIP J. Wireless Commun. Network. 2019, 53 (2019)
12. Lewis, J., Fowler, M.: Microservices (2014). http://martinfowler.com/articles/microservices.html
13. Longo, A., Zappatore, M., Bochicchio, M.A.: A cloud-based approach to dynamically manage service contracts for local public transportation. Int. J. Grid Util. Comput. 10(6), 694 (2019). https://doi.org/10.1504/IJGUC.2019.102750
14. Maamar, Z., Baker, T., Faci, N., Ugljanin, E., Al-Khafajiy, M., Burégio, V.: Towards a seamless coordination of cloud and fog: illustration through the internet-of-things. In: Proceedings of the 34th ACM/SIGAPP Symposium on Applied Computing (SAC'2019). Limassol, Cyprus (2019)
15. Maamar, Z., Baker, T., Sellami, M., Asim, M., Ugljanin, E., Faci, N.: Cloud vs edge: who serves the Internet-of-things better. Int. Technol. Lett. 1(5), e66 (2018). https://doi.org/10.1002/itl2.66
16. Maamar, Z., Faci, N., Sakr, S., Boukhebouze, M., Barnawi, A.: Network-based social coordination of business processes. Inf. Syst. 58, 56–74 (2016). https://doi.org/10.1016/j.is.2016.02.005

17. Maamar, Z., N., F., El Haddad, J., Yahya, F., Askar, M.: Multi-party contract management for microservices. In: Proceedings of the 17th International Conference on Software Technologies (ICSOFT'2022). Lisbon, Portugal (2022)
18. Marino, F., Moiso, C., Petracca, M.: Automatic contract negotiation, service discovery and mutual authentication solutions: a survey on the enabling technologies of the forthcoming IoT ecosystems. Comput. Netw. **148**, 176–195 (2019)
19. Mendez-Bonilla, O., Franch, X., Quer, C.: Requirements patterns for COTS systems. In: Proceedings of the Seventh International Conference on Composition-Based Software Systems (ICCBSS'2008). Madrid, Spain (2008)
20. Nieves, E., Hernández, G., Gil González, A., Rodríguez-González, S., Corchado, J.: Fog computing architecture for personalized recommendation of banking products. Expert Syst. with Appl. **140**, 112900 (2020)
21. Pan, J., Wang, J., Hester, A., AlQerm, I., Liu, Y., Zhao, Y.: EdgeChain: an edge-IoT framework and prototype based on blockchain and smart contracts. IEEE Internet Things J. **6**(3) 4719–4732 (2018)
22. Puliafito, C., Mingozzi, E., Longo, F., Puliafito, A., Rana, O.: Fog computing for the internet of things: a survey. ACM Trans. Internet Technol. **19**(2), 1–41 (2019)
23. Qin, Y., Sheng, Q., Falkner, N., Dustdar, S., Wang, H., Vasilakos, A.: When things matter: a data-centric view of the internet of things. CoRR abs/1407.2704 (2014)
24. Satyanarayanan, M., Bahl, P., Cáceres, R., Davies, N.: The case for VM-based cloudlets in mobile computing. IEEE Pervasive Comput. **8**(4) (2009)
25. Thramboulidis, K., Vachtsevanou, D., Kontou, I.: CPuS-IoT: a cyber-physical microservice and IoT-based framework for manufacturing assembly systems. Annu. Rev. Control. **47**, 237–248 (2019)
26. Valderas, P., Torres, V., Pelechano, V.: A microservice composition approach based on the choreography of BPMN fragments. Inf. Soft. Technol. **127**, 106370 (2020)
27. Varghese, B., Wang, N., Nikolopoulos, D., Buyya, R.: Feasibility of fog computing. arXiv preprint arXiv:1701.05451 (2017)
28. Weiser, M.: The computer for the 21st century. Newslett. ACM SIGMOBILE Mobile Comput. Commun. Rev. **3**(3), 3–11 (1999)
29. Zorzi, M., Gluhak, A., Lange, S., Bassi, A.: From today's Intranet of things to a future Internet of things: a wireless- and mobility-related view. IEEE Wireless Commun. **17**(6), 44–51 (2010)

A Decision Model Based on an Optimized Choquet Integral: Multifactor Prediction and Intelligent Agriculture Application

Yann Pollet[1]([✉]) [iD], Jérôme Dantan[2] [iD], and Hajer Baazaoui[3] [iD]

[1] CEDRIC EA4629, Cnam, Paris, France
yann.pollet@cnam.fr
[2] Interact UP 2018.C102, Institut Polytechnique UniLasalle, Mont-Saint-Aignan, France
[3] ETIS UMR 8051, CY University, ENSEA, CNRS, Cergy, France

Abstract. Smart farming aims at improving agriculture production by using artificial intelligence and smart devices and, in continuity, farming optimization aims at supporting autonomous decision-making to maximize crop yield. In this context, the question of predicting the future days of growth stages transition of a plant is still a challenge, as existing automated predictions are not accurate nor reliable enough to be effectively used in the farming process. We propose here an approach based on Choquet integral, performing an aggregation of multiple imperfect predictions into a more accurate and reliable one, considering the specific relevance of various prediction sources as well as interactions, synergies, or redundancies between them. To identify the numerous parameter values defining the Choquet-based decision model, we propose a generic approach of optimization based on observed history, ensuring a reduced sensitivity to parameters, thanks to a principle of less specificity. Our proposal defines so an evaluation function assigning to any potential solution a predictive capability, quantifying the conformance of its outputs to evidence, as well as an associated optimization process based on the satisfaction degrees regarding a set of stated inequalities. The case study concerns an implemented prototype that enables, for a given culture and several input sources, to help farmers, providing them with better predictions of the growth stages. We also analyze the reliability of the process, enabling the assignment of an objective probabilistic criteria to any provided prediction. The experimental results are very encouraging, the predicted day remaining stable despite presence of noise and local errors.

Keywords: Choquet integral · Decision model · Parameters identification · Smart farming applications

1 Introduction

Rapid population growth has increased the demand for food production and hence the pressure among farmers to meet customer demand. We consider here the agricultural domain, a strategic area where, today, a major issue consists in increasing field productivity while respecting the natural environment and farms sustainability, requiring the development of advanced decision support tools supporting the farmer's day-to-day decision process.

In this context, a key issue in maximizing crop efficiency is this of making reliable predictions regarding growth stage transitions of plants, especially dates of transitions from a present stage to the next one enabling the farmer to prepare and perform relevant actions at the best instant with a maximized impact on efficiency (e.g., triggering irrigation, adjusting water flow, adding precisely optimized quantity of intrants, ...). Such predictions should be based on various available sources of information, that deliver in practice more or less accurate and reliable information [9].

In this context, multi-criteria decision requires use of aggregation functions, such as fuzzy integrals, among those the well-known integral of Choquet. This latter is defined from a fuzzy measure representing not only the relative importance of the various criteria but also the possible interactions between them [2]. Choquet integral will be used here as an operator of aggregation, in charge of fusing multiple imperfect predictions into a more certain and accurate one, exploiting source diversity to get a more significant and reliable information for guiding decisions.

In this paper, we focus on the Choquet integral, proposing a parametric model for data aggregation. We put our interest on an application of smart farming, proposing a generic way to identify the parameters of a growth stage prediction model. We point out that in a previous work [7], we proposed a fuzzy decision support environment for smart farming ensuring better data structuration extracted from farms, and automated calculations, reducing the risk of missing operations.

Our aim here is to identify the parameters of a Choquet-based decision model using a training dataset including past data delivered by available sources jointed the corresponding observed evidence, proposing a set of optimized parameter values. Our proposal defines 1) a function enabling to evaluate the prediction capability of any potential solution based on a set of inequalities, standing for the evidence this model enables to satisfy, 2) an algorithm adapted from the classical gradient descent and providing a robust solution, 3) a way to objectively evaluate in operation the reliability of the made prediction in each case.

Our operator, based on Choquet integral, should apply ponderations to each information source, considering possible interactions, synergy complementarity, or, conversely, partial redundancy, between them. It will transform the input fuzzy sets delivered to sources into a new fuzzy set aggregating the input sources and delivering a global value of confidence based on several source-dependent inputs. The solution to our problem will be the optimum of our evaluation function, the obtained evaluation value quantifying both the ability of the solution to make right predictions and the robustness of this solution. This approach has been validated on data issued from a set of fields, on several years.

This paper focuses on a study in the agricultural domain aiming at improving smart technologies. The originality of our proposal relies on one hand on identifying a model only using conformance to stated inequalities, not requiring values of a function to be learnt, and on the other hand, on the robustness of the obtained solution due to its least specificity, reducing so the sensitivity to the defaults of training data.

The remainder of this paper is organized as follows. Section 2 presents the preliminaries and related works. Section 3 is dedicated to a formalization of our problem. Then, in Sect. 4, we detail our proposal and its main components, and present the algorithm enabling to identify the parameters of the Choquet integral. Section 5 presents a model of decision based on our approach and then, the obtain numerical results on the chosen case study and their interpretation are presented and discussed in Sect. 6. Finally, we conclude and present our future work in Sect. 7.

2 State of the Art and Motivations

In this section, we first present preliminaries, and an overview of the related research concerning Choquet integral and decision models along with our motivations and objectives, and we shall then consider related works.

2.1 Smart Farming Applications and Systems: Motivations

The present issue falls into the developments of Smart Applications and Systems, that aims at meeting the requirements of next generation agricultural processes, and more especially these of precision farming [13]. Smart farming approach consists in deploying computer-based systems enabling the control of all actions on a culture, based on information collected from terrain. The objective is to provide a smart support to the farmer, executing automatized actions at the right time (e.g., watering), or informing they of actions to be manually performed (e.g., adding a specified quantity of intrant).

In this context, a key aspect in smart farming is this of building estimations of present and future states of development of the controlled culture, based on available pieces of information, processing and consolidating them to obtain the best possible picture of reality at t instant, as well as projections into the future. Theses estimations should be reconsidered and rightly updated at any time with arrival of new pieces of information.

We consider here the case of surveillance of a culture with prediction of growth stages (*phenological stages*) of a plant [10]. The plant being in a stage S, the objective is to predict the future day of transition d toward the next stage S'. Each existing source delivering its own imperfect prediction, the system must build a relevant aggregation of the delivered data to deliver a better prediction, i.e., a more reliable and more accurate one.

The overall functional architecture of our prediction process is presented on the figure below. We have three levels, with 1) sensor and data acquisition level (including terrain sensors, aircraft and sattelite images acquisition, external data collection through web services invokation), 2) the level of prediction sources, i.e. the various algorithms in charge of performing exprimental or more complex predictions, and at last 3) the global aggregation level. The most general case being this of n sources of prediction, we shall consider here, as an illustrative example, the case of 3 input sources (cf. Fig. 1).

Commonly used predictions sources are:

- Empirical « Degree Days» calculation [13], based on a cumulation of daily observed min-max temperatures differences, quantity that should have to meet a given known threshold, specific to plant and to considered phase.

- NDVI (Normalized Difference Vegetation Index), processed from visible and Infrared reflectance extracted from satellite images.
- Interpolation from statistical tables.

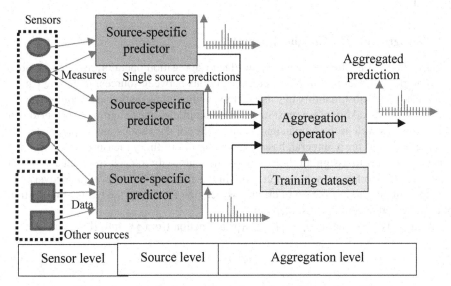

Fig. 1. Functional schema of growth stages prediction (from [9]).

An available dataset, containing evidence and past predictions, may be geometrically represented in of 2-dimensional factorial chart, thanks to a principal component analysis, giving typical results such as the simplified one (cf. Fig. 2).

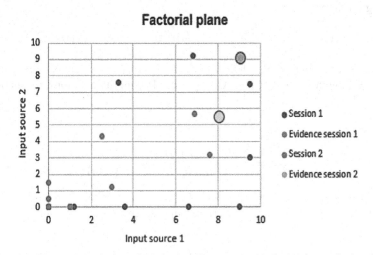

Fig. 2. Simplified representation of a Principal Component Analysis of a prediction dataset.

We can see there is no way to clearly separate transition and non-transition days by a simple hyperplane, or even by more complex classifiers, the reason being simply confidences delivered by sources are just relative values inside a given session of prediction (i.e., an instance of culture on a period), a level having no absolute quantitative meaning by itself.

2.2 Background: The Choquet Integral

Choquet integral is often adopted as multifactor agregation operator, as it has an ability to properly model multiple types of interactions between sources, including partial redundancy and substituability of some factors, with minimal hypothesis required on the nature of data. In addition, we must mention its simplicity of calculation to be perfomed at real time, as well as the human understandability of the various model parameters.

The notion of fuzzy integral, based on the concept of fuzzy measure [2], also called capacity, enables to assign a relative importance, not only to each individual decision criterion, but also for any subset of criteria. In the context of multi-criteria analysis, the weight or importance of the set of criteria association influences the entire combination of criteria, which could be also defined.

A capacity μ on the set $\mathcal{N} = \{1, ..., n\}$ is a function from $2^{\mathcal{N}}$ into IR^+, such as:

$$\mu(\emptyset) = 0 \tag{1}$$

$$\mu(\mathcal{N}) = 1 \tag{2}$$

$$\forall S \subseteq \mathcal{N}, \forall T \subseteq \mathcal{N}, S \subseteq T \Rightarrow \mu(S) \leq \mu(T) \text{ (monotony)} \tag{3}$$

The discrete Choquet integral related to the capacity μ is then defined as the function that associates to any n-uple $x = (x_1, ..., x_n) \in IR^n$ a value $C_\mu \in IR+$, defined by the following formula:

$$C_\mu(x_1, ..., x_n) := \sum_{i=1} i = n(\mu(A_{\sigma(i)}) - \mu(A_{\sigma(i+1)})).x_{\sigma(i)} \tag{4}$$

where σ is a permutation on $\mathcal{N}$ such as $X_{\sigma(1)} \leq ... \leq X_{\sigma(n)}$, and where $A_{\sigma(i)} := \{\sigma(i) ..., \sigma(n)\}, \forall i \in \mathcal{N}$, with, by convention, $A_{\sigma(n+1)} := \emptyset$. . To simplify notations, we shall write, for $i_1, ..., i_p, p \leq n$:

$$\mu(\{i\}) = \mu_i$$
$$\mu(\{i, j\}) = \mu_{i,j}, \quad (i \neq j) \tag{5}$$
$$\mu(\{i, j, k\}) = \mu_{i,j,k}(i \neq j, j \neq k, k \neq i)$$

In a decision process, x_i inputs will be the values attached to considered evaluation criteria. With $n = 1$, i.e., with just two criteria, the Choquet integral formula (4) becomes simply:

$$x_1 \leq x_2 \Rightarrow C_\mu(x_1, x_2) = (\mu_{1,2} - \mu_2) \cdot x_1 + \mu_2 \cdot x_2$$
$$x_1 > x_2 \Rightarrow C_\mu(x_1, x_2) = \mu_1 \cdot x_1 + (\mu_{1,2} - \mu_1) \cdot x_2 \tag{6}$$

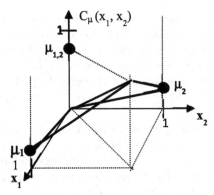

Fig. 3. Graph of a Choquet Integral, in the case of two variables on $[0, 1]^2$ domain.

as illustrated in Fig. 3, in the case where x_i values belong to $[0,1]$.

Graph of a C_μ function is always constituted of a set of hyperplanes sections defined on each convex polytope $0 \leq X_{\sigma(1)} \leq X_{\sigma(2)} \cdots \leq X_{\sigma(n)}$. The function C_μ is continuous, and derivable except on some singularities, the discrete Choquet integral being so the unique linear interpolation of a function defined on the vertices of the unit hypercube $[0,1]^n$, i.e., on points $M(1_S, 0_{N-S})$, $\forall S \subseteq \mathcal{N} = \{1, ..., n\}.$

A particular case of Choquet integral is the simple weighted sum $\sum_i \alpha_i \cdot x_i$ (with $\sum_i \alpha_i = 1$). In the most general case, with any values of capacity $\mu(S), S \subseteq \mathcal{N}$, Choquet integral generalises a classical weight vector. Limit cases of Choquet integral are the Min and Max operators, that respectively corrresponds to the limit capacities $\mu_i = \mu_{i,j} = \ldots = 1$ (Max operator) and $\mu_i = \mu_{i,j} = 0, \ldots$, except $\mu_\mathcal{N} = 1$(Min operator):

$$\text{Min}(x_1, \ldots, x_n) \leq C_\mu(x_1, \ldots, x_n) \leq \text{Max}(x_1, \ldots, x_n) \qquad (7)$$

The cross terms $\mu_{i,j}$, and more generally $\mu_{i,j,k}$, .., enable to consider pairs, or more generally subsets of non-additive criteria. In the case of a pair of criteria, we may have so:

- Synergistic criteria: $\mu_{i,j} > \mu_i + \mu_j$ (super-additive effect)
- Redundant criteria: $\mu_{i,j} < \mu_i + \mu_j$ (sub-additive effect)
- Independent (complementary) criteria : $\mu_{i,j} = \mu_i + \mu_j$ (additive effect)

The Choquet integral so enables the representation of non-additive criteria, i.e., with interactions between pairs or groups of more than two criteria. Its interest consists mainly in considering in decision possible relevant interactions between groups of factors.

2.3 Related Work

The Choquet integral is based on two fundamental concepts: (1) utility; a function which aims to model the preferences of the decision maker. Utility functions can be seen as making it possible to translate the values of the attribute into a satisfaction degree [4]. They are commensurable, monotonic and ascending because if an alternative a is preferred to b then u (a) $\geq$ u (b) [8]; (2) capacity: models the fuzzy measure on which the integral is based and summarizes the importance of the criteria (the weight vector traditionally used in additives) by aggregating utility functions. The learning ability of the Choquet integral has been demonstrated, mainly in [6]. Functions dealing with data mining issues such as least square and linear programming have been used in this context. Preference learning consists in observing and learning the preferences of an individual, precisely in particular when ordering a set of alternatives, to predict automatic scheduling of a new set of alternatives [7].

The Choquet integral learning function is based on a set of concepts that make it possible to leverage the consideration of user preferences (or decisions) and the interaction and/or synergy between the various criteria for data aggregation. Given a preferential ordering on a sample learning, the discrete Choquet integral enable to quantify, then learn, the relative weights of the different quality metrics.

In the literature, fuzzy integrals have been used for different purposes, for preferences or opinions fusion from a variety of sources, and several applications and extensions of fuzzy integrals have been developed. In [3], the authors have proven that the use of fuzzy neural network is more effective than the decision tree algorithms often used in the literature. The fuzzy neural network model allows precision improvement and less redundancy in decision-making.

In our previous work, we have proven that applying Choquet's integral to order data sources according to the user's preferences, is an interesting and challenging area of research and can lead to more relevant results [5]. One originality of the work described in this paper consists in the proposal of an evaluation function attaching to any potential solution a degree of acceptability, based on truth degrees of inequalities.

In [13] the importance of utilizing machine learning techniques in smart farming was demonstrated for end-users and experts in agriculture. The data mining techniques applied in smart farming problems offer numerous solutions to farmers in a variety of applications in the farming industry. The authors focus on yield forecasting, harvest time, crop information and best variety to plant next season, which can be provided to different end-users and experts. In [14], the authors distinguished the categories of cocoa beans and the differences between them. The proposal aims at adaptively accumulating contextual representations and introduces a contextual memory cell to progressively select contextual statistics. The authors simultaneously correlate contextual relationships to guide high-level representation retaining more detailed information, which helps to discriminate small variations in smart farming application task management. In [15] the authors proposed a Pythagorean fuzzy set (PFS) with Choquet Integral model integrated for vertical farming technology evaluation. They characterize the most feasible option from a group of vertical farming technologies considering a group of decision makers' opinions. The Vertical farming alternatives are assessed, and a suitable option is detected for the farm.

To meet the related works limitations, the originality of our proposal lies in answering famers' requirements by defining an approach of optimization, based on observation history, ensuring a reduced sensitivity to input data thanks to a principle of less specificity. A function assigning to any potential solution a predictive capability, quantifying the conformance of its outputs to evidence, as well as an associated optimisation process based on a degree of satisfaction regarding a set of stated inequalities.

3   Problem Statement

Considering a crop with n prediction sources, information delivered by a source will consists in a sequence of confidence levels $x_i(d) \in [0, 1]$ attached to future days 1, ..., D, given a temporal horizon of D days. $x_i(d)$ reflect the belief of the ith source regarding the occurrence of transition from the present phenological stage to the next one exactly at d day (cf. Fig. 4). We have so as many functions $d \in \{1, ..., D\} \rightarrow x_i(d) \in [0, 1]$ as prediction sources i = 1, ..., n, and $x_i(d)$ can be seen as a membership function of a fuzzy subset of $\{1, ..., D\}$, 0 meaning a null confidence, and 1 the maximum one.

No hypothesis is made on confidence levels semantics. One must point out these levels are not probabilities, only inequalities between two values issued from the same source at the same session of prediction being here significant. Note the case with several days having all a 1 value is possible, reflecting an inaccuracy of the prediction.

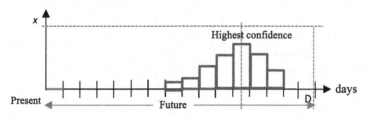

Fig. 4. A fuzzy prediction on a temporal horizon of D days (from [9]).

We use Choquet integral as an operator of aggregation, in charge of fusing the later n fuzzy predictions into a more certain and accurate one. It is expected from the combination of partially independent sources a more significant and reliable prediction for guiding decision. This operator will have to apply proper ponderations to each information source, considering possible, a priori unknown, interactions, synergy complementarity, or, at contrary, partial redundancy, between them. The Choquet integral will transform n fuzzy subsets into a result fuzzy subset, aggregating the n input sources. Our goal is to enable an automated estimation of Choquet integral coefficients based on a recorded history, i.e., on a set of past source prediction sessions in addition to the corresponding observed evidence at the same session.

$X = (x_1, ..., x_n)$ denoting a confidence vector, n being the number of sources, the training dataset consists in P sessions regarding the same plant, a session being related to a field at a given time period. For each session, we have a sequence of X(d), prediction vectors for days d = 1, ..., D, in addition to d_{Tr}, the real day of transition, unknow at prediction time but a posteriori observed for this session.

Available information may be expressed with a set of R = (D-1).P inequalities:

$$C_\mu(X_k) < C_\mu\left(X_{evidence(k)}\right) \qquad (8)$$

with k and evidence(k) $\in$ [1, D.P], evidence(k) $\neq$ k being the d_{Tr} transition day for the session containing day k.

Our problem is to learn a μ capacity, i.e. the values of the $2^n - 2$ parameters μ_i, $\mu_{i,j}$, $\mu_{i,j,k}$, $\cdots$ satisfying the above inequalities. Despite some of them may be trivially satisfied by any Choquet integral, i.e., for any μ, we keep them as input data of our problem, intensities of differences being considered here as significant pieces of information. It is the same for inequalities implicitly satisfied by transitivity, e.g., $C_\mu(X) < C_\mu(Z)$, if $X < Y$ and $C_\mu(Y) < C_\mu(Z)$.

Based on Choquet integral definition (4), input information may be expressed under the form of R inequalities, applying on linear expressions:

$$a_1^k \cdot \mu_1 + \ldots + a_n^k \mu_n + a_{1,1}^k \cdot \mu_{1,2} + \ldots + a_{n-1,n}^k \cdot \mu_{n-1,n} + \ldots + a_{1,\ldots,n}^k \cdot \mu_{1,\ldots,n} > 0, k = 1, \ldots, R \tag{9}$$

That is, using a matrix notation:

$$[A]_{k \cdot [\mu]} > 0, k = 1, \ldots, R \tag{10}$$

where $[A]_k$ is the $(2^n\text{-}1)$ row vector $\left[a^k, \ldots, a_n^k, a_{1,1}^k, \ldots, a_{n-1,n}^k, \ldots\ldots, a_{1,\ldots,n}^k \right]$ and $[\mu]$ the $(2^n\text{-}1)$ column vector $\left[\mu_1, \ldots, \mu_n, \mu_{1,1}, \ldots, \mu_{n-1,n}, \ldots, \mu_{1,\ldots,n} \right]$

That we may denote:

$$[A] \cdot [\mu] > 0 \tag{11}$$

$[A]$ being the rectangular matrix build with rows $[A]_k$.

And coefficients μ_i, $\mu_{i,j}$, $\mu_{i,j,k}$, etc., satisfying the minimal set of constraints:

$$\mu_i \leq \mu_{i,j}, \forall i, j; i \neq j$$
$$\mu_{i,j} \leq \mu_{i,j,k}, \forall i, j, k; i \neq j, j \neq k, k \neq i \tag{12}$$
$$\ldots$$

With $\mu_i \geq 0$, $\forall i$, and $\mu_{1,\ldots,n} = 1$

that may be more concisely expressed by:

$$\mu(S) \leq \mu(S') ; |S'| = |S| + 1, S \subset S' \tag{13}$$

$$\text{with } \mu(\emptyset) = 0 \text{ and } \mu_{1,\ldots,n} = \mu(2^N) \leq 1$$

We have here no values regarding a function to be learnt, but only a set of statements regarding inequalities. So, a direct identification method of the Choquet integral is not applicable. For building the solution, we are expecting 1) a scalable algorithm, i.e., that will be efficient for a huge training dataset with a time of execution linearly increasing with respect to the number of sessions P. In addition, 2) we consider data as potentially inaccurate, the solution having to be robust in case of conflicting examples, i.e., able to tolerate some local "nearly satisfied" inequalities. At last, 3) we are expecting a solution easily improvable by increments when new data are acquired.

4 Proposed Approach

Except in singular cases, inequalities (9) and (12) have either zero or an infinity of solutions. In practice, as numerous x_i, provided by sources are not perfect values, local violations of a inequalities (2) should be accepted. So, we do not consider only exact solutions, but all potential solutions with a μ vector satisfying the only strict inequalities (5) related to a regular capacity definition. On this domain of potential solutions, we shall optimize an evaluation function reflecting the expected characteristics considered above, to get the best solution.

4.1 Evaluation Function

Considering a given μ capacity, the empirical distribution of $[A]_k.[\mu]$ values on $[-1, 1]$, associated to a dataset, looks as the following histogram (cf. Fig. 5). We must choose as solution the μ capacity such as this distribution has the less as possible negative values (i.e., the most possible number of correct predictions), and so the greatest as possible positive values, according to a principle of lowest specificity of the expected solution. This is illustrated on the Fig. 5, case 2 being better than case 1, ideal case being this where all $[A]_k.[\mu]$ are exactly equal to 1.

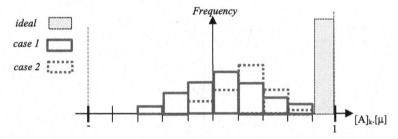

Fig. 5. Several fuzzy predictions on a temporal horizon of D days.

To meet such an expected distribution of $[A]_k.[\mu]$ values, we choose to minimize an additive cost function having the following form:

$$\Phi(\mu) = \sum_{k=1, \dots, R} \varphi([A]_k[\mu]) \tag{14}$$

where φ is a function : $[-1, 1]^m \to \mathbb{R}+$ continue, strictly decreasing, and C1 class, with:

$\varphi(1) = 0$ (case of a perfect compliance to required inequality).

$\varphi(x)$ being maximum for $x = -1$ (worst ordering).

φ being in addition strictly convex.

The fact that $\forall \delta x > 0$, $\varphi(-\delta x) + \varphi(\delta x) > 2.\varphi(0)$, resulting from convexity, will give us the guarantee that a local ordering defect corresponding to $-\delta x$ is not compensated by a positive margin of same intensity δx.

So, we can choose a local cost function:

$$\varphi(x) = -L \cdot \log_2(1/2.(x+1))\$, with\$L \in IR^+ + \qquad (15)$$

Normalizing the expression of $\varphi(x)$ with respect to R, number of inequality statements, we get:

$$\Phi(\mu) = -(1/R) \cdot \sum\nolimits_{k=1,\ldots,R} \log_2(1/2 \cdot ([A]_k.[\mu] + 1)) \qquad (16)$$

This quantity quantifies the average "degree of order" with respect to evidence present in results delivered by C_μ integral, expressing thus the predictive capability of C_μ with the chosen μ capacity. This order reflects both the crispness of the aggregated prediction and its degree of matching with observed reality.

We can remark φ is infinite for $x = -1$, i.e.:

$$\lim\nolimits_{\delta \to -1} \varphi(\delta) = +\infty \qquad (17)$$

corresponding to the case of a worst ordering, Fig. 6 showing the graphical representation of φ function.

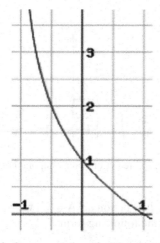

Fig. 6. Graphical representation of $\varphi(x) = \log_2(1/2.(x+1))$.

This definition of Φ appears as a particular case of a more general family of functions:

$$\Phi_v(\mu) = -(1/R) \cdot \sum\nolimits_{k=1,\ldots,R} \log_2\left(v\left([A]_{k\cdot[\mu]}\right)\right) \qquad (18)$$

$v(\delta)$ being a fuzzy comparator, i.e. a non-decreasing function associating to any $\delta = [A]_k \cdot [\mu] \in [-1, 1]$ a value $\in [0,1]$, standing for the degree of truth of an assertion $[C_\mu(X_d) < C_\mu(X_{Evidence(d)})]$. v may be, for example, $v(\delta) = 1/2 \cdot \lambda \cdot (1 + erf((\sqrt{2} \cdot \delta))$, where erf is the Gauss error function, enabling us to take into account a known inaccuracy of input values x. Our first expression corresponds just to the case where v is just the

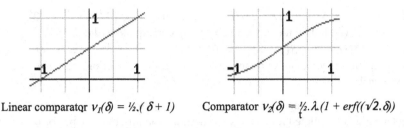

Linear comparator $v_1(\delta) = \frac{1}{2}.(\delta + 1)$ Comparator $v_2(\delta) = \frac{1}{2}.\lambda.(1 + erf((\sqrt{2}.\delta))$

Fig. 7. Graphical representation of two comparators.

linear comparator $v(\delta) = 1/2 \cdot (\delta + 1)$, Fig. 7 giving a comparison of the two definitions of v comparator:

Note that another choice for Φ would be an energy-like functions having the following definition.

$$\Phi(\mu) = \sum_{k=1,...,R} (Exp(-K.1/2 \cdot ([A]_k.[\mu] + 1)) - Exp(-K)) \qquad (19)$$

Note also that these functions may be approximated by a family of simple quadratic functions such as, for example:

$$\Phi(\mu) = \sum_{k=1,...,R} ([A]_k.[\mu] - 1) \cdot ((2 - 4 \cdot \alpha) \cdot ([A]_k.[\mu] - 1) \qquad (20)$$

where α is the expected value of the function φ at $x = 0.5$.

4.2 A Measure of Order

More generally, one can associate to any fuzzy prediction y, y(d), d = 1, ..., D, either coming from a single source, either issued from a multisource aggregation process, a quantity S reflecting it actual lack of information in comparison to independently observed evidence, value standing for a quantity of disorder. It is given by the formula (15), evaluated on the only considered session of prediction, i.e., on the fuzzy subset y given as input:

$$S(y) = (1/(D - 1)). \sum_{d=1,...,D,\, d \neq dp} \varphi\big(y(d_p) - y(d)\big) \qquad (21)$$

where $y(d_p)$ is the prediction regarding the day of transition d_p, and where $\varphi(\delta y) = -log2(1/2 \cdot (\delta y + 1))$. We can equivalently consider a quality factor defined by:

$$Q(y) = 2^{-Sys)} \in [0, 1] \qquad (22)$$

$Q(y) = 1$ standing for a perfect prediction and $Q(y) = 0$ for the worst possible one.

Let's define $d_0(y)$, the day index maximizing y(d), i.e., $d_0(y) = Arg(Sup\{y(d), d = 1, D\})$. We have:

- If $0 \le S(y) \le 1/(D - 1)$, i.e., if $Q(y) \in [2^{1/(D-1)}, 1] = [Q_2(D), 1]$, then the real transition day d = evidence necessary correspond to d_0, and the prediction evidence = $d_0(y)$ is necessarily right.

- If $1/(D-1) \leq S(y) \leq (D-2)/(D-1)$, i.e., if $Q(y) \in \left[2^{(D-2)/(D-1)}, 2^{1/(D-1)}\right] = [Q_1(D), Q_2(D)]$, then the transition day may correspond to d_0.
- If $(D-2)/(D-1) \leq S(y) \leq 1$, i.e., if $Q(y) \in \left[0, 2^{(D-2)/(D-1)}\right] = [0, Q_1(D)]$, then the transition day cannot correspond to d0, and the prediction *evidence* = $d_0(y)$ is necessarily wrong.

$\Phi(\mu)$ appears as the average value of S(y) on the given training dataset. It represents the expected value of S related for any new prediction, quantify thus the performance of the aggregation operator prediction.

The function $\Phi(\mu)$ being strictly convex, as a sum of strictly convex functions, and so, having a unique minimum, we use at first a simple gradient descent method to minimize it. We combine this basic method with the use of a penalization function to keep candidate solutions strictly inside the limits of the domain defined by the canonical constraints (5).

4.3 Gradient Descent

The solution is a(2^n-1)-dimension vector $[\mu] = [\mu_1, \ldots, \mu_n, \mu_{1,1}, \ldots, \mu_{n-1,n}, \ldots, \mu_{1,\ldots,n}]$, denoted here $[m] = [m_1, m_2, \ldots, m_{2^n-1}]$, minimizing Φ. Φ may be expressed as:

$$\Phi(m) = -L \cdot \sum_{k=1,\ldots,R} \log\left(1 + \sum_{i=1,\ldots,2^n-1} a_{k,i} \cdot m_i\right) \tag{23}$$

where $a_{k,i}$ is the ith component of $[A]_k$, and where $L = 1/(R.Log(2))$

The jth component of the gradient being:

$$\partial\Phi/\partial n_j(m) = -L \cdot \sum_{k=1,\ldots,R} a_{k,j}/\left(1 + \sum_{i=1,\ldots,2^n-1} a_{k,i} \cdot m_i\right) \tag{24}$$

First, we calculate, for each statement of inequality k, the 2^n-1 values $a_{i,k}$. Then, a loop calculates successive iterations m_p of the m vector, according to the formula:

$$m_{p+1} = m_p - \varepsilon_p.\text{grad}(m_p) + \Psi(m_p) \tag{25}$$

where grad(m_p) is the gradient vector $[\partial\Phi/\partial m_j(m_p)]$, and where $\Psi(m_p)$ represents a penalizations related to domain frontiers associated to the constraints $\mu_i \geq 0$, $\mu_{i1,i2} \geq \mu_{i1}$, $\mu_{i1,i2,i3} \geq \mu_{i1,i2}$, ..., and ε_p being a step size with an initial value ε_0, and possibly updated at each iteration. The iteration loop stops when $\|m_{p+1} - m_p\| < \eta$, where is η is a predefined value.

4.4 Penalization and Projected Gradient

We consider the frontiers of solution domain with the use of a penalization function $m \to \Psi(m)$, defined as:

$$\psi(m) = \sum_{i=1,\ldots,n} \theta(\mu_i) + \sum_{S \subseteq N, S=\emptyset, S \neq N, \{i\} \cap S = \emptyset} \theta(\mu_{S \cup \{i\}} - \mu_S) \qquad (26)$$

where θ is continuous and derivable, $\theta(x) \approx 0$ for $x > 0$, $\theta(x)$ being large positive for $x < 0$. E.g., for n = 2, to express the required constraints $\mu_1 \geq 0$, $\mu_2 \geq 0$, $\mu_1 \leq \mu_{1,2}$, $\mu_2 \leq \mu_{1,2}$ and $\mu_{1,2} \leq 1$ we shall have:

$$\Psi([\mu_1, \mu_2, \mu_{1,2}]) = \theta(\mu_1) + \theta(\mu_2) + \theta(\mu_{1,2} - \mu_1) + \theta(\mu_{1,2} - \mu_2) + \theta(1 - \mu_{1,2}) \qquad (27)$$

We use here a simple exterior penalization $\theta(x) = \min(x, 0))^2/(2 \cdot \gamma)$, γ being a parameter in relationship with the expected result accuracy (e.g., $\eta = 0.01$).

As convergence process may be long, especially when the optimum solution is on the domain frontier, i.e. on one of the canonical hyperplanes $\mu_i = 0, \ldots, \mu_{i1,\ldots,ip} = \mu_{i1,\ldots,ip,ip+1}, \ldots, \mu_{i,\ldots,in} = 1$, instead of a penalization, we decided to use an adaptation of projected gradient method, that is simple in our case where domain is a convex polytope closed by a set of canonical hyperplanes.

At each iteration, we evaluate the quantities:

$$\omega_i(\mu) = \mu_i, \ldots.$$
$$\omega_{i1,\ldots,ip,ip+1}(\mu) = \mu_{i1,\ldots,ip,ip+1} - \mu_{i1,\ldots,ip}, \ldots, ip, \ldots. \qquad (28)$$
$$\omega_{i1,\ldots,in}(\mu) = 1 - \mu_{i1,\ldots,in}, \ldots$$

a negative ω value meaning that the candidate solution vector m_p is out of the domain. In this case, the actual step ε_p is adapted in such a way that candidate solution is put just on the frontier. Then, at the next iteration, gradient grad(m_p) is replaced by grad(mp)^{proj}, orthogonal projection of grad(mp)^{proj}, on the considered hyperplane, ensuring that the candidate solution will remain inside the domain.

5 Decision Model

Once the training achieved on the available dataset and having got, as a result, the values of our μ capacity, the decision model will be used in operation. For each new session, i.e., for each new multisources n-vector input data X, X(d), d = 1, ..., D, the Choquet integral will deliver a fuzzy dataset defined by the membership function $y(d) = C_\mu(X(d))$, d = 1, ..., D, and our decision model will propose as awaited transition day this of maximum confidence:

$$d_{Pred}(X) = Arg\left(Sup\{C_\mu(X(d)), d = 1, \ldots, D\}\right) \qquad (29)$$

The user having no idea about the reliability of this result, and the actual quality of it depending on the statistical distribution of Q on the dataset, the problem is now to provide the user with a quantity that will objectively reflect the confidence they can have in the proposed day.

Figure 8 shows a typical statistical distribution of the Q quantity on a training dataset, with 1) the global distribution of inputs on Q values, 2) the distribution of successful predictions and 3) the distribution of wrong predictions (presented here in the case of D = 11 days).

Using the values $C_\mu(X(d))$ delivered by the Choquet integral, we first calculate a quality of the prediction, evaluated with regards to the predicted day d_{pred}:

$$Q^*(y) = 2^{-S^*(y)}, \ with \ S^*(y) = 1/(D-1) \cdot \sum_{d=1,\ldots,D,\, d\neq dPred} \varphi(y(d_{Pred}) - y(d)) \tag{30}$$

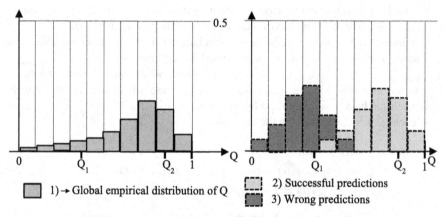

1) → Global empirical distribution of Q

2) Successful predictions

3) Wrong predictions

Fig. 8. Empirical distribution of Q quantity on a dataset.

We consider then the probability density p(q) of Q, the conditional probability densities of sucessful and wrong predictions $p_S(q)$ and $p_W(q)$, and, at last, the global probabilities of sucessful and wrong predictions P_S and P_W.

Using Bayes' theorem, the conditional probability of a sucessuful prediction given the known present value q of Q* is immediately given by:

$$P(success \,|q) = p_s(q) \cdot P_s/(p_s(q) \cdot P_s + p_w(q) \cdot P_w) \tag{31}$$

That give the probability of the system estimation to be the real still unknow day of transition. Here, the required densities of probabilities are simply estimated by intervals of values [qi, qi + 1], after solution delivery at the last step of the algoritm.

6 Case Study and Experimental Evaluation

Our goal is to deliver to farmers estimated future states of their culture regarding its development, maintaining and improving this estimation over time. More specifically, evaluation of the proposed approach is led in the context of crop monitoring, aiming at predicting the growth stages of a plant. So, in each stage, we propose to predict the transition day regarding the next development stage of a plant. As already pointed out, knowing with a sufficient advance the day of transition from a growth stage to the next one is a very important issue for farmers, who have to to plan the sequence of actions to be taken with the right timing (e.g. fertilization, watering, other treatments, …).

6.1 Experimental Setup

As an illustrative example, we base our experiment on three sources of input, which are the classical empirical calculation, a statistical model of the plant, and an observation by digital image processing [13].

The case study concerns cultivation of winter wheat in Normandy, which is a region with a temperate oceanic climate in France. This case is based on data issued from data recorded over several years mixed with data issued from simulation models.

In the considered example, we are at the beginning of stage 8 (maturity) and we are trying to predict the end of ripening and therefore the beginning of stage 9 (senescence), in order to harvest wheat at the best moment. The prototype was developed in Python version 3.9.12 programming language.

To assess the robustness of our algorithm, we placed as inputs sensor confidence data, parametrized as follows:

- The day of maximum confidence, drawn pseudo-randomly according to a Gaussian centred on the day in question and with a sigma standard deviation called bias.
- The spread of the source over adjacent days (accuracy of the source), which is calculated using the function f which associates x with:

$$f(x) = e^{-k.|x-day|} \tag{33}$$

With:

- Day: day this of maximum confidence
- k: accuracy ("spreading coefficient") of the function. The larger k is, the more accuracy the source (the spread is less important).

- Noise: variation of the confidence drawn randomly according to a Gaussian of standard deviation fixed in advance. For each day, the confidence value corresponds to the starting confidence, to which we add the noise, which is drawn randomly until we obtain a positive value.

The first three parameters (day of maximum confidence, bias and accuracy) correspond to the configuration of the sources along the x axis (knowing that the triangular shape of the source, in y, is also fixed by these parameters). Finally, the last parameter (noise) corresponds to the variation in y of the source (noise). Figure 9 illustrates an example of data source.

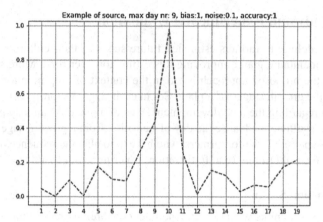

Fig. 9. Example of data source.

6.2 Simulation Protocol

As a control, before of each simulation set, we first performed the algorithm on zero bias and non-noisy sources. The spread is previously chosen and fixed for each of the following simulation set.

For comparison and justification for using the Choquet integral, we also applied our algorithm to a simple weighted sum (calculation of weights μ_1, μ_2, μ_3), for identical noisy or non-noisy sources. We performed simulations with noisy inputs 50 times per fixed bias/accuracy/noise values. For each simulation set, we evaluated performance with the following descriptive statistics about the predicted day of passage (cf. Table 1).

Table 1. Computed indicators.

Indicator	Control data source or simulations	Description
Type	Both	Weighted sum or Choquet integral
Day target (without noise)	Control data sources	Day predicted by the algorithm with unbiased and noise-free control data sources
Max value (without noise)	Control data sources	Maximum confidence value with unbiased and noise-free control data sources
Avg predicted day	Simulations	Average predicted day
Std deviation pred day	Simulations	Average standard deviation of predicted day

(*continued*)

Table 1. (*continued*)

Indicator	Control data source or simulations	Description
Min pred day, Max pred day	Simulations	Resp. Minimum and maximum predicted days by the algorithm during the simulations
Avg max integral value	Simulations	Average maximum confidence of predicted days
Avg evaluation	Simulations	Average evaluation function value (please refer to 4.1). We chose an evaluation function in the form: $$\Phi(\mu) = 2^{-\Sigma k=1,...,R\log 2(1/2.([A]k\cdot[\mu]+1))} \quad (34)$$ The indicator is between 0 and 1. The closer this indicator is to 1, the better the prediction quality. On the contrary, the closer the indicator is to 0, the worse the quality
Avg source 1 quality, Avg source 2 quality, Avg source 3 quality, Avg result model quality	Simulations	The average quality resp. For each source and for the computed result model (Choquet or Weighted sum). Please refer to part 6
Source 1 ratio, Source 2 ratio, Source 3 ratio, Result model ratio	Simulations	Ratio of right predicted day/ number of simulations resp. For each source and for the computed result model (Choquet or Weighted sum). Please refer to part 6

In summary, the simulation protocol is set as follows:

- A precision value is fixed (identical for each source).
- We set a transition day.
- We generate the three data sources.
- We run the program for calculating the coefficients:

  - for the Choquet integral.
  - for the weighted sum.

- We fix a bias and a noise.
- We perform the following 50 simulations:

  - We regenerate the 3 sources of biased and noisy data.
  - We run the program for calculating the coefficients:

    - for the Choquet Integral.

    – for the weighted sum.

• The descriptive statistics are calculated on the 50 simulations carried out.

6.3 Results

In this section, we present the results obtained under the form of graphs and summary tables. We performed simulations with noisy inputs 50 times per fixed bias/accuracy/noise values.

Simulation 1: Transition day: 9, runs: 50, bias: 0.8, noise: 0.1, accuracy: 0.5, deviation between the confidence maximums of each source: 1 (cf. Figs. 10, 11, and Table 2).

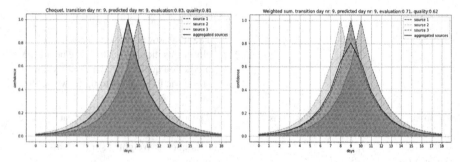

Fig. 10. Graphs with control data sources and both Choquet/weighted sources results.

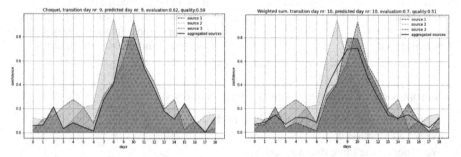

Fig. 11. Example of simulation result (nr 2 out of 50) with biased/noisy data.

Table 2. Experimental results (1st simulation set).

Type	Control data sources		Predicted day (calculated on 50 simulations)				Avg max integral value	Avg evaluation	Avg quality				Ratio of right day prediction			
	Day target (without noise)	Max value (without noise)	Avg	Std dev	Min	Max			Source 1	Source 2	Source 3	Result model	Source 1	Source 2	Source 3	Result model
Weighted sum	9	0.81	9.04	0.69	8	10	0.75	**0.69**	0.6	0.48	0.45	**0.5**	0.56	0.22	0.1	**0.52**
Choquet	9	1.0	8.94	0.65	8	10	0.88	**0.83**	0.6	0.48	0.45	**0.59**	0.56	0.22	0.1	**0.58**

Simulation 2: Transition day: 9, runs: 50, bias: 0.8, *noise: 0.2,* accuracy: 0.5, deviation between the confidence maximums of each source: 1. Graphs with control data sources and both Choquet and weighted sources results appear as identical to those of the previous simulation (cf. Fig. 12 and Table 3).

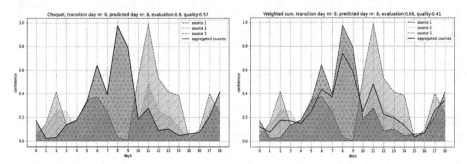

Fig. 12. Example of simulation result (nr 8 out of 50) with biased/noisy data.

Table 3. Experimental results (1st simulation set).

Type	Control data sources		Predicted day (calculated on 50 simulations)				Avg max integral value	Avg evaluation	Avg quality				Ratio of right day prediction			
	Day target (without noise)	Max value (without noise)	Avg	Std dev	Min	Max			Source 1	Source 2	Source 3	Result model	Source 1	Source 2	Source 3	Result model
Weighted sum	9	0.81	8.9	1.14	7	13	0.73	**0.67**	0.48	0.45	0.44	**0.43**	0.36	0.16	0.26	**0.36**
Choquet	9	1.0	8.78	1.17	7	13	0.85	**0.79**	0.48	0.45	0.44	**0.48**	0.36	0.16	0.26	**0.36**

Simulation 3: Transition day: 9, runs: 50, *bias: 1.2*, noise: 0.1, accuracy: 0.5, deviation between the confidence maximums of each source: 1. Graphs with control data sources and both Choquet/weighted sources results are identical to those of the previous simulation (cf. Fig. 13 and Table 4).

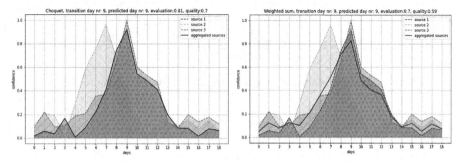

Fig. 13. Example of simulation result (nr 16 out of 50) with biased/noisy data.

Table 4. Experimental results (1st simulation set).

Type	Control data sources		Predicted day (calculated on 50 simulations)				Avg max integral value	Avg evaluation	Avg quality				Ratio of right day prediction			
	Day target (without noise)	Max value (without noise)	Avg	Std dev	Min	Max			Source 1	Source 2	Source 3	Result model	Source 1	Source 2	Source 3	Result model
Weighted sum	9	0.81	8.92	1.11	6	12	0.74	**0.7**	0.53	0.47	0.5	**0.47**	0.38	0.24	0.28	**0.38**
Choquet	9	1.0	8.82	1.13	6	12	0.91	**0.82**	0.53	0.47	0.5	**0.53**	0.38	0.24	0.28	**0.38**

Simulation 4: Transition day: 9, runs: 50, bias: 0.8, noise: 0.1, **_accuracy: 2,_** deviation between the confidence maximums of each source: 1 (cf. Figs. 14, 15 and Table 5).

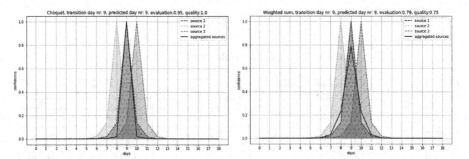

Fig. 14. Graphs with control data sources and both Choquet/weighted sources results.

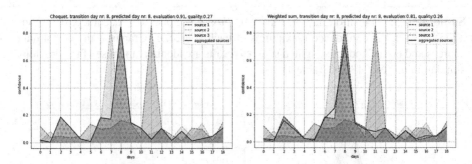

Fig. 15. Example of simulation result (nr 4 out of 50) with biased/noisy data.

Table 5. Experimental results (1st simulation set).

Type	Control data sources		Predicted day (calculated on 50 simulations)				Avg max integral value	Avg evaluation	Avg quality				Ratio of right day prediction			
	Day target (without noise)	Max value (without noise)	Avg	Std dev	Min	Max			Source 1	Source 2	Source 3	Result model	Source 1	Source 2	Source 3	Result model
Weighted sum	9	0.79	9.15	0.73	8	11	0.82	**0.83**	0.6	0.44	0.46	**0.57**	0.6	0.3	0.35	**0.6**
Choquet	9	1.0	9.15	0.73	8	11	0.88	**0.9**	0.6	0.44	0.46	**0.6**	0.6	0.3	0.35	**0.6**

Simulation 5: Transition day: 9, runs: 50, bias: 0.8, noise: 0.1, accuracy: 0.5, deviation between the confidence maximums of each source: 3 (cf. Figs. 16, 17, Table 6).

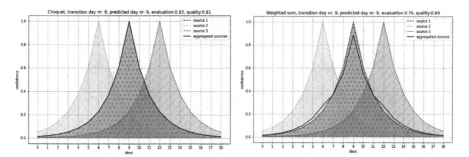

Fig. 16. Graphs with control data sources and both Choquet/weighted sources results.

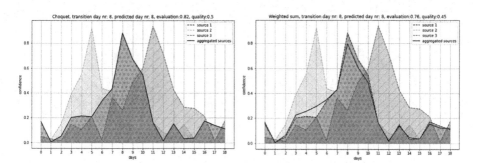

Fig. 17. Example of simulation result (nr 5 out of 50) with biased/noisy data.

Table 6. Experimental results (1st simulation set).

Type	Control data sources		Predicted day (calculated on 50 simulations)				Avg max integral value	Avg evaluation	Avg quality				Ratio of right day prediction			
	Day target (without noise)	Max value (without noise)	Avg	Std dev	Min	Max			Source 1	Source 2	Source 3	Result model	Source 1	Source 2	Source 3	Result model
Weighted sum	9	0.88	9.22	0.81	8	11	0.88	**0.79**	0.57	0.32	0.33	**0.54**	0.48	0.0	0.0	**0.48**
Choquet	9	1.0	9.14	0.92	6	11	0.89	**0.81**	0.57	0.32	0.33	**0.56**	0.48	0.0	0.0	**0.48**

Simulation 6: Transition day: 6, runs: 50, bias: 0.8, noise: 0.1, accuracy: 0.5, deviation between the confidence maximums of each source: 3 (cf. Figs. 18, 19, and Table 7).

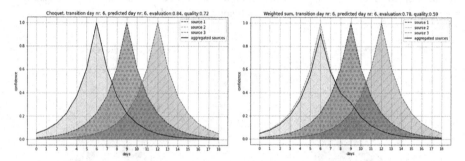

Fig. 18. Graphs with control data sources and both Choquet/weighted sources results.

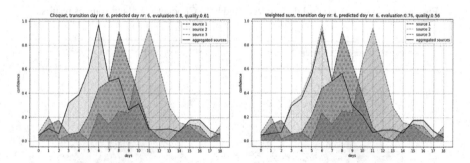

Fig. 19. Example of simulation result (nr 16 out of 50) with biased/noisy data.

Table 7. Experimental results (1st simulation set).

Type	Control data sources		Predicted day (calculated on 50 simulations)				Avg max integral value	Avg evaluation	Avg quality				Ratio of right day prediction			
	Day target (without noise)	Max value (without noise)	Avg	Std dev	Min	Max			Source 1	Source 2	Source 3	Result model	Source 1	Source 2	Source 3	Result model
Weighted sum	6	0.91	5.86	0.89	4	8	0.91	0.8	0.17	0.4	0.15	0.38	0.0	0.42	0.0	0.42
Choquet	6	1.0	5.86	0.89	4	8	0.93	0.82	0.17	0.4	0.15	0.39	0.0	0.42	0.0	0.42

6.4 Discussion

Experimental results show the mean prediction quality for the Choquet integral is always higher than this of a classical weighted sum, independently from input values, validating the choice of the Choquet integral as aggregation operator. The prediction rate seems low at first, but this is explained by the bias attached to the day of maximum confidence of each source, which is different at each stage of the simulation.

Finally, the quality of prediction as well as the ratio of right day prediction of our Choquet-based decision model are systematically superior or equal (the rare times it is not the case can be weighed against the significance of certain calculations) to those of the different sources separately considered, that tends to validate the interest of our approach.

According to the calculations, the noise and then the bias that have the greatest impact on the quality of prediction and the ratio of right day prediction. However, the descriptive statistics seem to show a certain robustness of the algorithm, even with noisy signal. The average predicted day does not seem to vary significantly.

7   Conclusion and Future Work

In this paper, we proposed a Choquet-based decision model associated to an original parameter identification process, enabling to consider possible non-additivity such as partial redundancy and the synergies between various input criteria. Using our approach, we are able to identify the values of the decision model parameters, considering an input training dataset from which we derivate a set of preference constraints the model has to conform with. A measure enabling to evaluate a prediction capability, attaching to any potential solution a degree of order, have been detailed. The results of experiments are promising, as they provide better right day prediction ratios than those obtained by both classical weighted sum approach and use of one data source considered separately. Our approach provides in addition a useful quality of robustness due to the principle on which the evaluation function used in our identification process relies.

The case study concerns smart farming, and the implemented prototype allows, for a given culture and several input sources, to assist farmers, predicting growth stages of a culture. This case study concerns the cultivation of winter wheat in Normandy. Indeed, for a given culture, several sources of input are considered, mainly the classical empirical calculation called "growing degree-days", a statistical model of the plant and digital image processing. The experimental results are very encouraging, the predicted days being stable despite the variation of the noise attached to inputs.

The proposed algorithm is currently extended to integrate more sophisticated entropy criteria in the evaluation function, future work including an extension of the proposal supporting the bi-capacities, which emerge as a natural generalization of capacities in such context and could be interesting to integrate information that may go to against a phase transition over a given period.

The number of inputs to be considered being potentially high, another extension of our work concerns, among those, an algebraic approach enabling to a priori reduce the dimension of the problem, and so reduce the number of Choquet parameters to be identified, enabling so to consider larger source sets with less calculations.

At last, another extension of this work is this of considering additional inputs in decision model, taking into account context specificities about a field or a region (e.g. climate, quality of soil, ...). The goal is to dispose of models with larger domains of validity, i.e., appliable to larger sets of fields and cultures, one issue being the impossibility of a direct integration of such variables as input of the integral due to nonlinear effects, requiring the study of non-linear and fuzzy extensions of our Choquet-based decisions model.

References

1. Siami, M., Naderpour, M., Lu, J.: A Choquet fuzzy integral vertical bagging classifier for mobile telematics data analysis, FUZZ-IEEE, 1–6 (2019)
2. Sugeno, M.: Theory of fuzzy integrals and its applications. Ph.D. Thesis, Tokyo Institute of Technology (1974)
3. de Campos Souza, P.V., Guimarães, A.J.: Using fuzzy neural networks for improving the prediction of children with autism through mobile devices. ISCC, 1086–1089 (2018)
4. Kojadinovic, I., Labreuche, C.: Partially bipolar Choquet integrals. IEEE Trans. Fuzzy Syst. **17**(4), 839–850 (2009)
5. Dantan, J., Baazaoui-Zghal, H., Pollet, Y: Decifarm: A fuzzy decision-support environment for smart farming. ICSOFT, 136–143 (2020)
6. Grabisch, M., Labreuche, C.: A decade of application of the Choquet and Sugeno integrals in multi-criteria decision aid. 4OR 6, 1–44 (2008)
7. Fürnkranz, J., Hüllermeier, E., Rudin, C., Slowinski, R., Sanner, S.: Preference learning (dagstuhl seminar 14101), Dagstuhl Reports **4**(3), (2012)
8. Labreuche, C.: On the completion mechanism produced by the Choquet integral on some decision strategies. IFSA/EUSFLAT Conference
9. Pollet Y., Dantan J., Baazaoui H.: Multi-factor prediction and parameters identification based on choquet integral: smart farming application. In: Proceedings of the 17th International Conference on Software Technologies (ICSOFT 2022)
10. Kang, F.: Plant growth models and methodologies adapted to their parameterization for the analysis of phenotypes. Thesis. Ecole Centrale Paris (2013). English (tel-01164965)
11. Christodoulou, P., Christoforou, A., Andreou, A.S.: A hybrid prediction model integrating fuzzy cognitive maps with support vector machines. Cyprus University of Technology. https://doi.org/10.5220/0006329405540564
12. Fakhar, K., El Arousi, M., Nabil Saidi, M., Aboutajdine, D.: Biometric score fusion in identification model using the Choquet integral. https://doi.org/10.1109/EITech.2015.7162955

13. De Alwis, S., Hou, Z., Zhang, Y., Hwan Na, M., Ofoghi, B.: Atul Sajjanhar: a survey on smart farming data, applications and techniques. Comput. Ind. **138**, 103624 (2022)
14. Bai, C.-H., Prakosa, S.W., Hsieh, H.-Y., Leu, J.-S., Fang, W.-H.: Progressive contextual excitation for smart farming application. In: Tsapatsoulis, N., Panayides, A., Theocharides, T., Lanitis, A., Pattichis, C., Vento, M. (eds.) CAIP 2021. LNCS, vol. 13052, pp. 332–340. Springer, Cham (2021). https://doi.org/10.1007/978-3-030-89128-2_32
15. Büyüközkan, G., Göçer, F., Uztürk, D.: A novel Pythagorean fuzzy set integrated Choquet integral approach for vertical farming technology assessment. Comput. Ind. Eng. **158**, 107384 (2021)

A New Simulation Tool for Sensor Networks Based on an Energy-Efficient and Fault-Tolerant Methodology

Hanene Rouainia[1](✉) , Hanen Grichi[2,3] , Laid Kahloul[4] ,
and Mohamed Khalgui[3,5]

[1] Faculty of Sciences of Tunis, El-Manar University, Tunis, Tunisia
hanene.rounainia@fst.utm.tn
[2] Faculty of Sciences of Bizerte (FSB), University of Carthage, Bizerte, Tunisia
[3] School of Electrical and Information Engineering, Jinan University, Zhuhai, China
[4] LINFI Laboratory, Computer Science Department, Biskra University,
Biskra, Algeria
[5] INSAT Institute, University of Carthage, Tunis, Tunisia

Abstract. Recently, reconfigurable wireless sensor networks (RWSNs) have attracted a lot of attention in research and industrial communities. They became more complex and dynamic systems which led to the emergence of many challenges. The lack of energy, real-time constraints, and software and hardware failures are the most important challenges in RWSNs. Indeed, several solutions have proposed to come up with these challenges. To avoid huge costs in terms of money, time, and effort of real experimentation, networks' simulation tools have become an essential necessity to study the impact of the proposed solutions. In this work, we propose a new energy-efficient and fault-tolerant methodology that composed of a set of solutions summarized in the use of mobile sink nodes (MSNs), application of the mobility, resizing, and test packet technique using a multi-agent architecture and an energy-efficient routing protocol. Moreover, we propose a new discrete-event simulation tool named *RWSNSim* designed for sensor networks (WSNs & RWSNs). We present its description, modeling, and provided services. The proposed simulation tool allows simulating sensor networks with and without application of the proposed methodology. Finally, we simulate a case study using *RWSNSim* in a 3D environment which proves the effectiveness of the proposed methodology and demonstrate the efficiency of the suggested simulation tool.

Keywords: Sensor networks · WSNs · RWSNs · Multi-agent architecture · Mobility · Resizing · Mobile sink node · Hardware & Software failures · Test packet technique · Energy-efficient · Fault-tolerant · RWSNSim · Simulation tool

1 Introduction

In recent years, wireless sensor networks (WSNs) have gained worldwide attention in research and industrial communities. They have a wide variety of applications from small-size to large-scale systems and provide unlimited future potentials in a variety of areas such as medical, agricultural, environmental monitoring, smart transportation and

H.-G. Fill et al. (Eds.): ICSOFT 2022, CCIS 1859, pp. 68–97, 2023.
https://doi.org/10.1007/978-3-031-37231-5_4

intelligent home [5,22,47]. WSNs deploy a set of multi-functional and battery-operated devices known as sensor nodes (SNs). They have considerable characteristics such as low cost, small size, low computing resources, and limited processing. SNs can sense both physical and chemical measurements in the surrounding environment such as temperature, humidity, and gases. They communicate with each other through wireless communication and work cooperatively to transmit a volume of data to a central station, process the sensing data, and execute a set of tasks [1,38,39].

In fact, there are several challenges in WSNs such as lack of energy problem, real-time constraints, and hardware/software failures [2,16]. The mentioned problems occur because of several factors like SNs use limited energy resources, WSNs work under many types of renewable energy resources which are not frequently available, SNs are fragile and prone to failures, communication volume, human effects, and harsh environmental conditions [11,37,38].

To resolve the mentioned problems, many solutions and techniques are proposed such as reconfiguration, mobility, resizing of zones, energy-efficient and fault-tolerant routing protocols [17,42]. Reconfigurable wireless sensor networks (RWSNs) are WSNs with the possibility to execute reconfiguration scenarios thanks to the existence of additional specific devices (i.e., software and hardware agents, mobile SNs, and MSNs) [15,37,39].

Indeed, there are several energy-efficient routing protocols in WSNs such as e-NL BEENISH (extended-Network Lifetime Balanced Energy Efficient Network Integrated Super Heterogenous Protocol) [43], WBM-TEEN (Well Balanced with Multihops intra-cluster Threshold sensitive Energy Efficient sensor Network protocol) [26], and LEACH (Low Energy Adaptive Clustering Hierarchy) [49]. Otherwise, there are also many fault-tolerant routing protocols for WSNs such as PFTP (Proactive Fault Tolerant Routing Protocol) [32], CFTR (Cluster-based Fault-Tolerant Routing protocol) [25], and FTCM (Fault-Tolerant Clustering-based Multi-path algorithm) [23].

In order to evaluate the proposed solutions and techniques and conclude their impact on the networks' efficiency, the researchers have two choices: real experimentations or simulation. Since the expensive cost, effort, time, and complexity implicated in the real experimentations which associated with the construction and the implementation of WSNs & RWSNs, the developers prefer to get an overview about feasibility and behavior of RWSNs before hardware implementation [39]. Indeed, the analysis and evaluation of the performance of the proposed solutions and techniques through real experimentations are not feasible, complex, and very expensive. As result, to keep up with these challenges, several simulation tools [27] are proposed. They provide many advantages like low cost, giving real-time results, and easy development.

In this work, we present an extended version of the paper [39] with a simplified explanation of the suggested methodology in [38] with some improvements. Briefly, we present an energy-efficient and fault-tolerant methodology which is a unified methodology permits the use of a set of solutions and techniques in energy and time-saving manner to resolve the mentioned problems. The proposed solutions are summarized as follows: i) using a multi-agent architecture which allows to handle the execution of the reconfiguration scenarios, ii) using mobile sink nodes, iii) applying the mobility of mobile entities in a 3D environment which permits to reduce the consumed energy in the network, iv) applying the geographic resizing of zones in a 3D environment which guarantees a good coverage of the largest possible area in the network, and v) using the test packet technique which permits to detect and isolate the malfunctioning entities in the network [38]. Moreover, we suggest a new discrete-event simulation tool called *RWSNSim* which permits the construction of WSNs and RWSNs, saving them in a database, using two routing protocols (LEACH and WBM-TEEN), plotting the simulation graph, showing the execution report of each monitoring time, drawing the resulting line charts after the simulation, and comparing between the different networks and simulations. The proposed simulation tool permits also to apply the suggested methodology [39,41].

The rest of this work is organized as follows. After the introduction section, we present the state of the art in Sect. 2. Then, we resume a background about sensor networks, energy issue, and hardware & software failures of networks' entities in Sect. 3. Morover, the proposed methodology is formalized and detailed in Sect. 4. Furthermore, the suggested simulation tool is described and reported in Sect. 5. Section 6 presents a case study simulated using *RWSNSim* to validate and evaluate the performance of the proposed methodology and simulation tool. Finally, the conclusion is drawn in Sect. 7.

2   State of the Art

The work in [17] proposed an approach based on an intelligent multi-agent distributed architecture using the three forms of reconfiguration (software, hardware, and protocol reconfiguration). The suggested architecture composed of five types of agents: coordinator, supervisor, scheduler, battery manager, and reconfiguration manager. Each agent has specific responsibilities in the system.

In [15], reconfiguration is considered as an efficient and effective solution to resolve the energy problem in WSNs because it makes the WSN satisfy the real-time and energy constraints taking into consideration the system performance optimization. While the paper [10] proposes a new pipelined approach to execute a set of reconfiguration scenarios that need to be applied without altering the performance of the pipeline.

On the other side, the paper [6] proposes a mobile data collection scheme based on the high maneuverability of the unmanned aerial vehicles (UAVs) considering them as MSNs in WSN water monitoring. They transmit data wirelessly to collect monitoring node data efficiently and flexibly. Otherwise, the paper [48] proposes an energy efficient routing schema combined with clustering and sink mobility technologies in WSNs. Otherwise, the authors in [6] propose a new method to find an efficient location service for MSNs using the surplus energy of a solar-powered WSN. The paper [31] studies the energy-efficient routing method with a support for multiple MSNs to effectively alleviate the hot spot problem, as the sink node can move along certain paths, resulting more even distribution of the hot spot nodes. Finally, the authors of [44] propose an intelligent method to discover the optimal path for MSNs using a modified traveling salesman problem (MTSP).

The papers [28,33] propose the mobility as a solution to minimize the total distance between SNs which permits to decrease the energy consumption to keep the network alive as long as possible. The authors of [3] propose a zone-based sink mobility (ZBSM) approach which permits the mitigation of the energy hole problem and optimal sink node placement thanks to the zone formation along with controlled sink mobility.

To avoid network portioning problems, the sink decides to move toward strongly loaded zone (SLZ) which can be selected using Fuzzy Logic.

Otherwise, the work in [18] suggests the geographic resizing of zones as a solution to the lack of energy and coverage of zones problems in WSNs. Moreover, the paper [9] proposes a data dissemination protocol named hexagonal cell-based data dissemination (HexDD) which exploits a virtual infrastructure and considers dynamic conditions of multiple sinks and sources. The proposed protocol is a fault-tolerant protocol which permits to bypass routing holes created by imperfect conditions of wireless communication in the network. While the authors of [15] tend to apply the resizing of zones and the 3D mobility of mobile SNs into a run-time power-oriented methodology which permits to conserve more energy during the communication among network elements and increase the network lifetime.

On the other hand, many researches suggest energy-efficient routing protocols as effective solutions to the lack of energy problem in WSNs. In fact, there are several energy-efficient routing protocols such as the Balanced Energy Efficient Network Integrated Super Heterogeneous Protocol (BEENISH), extended-Network Lifetime BEENISH (e-NL BEENISH), Information Quality Aware Routing protocol (IQAR), and Low-Energy Adaptive Clustering Hierarchy (WBM-TEEN) [20,21,43,46,49].

In the same context, there are many fault-tolerant routing protocols which are used to treat the software & hardware failures such as Efficient Fault-Tolerant Multipath Routing Protocol (HDMRP), Proactive Fault Tolerant Routing Protocol (PFTP), and Energy-Efficient and Fault-Tolerant Routing Protocol for Mobile Sensor Network (FTCP-MWSN) [24,49].

Table 1 presents a discussion about the contribution of some of the mentioned related works and the suggested methodology in this work in terms of the proposed solutions.

Table 1. Discussion about the contribution of some of the mentioned related works and the suggested methodology.

Work	MAA	REC	MOB	RES	MSNs	EERP	FTRP&Tech
[15]	✓	✓	✓	✓	✗	✗	✗
[6]	✗	✓	✓	✗	✓	✗	✗
[31,48]	✗	✓	✓	✗	✓	✓	✗
[3]	✗	✓	✓	✗	✓	✗	✗
[9]	✗	✗	✗	✓	✗	✗	✓
[38]	✓	✓	✓	✓	✓	✓	✓
							Only for time-driven routing protocols
Suggested methodology	✓	✓	✓	✓	✓	✓	✓

MAA: multi-agent architecture, **REC**: reconfiguration, **MOB**: mobility, **RES**: resizing, **MSNs**: mobile sink nodes, **EERP**: energy-efficient routing protocol, **FTRP&Tech**: fault-tolerant routing protocol & techniques.

Through Table 1, we conclude that the proposed methodology permits the application of several effective solutions in energy and time-saving manner which leads to achieving a high success rate in extending the lifetime of the network compared with other related works.

Indeed, many simulation tools of sensor networks have been proposed by academic and commercial communities such as NS-3, JavaSim, OMNet++, GloMoSiM, and RWiN-Environment [27,34].

NS-3 (Network Simulator-3) [29] is a discrete-event simulator designed for Internet systems. It was launched in June 2008 as an open-source project and licensed under the GNU GPLv2 license. It was targeted primarily at research and educational uses and maintained by a worldwide community. The latest version of NS-3 is NS-3.35 which provides several improvements such as IPv6 support for NixVectorRouting and a group mobility helper. It is released in October 1, 2021.

J-Sim (JavaSim) simulator [19] is a general purpose simulator started in year 1997 and used by various commercial and academic organizations. It is an object-oriented simulation package based upon C++SIM. J-Sim permits executing several script-based languages such as Python and Perl thanks to the use of a script interface. It provides a framework for WSN simulation using INET, ACA, and Wireless Protocol stack. The latest version of J-Sim is 2.2.0 GA which is released in January 4, 2020.

OMNet++ [30] is a powerful object-oriented discrete-event simulator which was launched in September 1997 and has a large number of users in educational, academic, and research-oriented commercial institutions. It is designed for the simulation of distributed and parallel systems, computer networks, performance evaluation of complex software systems, and modeling of multiprocessors. It is a modular, extensible, and component-based open-architecture simulation framework. The current version of OMNet++ is 5.7 which is released in October 6, 2021.

GloMoSiM (Global Mobile Information System) simulator [12] is a discrete-event scalable simulation software developed by Parallel Computing Lab at UCLA. It is designed for large-scale wireless network systems using parallel discrete-event simulation provided by Parsec. It supports three communication protocols: traditional Internet protocols, multi-hop wireless communication, and direct satellite communication. GloMoSiM uses Parsec compiler to compile the simulation of protocols. It allows the simulation of networks which contain thousands of heterogeneous nodes and communication links.

RWiN-Environment (Reconfigurable Wireless Network Environment) [40] is a graphical tool developed in the research laboratory LISI at the University of Carthage in Tunisia. It is develop for the modeling, formal verification, validation, simulation, code generation and implementation of RWSNs. It also permits evaluating the services of the RWiN-Methodology which is proposed to construct, analyse, develop, and verify an RWSN system in order to reduce the consumed energy by the network elements [14]. It is intended for a large community that allows RWSN designers to develop safety systems. RWiN-Environment is able to treat all forms of reconfiguration together and simulate and validate reconfigurable systems in the same environment, reduce the formal verification time, deploy the obtained code generation on STM32F4 microcontrollers, and save the obtained graphics which allows the study of the history of all RWSN implementations [13].

Table 2. Comparison of some simulation tools [39].

Name	Type	Prog. Lang.	License	GUI	Scalability	Portability	Designed for (WSNs or RWSNs)
NS-3	Discrete event	C++, Python	Open source	Limited	Large	Yes	WSNs
JavaSim	Discrete event	Java	Open source	Medium	Medium	Yes	WSNs
OMNet++	Discrete event	C++	Open source	Excellent	Large	Yes	WSNs
GloMoSiM	Discrete event	C	Open source	Limited	Large	Yes	WSNs
RWiN-Environment	Discrete event	Java	Open source	Excellent	Medium	Yes	RWSNs
RWSNSim	Discrete event	Java	Open source	Excellent	Medium	Yes	WSNs, RWSNs

Table 2 presents a comparison of the mentioned simulation tools according to general parameters.

Through Table 2, we remark that the most obvious strength of the proposed simulation tool is its ability to simulate both WSNs and RWSNs. For that, the proposed simulation tool *RWSNSim* is considered as the first simulation tool designed to simulate both WSNs and RWSNs. Moreover, it has also other strengths summarized as follows: license, graphical user interface (GUI), and portability.

3 Background

We present in this section a semi-formal description of the components and architecture of sensor networks. Then, we describe the energy issue by formalizing the energy model and problem. Finally, we detail the software & hardware problems in sensor networks [38].

3.1 WSN Architecture

A wireless sensor network *(W)* in a 3D environment is composed of:

1. A base station *BS*,
2. A set of zones formalized by: $S_Z(W) = \{ \bigcup_{k=1}^{Nb_Z(W)} \{Z_k\}\}$ where $Nb_Z(W)$ is the number of zones in W and Z_k is a zone in W,
3. Each zone Z_k contains:
   - A gateway G_k,
   - A set of fixed sensor nodes formalized by: $S_N(Z_k) = \{ \bigcup_{i=1}^{Nb_N(Z_k)} \{N_{i,k}\}\}$, where $N_{i,k}$ is a sensor node in Z_k and $Nb_N(Z_k)$ is the total number of sensor nodes in Z_k.

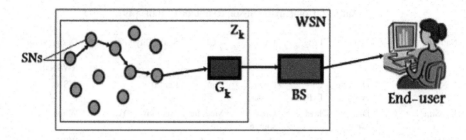

Fig. 1. WSN Architecture.

Figure 1 shows the architecture of a WSN.

Each sensor node in W has a sensing unit composed of: *i)* a set of sensors formalized by $S_{Sens}^{N_{i,k}} = \{Sens_{j,N_{i,k}}|i \in [1..Nb_N(Z_k)], \quad k \in [1..Nb_Z(W)] \quad and \quad j \in [1..Nb_{Sens}(N_{i,k})]\}$ where $Sens_{j,N_{i,k}}$ is a sensor in $N_{i,k}$ and $Nb_{Sens}(N_{i,k})$ is the total number of sensors in $N_{i,k}$ and *ii)* an analog to digital converter (ADC). These sensors are designed for sensing the chemical and physical conditions in the surrounding environment such as temperature, gases, humidity, light, luminosity, pressure, etc. It contains also a transceiver unit connected with an antenna, a processing unit composed of a microcontroller, and an external memory. Each sensor node contains also a power unit composed of two batteries. The first one is the principal battery $B_{pr}(N_{i,k})$ and the second one is the additional battery $B_{add}(N_{i,k})$. The principal battery is rechargeable by the additional battery and this last one is rechargeable from the harvesting energy. Finally, to generate the harvesting energy, each sensor node has a power generator connected with the harvesting energy module [4,32,35,36,45].

Each entity E in W has three coordinates $\{(x_E, y_E, z_E)|E \in \{S_N(W), S_G, BS\}\}$, where $S_N(W)$ is the set of sensor nodes in W and S_G is the set of gateways in W. These coordinates represent the position of E in W.

3.2 RWSN Architecture

A reconfigurable wireless sensor network *(R)* in a 3D environment is composed of:

1. A base station *BS*,
2. A controller agent Ag_{Ctrl}
3. A set of zones formalized by: $S_Z(R) = \{ \bigcup\limits_{k=1}^{Nb_Z(R)} \{Z_k\}\}$ where $Nb_Z(R)$ is the number of zones in R and Z_k is a zone in R,
4. Each zone Z_k contains:
   - A zone agent Ag_k,
   - A set of MSNs formalized by $S_{SN}(Z_k) = \{SN_{m,k}| \quad k \in [1..Nb_Z] \quad m \in [1..Nb_{SN}(Z_k)]\}$, where $SN_{m,k}$ is a mobile sink node in Z_k and $Nb_{SN}(Z_k)$ is the number of MSNs in Z_k,
   - A set of sensor nodes formalized by: $S_N(Z_k) = \{ \bigcup\limits_{i=1}^{Nb_N(Z_k)} \{N_{i,k}\}\}$, where $N_{i,k}$ is a sensor node in Z_k and $Nb_N(Z_k)$ is the total number of SNs in Z_k,
   - There are two types of SNs: fixed and mobile ones. The fixed SNs are formalized by $S_{FN}(Z_k) = \{N_{i,k}| \quad k \in [1..Nb_Z] \quad i \in [1..Nb_N(Z_k)]\}$. The mobile SNs

are formalized by $S_{MN}(Z_k) = \{N_{i,k}|\quad k \in [1..Nb_Z]\quad i \in [1..Nb_N(Z_k)]\}$. We denote that $S_{MN} \cup S_{FN} = S_N\quad and\quad S_{MN} \cap S_{FN} = \emptyset\}$.

Figure 2 displays the architecture of an RWSN.

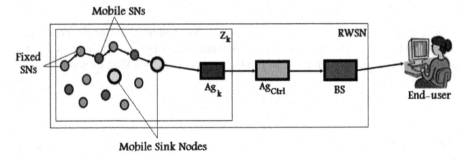

Fig. 2. RWSN Architecture.

Indeed, the fixed sensor nodes in R are the same in W. Otherwise, the mobile SNs contain the same components as fixed SNs with two additional components: a location finder and a mobilizer. The location finder is used to identify the position of the mobile SNs. While the mobilizer permits them to move easily in the network.

Otherwise, MSNs have the same components as mobile SNs with two high-charge level batteries and without the sensing unit. They play the role of gateway between sensor nodes and zone agents [36,45].

Each fixed entity E_f in R has three coordinates formalized by $\{(x_{E_f}, y_{E_f}, z_{E_f})|$ $E_f \in \{S_{FN}(R), S_{Ag_k}, Ag_{Ctrl}, BS\}\}$, where S_{Ag_k} is the set of zone agents in R. These coordinates represent the position of E_f in R. While each mobile entity E_m in R has three original coordinates formalized by $\{(x_{E_m}, y_{E_m}, z_{E_m})|E_m \in \{S_{MN}(R), S_{SN}\}\}$. These coordinates represent the original position of E_m in R. Each mobile entity E_m in R has also three actual coordinates formalized by $\{(x'_{E_m}, y'_{E_m}, z'_{E_m})|E_m \in \{S_{MN}(R), S_{SN}\}\}$ which represent the actual position of E_m after its last executed mobility task.

Finally, the charge capacity of each entity E in W and R is formalized by $capacity(E) = capacity(B_{pr}(E)) + capacity(B_{add}(E))$. While the total charge of each entity E in W and R is formalized by $C(E) = C(B_{pr}(E)) + C(B_{add}(E))$.

3.3 Energy Model in RWSNs

In each period ρ, each entity E in R executes a set of tasks which is formalized by $T_\rho(E) = \{\tau_1, \tau_2, ..., \tau_{Nb_\tau(E)}\}$, where $Nb_\tau(E)$ is the total number of tasks that executed by E during ρ. Each task τ_a is associated with a trilogy formalized by $Tr_{\rho,\tau_a}(E) = \{t_{exec}(\tau_a), e_c(\tau_a), p_{\tau_a}\}$ such that $t_{exec}(\tau_a)$ is the execution time of τ_a, $e_c(\tau_a)$ is the energy consumed by E to execute τ_a, and p_{τ_a} is a function formalized by:

$$p_{\tau_a} = \begin{cases} n \text{ if } \tau_a \text{ is executed } n \text{ times} \\ 0 \text{ if not} \end{cases} \tag{1}$$

Indeed, we can predict the approximate value of the consumed energy by each entity E in R during ρ using the following formula:

$$EC_{[\rho]}(E) = \int_{t_x}^{t_y} \sum_{a=1}^{Nb_\tau^E} (p_{\tau_a}(E) \times e_c(\tau_a(E)))dt + \epsilon \qquad (2)$$

where $\rho = |t_y - t_x|$, Nb_τ^E is the number of tasks executed by E during the period ρ.

Otherwise, we can predict also the approximate value of the produced energy by the additional battery in each entity E in R during ρ using the following formula:

$$EP_{[\rho]}(E) = \int_{t_x}^{t_y} \sum_{t_i}^{t_j} [e_{prod} \times (t_j - t_i)] \qquad (3)$$

where e_{prod} is the produced energy in each time unit, $t_x \leq t_i \leq t_y, t_x \leq t_j \leq t_y$ and $\rho = |t_y - t_x|$.

3.4 Energy Problem in Sensor Networks

In fact, sensor networks are designed for specific applications which range from small-size healthcare surveillance systems to large-scale environmental monitoring systems. In recent years, several challenges appear in sensor networks where the energy problem is the most important challenge [38].

The lack of energy problem in sensor networks is a disturbing problem, especially in crucial domains such as medical, nuclear, and the prediction of natural disasters. Indeed, sensor networks operate using renewable energy resources which are characterized by the oscillating presence in the surrounding environment such as solar energy, wind energy, hydropower, and bioenergy. For that, we explain the energy problem in the following.

We assume that the energy production times can interfere with the energy consumption times. But in several periods renewable energy cannot be available. For that, we consider that the harvesting energy is unavailable in the period $\rho = t_b - t_a$ which can be a long period. Therefore, the energy produced by the harvesting energy module in each entity E in the network is almost equal to zero ($EP_\rho \approx 0$). While the energy consumed by the active entities in the network increases with time ($EC_\rho >> 0$) (Fig. 3). As a result, the total charge of the remaining active entities will reach the threshold β which is a threshold for the energy charge in each entity E in the network and it is used to deactivate the entity E ($C(E) \leq \beta$).

As more time passes, the distance between the remaining active entities in the network will be expanded which leads to increasing the consumed energy by these entities which speed up their deactivation. As a result, more entities will be deactivated and the network can stop working until human intervention or the return of harvesting energy.

3.5 Software and Hardware Failure Problems

In fact, wireless sensor networks are mainly composed of a set of sensor nodes that are fragile and prone to many failures such as software & hardware failures, unreliable

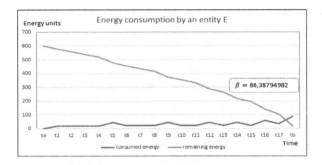

Fig. 3. Energy consumption by an entity E.

wireless connections, and malicious attacks. These failures make the network performance degrade significantly during its lifespan. The probability of sensor node failures increases because of several factors such as increasing the number of sensor nodes and deploying them in dangerous environments. SNs may fail because of many reasons such as lack of energy and failure of one of the sensor node components. They may also sense and transmit incorrect data. Otherwise, the network topology can be affected because of link failures which may cause some delays in data communication. In WSNs, every failure affects the efficiency of the network by disrupting the execution of the data transmission process and reconfiguration scenarios. For that, fault detection in WSNs is an efficient solution that has to be precise to avoid negative alerts, and rapid to limit loss. In this work, we treat the software/hardware failures that disrupt the receiving and sending tasks executed by the different network entities. We use a test packet technique that permits detecting the malfunctioning entities in the network and isolating them [7,8,50].

4   New Energy-Efficient and Fault-Tolerant Methodology in RWSNs

In this section, we formalize a set of constants, variables, and functions that are used to describe and treat the energy problem and the hardware & software failures. Then, we formalize the different rules that are used in the suggested methodology to regulate the application of the proposed solutions and techniques.

4.1   Terminology

Table 3 presents the most executed tasks by the entities in RWSNs.

Firstly, we propose a set of constant and variable thresholds and a set of functions to describe the energy problem in RWSNs. They are summarized as follows:

- α_E: is a constant threshold for the energy charge in each entity E in the network where $E \in \{Ag_{Ctrl}, S_{Ag_k}, S_{SN}, S_N\}$. It is used by agents to activate the inactive entities in the network. While, $\alpha_{N_{i,k}}$ is used by zone agents to determine the poor

Table 3. Set of the most energy-consuming tasks executed by different entities in R.

E	$\tau_a(E)$	Description
$E \in \{Ag_{Ctrl},$ $S_{Ag_k}, S_{SN}, S_N\}$	$\tau_{Recept}(E)$	Receiving packets from predecessors.
	$\tau_{Send}(E)$	Sending packets to successors.
$Ag \in S_{Ag}$	$\tau_{Deact}(Ag)$	Deactivate the entity E which is controlled by Ag.
	$\tau_{Act}(Ag)$	Activate the entity E which is controlled by Ag.
Ag_{Ctrl}	$\tau_{Res}(Ag_{Ctrl})$	Apply the resizing of zones.
	$\tau_{Iso}(Ag_{Ctrl})$	Isolate the malfunctioning zone agent Ag_k.
	$\tau_{Mob}(Ag_k)$	Apply the mobility of mobile entities.
Ag_k	$\tau_{Iso}(Ag_k)$	Isolate the malfunctioning entity E where $E \in \{S_N, S_{SN}\}$.
	$\tau_{Org}(Ag_k)$	Organize the sensor nodes in Z_k in subzones into clusters.
$E \in \{S_{SN}, S_{MN}\}$	$\tau_{Move}(E)$	Moving to another position in Z_k.
$N_{i,k} \in S_N$	$\tau_{Sens}(N_{i,k})$	Sensing the physical and chemical conditions of the surrounding environment by $Sens_{j,N_{i,k}}$.

SNs in their zones in terms of energy charge and to apply the mobility. α_E is formalized by:

$$0.15 \times capacity(E) \leq \alpha_E \leq 0.2 \times capacity(E) \tag{4}$$

– β_E: is a variable threshold for the energy charge in each entity E. It is used by the agent that controls E to deactivate it. It is formalized by:

$$\beta_E = EC_{[\rho]}(E) \tag{5}$$

where $E \in \{Ag_{Ctrl}, S_{Ag_k}, S_{SN}, S_N\}$ and ρ is the period that is required for one monitoring time.

– γ: is a constant threshold for the number of active SNs in each zone Z_k. It is used by zone agents to apply the mobility of mobile SNs. It is formalized by:

$$0.3 \times Nb_N(Z_k) \leq \gamma \leq 0.4 \times Nb_N(Z_k) \tag{6}$$

– λ: is a constant threshold for the number of active SNs in each zone Z_k. It is used by Ag_{Ctrl} to apply the resizing of zones. It is formalized by:

$$0.15 \times Nb_N(Z_k) \leq \lambda \leq 0.2 \times Nb_N(Z_k) \tag{7}$$

– $state(E)$: is a boolean function that indicates the state of the entity E. It is formalized by:

$$state(E) = \begin{cases} 1 \ \ if \ \ E \ \ is \ \ active \\ \ \ \ \ \ \ \ 0 \ \ if \ \ not \end{cases} \tag{8}$$

where $E \in \{Ag_{Ctrl}, S_{Ag_k}, S_{SN}, S_N\}$

– $isFree(E)$: is a boolean function that indicates the recent movements of a mobile entity E. It is formalized by:

$$isFree(E) = \begin{cases} 0 \ \ if \ \ E \ \ has \ \ moved \ \ recently \ \ as \ \ close \ \ to \\ \ \ \ \ \ \ \ \ \ \ \ \ \ a \ \ poor \ \ sensor \ \ node \ \ N_{a,k} \\ 1 \ \ if \ \ not \end{cases} \tag{9}$$

where $E \in \{S_{SN}, S_{MN}\}$

- $isMalFun(E)$: is a boolean function that indicated if the entity E is a malfunctioning entity or not. It is formalized by:

$$isMalFun(E) = \begin{cases} 1 \;\; if \;\; E \;\; is \;\; aMalfunctioning \;\; entity \\ \qquad\qquad\qquad\qquad 0 \;\; if \;\; not \end{cases} \quad (10)$$

where $E \in \{Ag_{Ctrl}, S_{Ag_k}, S_{SN}, S_N\}$

- $EPres(N_{i,k})$: is a boolean function that indicates if the energy problem of a poor sensor node $N_{i,k}$ is resolved recently. It is formalized by:

$$EPres(N_{i,k}) = \begin{cases} 1 \;\; if \;\; the \;\; energy \;\; problem \;\; of \;\; N_{i,k} \\ \qquad\qquad\qquad is \;\; resolved \;\; recently \\ \qquad\qquad\qquad\qquad 0 \;\; if \;\; not \end{cases} \quad (11)$$

- $Nb_{Act}(N_{i,k}, Z_k)$: is the total number of active SNs in a zone Z_k. It is formalized by:

$$Nb_{Act}(N_{i,k}, Z_k) = \sum_{i=1}^{Nb_N(Z_k)} state(N_{i,k}) \quad (12)$$

- $Nb_{Act}(SN_{m,k}, Z_k)$: is the total number of active MSNs in a zone Z_k. It is formalized by:

$$Nb_{Act}(SN_{m,k}, Z_k) = \sum_{i=1}^{Nb_{SN}(Z_k)} state(SN_{m,k}) \quad (13)$$

Moreover, we propose a set of variables that are used to detect the malfunctioning entities in the network and isolate them. They are summarized as follows:

- δ: is a percentage factor that must be defined by the administrator of the network to fix the waiting time to receive the sensing data in time-driven routing protocols or the acknowledge messages in both time-driven and event-driven routing protocols.
- $t_{rep_1}(E)$: is the response time of the entity E when receiving a request for sensing data.
- $dl_1(E_1, E_2)$: is a deadline for the receiving task when E_2 sends a request for sensing data from E_1.
- $t_{rep_2}(E_1)$: is the response time of the entity E_1 when receiving a test packet from E_2.
- $dl_2(E_1, E_2)$: is a deadline for the receiving task when E_2 sends a test packet to E_1 and waits for the acknowledge message. It is used by E_2 to accurately detect the malfunctioning entity.

Otherwise, we suggest a set of variables that permit to Ag_{Ctrl} and BS to send alert messages and call human intervention. They are summarized as follows:

- $Nb_{flrN}(Z_k)$: is the number of malfunctioning SNs in Z_k.
- $Nb_{flrSN}(Z_k)$: is the number of malfunctioning sink nodes in Z_k.
- $Nb_{flrAg}(R)$: is the number of malfunctioning zone agents in R.

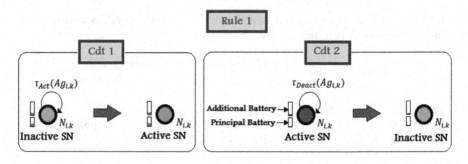

Fig. 4. Illustration diagram of an example of **Rule 1**.

- $flrN$: is a constant threshold for the number of malfunctioning SNs in Z_k. It's value is formalized by $flrN \geq 0.1 \times NbN(Z_k)$.
- $flrSN$: is a constant threshold for the number of malfunctioning MSNs in Z_k. It's value is formalized by $flrSN \geq 0.2 \times NbSN(Z_k)$.
- $flrAg$: is a constant threshold for the number of malfunctioning zone agents in R. It's value is formalized by $flrAg \geq 0.1 \times NbZ$.

4.2 Rules

Indeed, we propose a set of rules to distribute the different responsibilities in the network, regulate the application of different reconfiguration scenarios, and realize the proposed solutions and techniques in the suggested methodology. They are formalized as follows:

- **Rule 1:** Activation & Deactivation of the network entities (Fig. 4).
  - **Cdt 1:** $if\,(C(E) \geq \alpha_E\,\&\,state(E) = 0\,\&\,isMalFun(E) = 0)\,then$ the agent Ag that controls the entity E decides to activate it. As a result, the following task must be executed by Ag:

$$\tau_{Act}(Ag) = Activate(E)$$

where $Ag \in S_{Ag}$ and $E \in \{Ag_{Ctrl}, S_{Ag_k}, S_{SN}, S_N\}$.
  - **Cdt 2:** $if\,(C(E) \leq \beta_E\,\&\,state(E) = 1)\,then$ the agent Ag that controls the entity E decides to deactivate it. As a result, the following task must be executed by Ag:

$$\tau_{Deact}(Ag) = Deactivate(E)$$

where $Ag \in S_{Ag}$ and $E \in \{Ag_{Ctrl}, S_{Ag_k}, S_{SN}, S_N\}$.
- **Rule 2:** Application of mobility (Fig. 5).
  - **Cdt 1:** $if\,(state(N_{i,k}) = 1\,\&\,C(N_{i,k}) \leq \alpha_{N_{i,k}}\,\&\,EPres(N_{i,k}) = 0\,\&\,Nb_{Act}(N_{i,k}, Z_k) > \gamma\,\&\,N_{i,k} \in SZ_{m,k})\,then$ Ag_k decides to apply the mobility of $SN_{m,k}$ taking into consideration the following subcondition:
    * **Cdt 1.1:** $if\,(isFree(SN_{m,k}) = 1)\,then$ Ag_k and $SN_{m,k}$ must execute the following tasks:

$$\tau_{Mob}(Ag_k) = ApplyMobility(SN_{m,k})$$
$$\tau_{Move}(SN_{m,k}) = MoveTo(NewPosition)$$

- **Cdt 2:** $if\ (state(N_{i,k}) = 1\ \&\ C(N_{i,k}) \leq \alpha_{N_{i,k}}\ \&\ EPres(N_{i,k}) = 0\ \& Nb_{Act}(N_{i,k}, Z_k) \leq \gamma\ \&\ N_{i,k} \in SZ_{m,k})\ then\ Ag_k$ decides to apply the mobility according to the following subconditions:

  * **Cdt 2.1:** $if\ |N_{i,k}SN_{m,k}| \leq |N_{i,k}E|\ then\ Ag_k$ decides to apply the mobility considering the following cases:

    · *Case 1:* $if\ (isFree(SN_{m,k}) = 1)\ then\ Ag_k$ applies the mobility of $SN_{m,k}$ according to **Cdt 1.1** without considering **Cdt 1**.

    · *Case 2:* $if\ (isFree(SN_{m,k}) = 0)\ then\ Ag_k$ applies the mobility of $N_{a,k}$ according to **Cdt 2.2** without considering **Cdt 2**.

    such that $E \in \{SN_{m,k}, N_{a,k}\}$ where $N_{a,k}$ is the closest active mobile SN to $N_{i,k}$

  * **Cdt 2.2:** $if\ (|N_{i,k}SN_{m,k}| > |N_{i,k}Nb_{,k}|\ then\ Ag_k$ applies the mobility taking into consideration the following cases;

    · *Case 1:* $if\ (isFree(N_{a,k}) = 1\ \& C(N_{a,k}) > [\int_{t_x}^{t_y}(e_c(\tau_{Move}(N_{a,k}))dt + \alpha_{N_{a,k}} + \epsilon)])\ then\ Ag_k$ applies the mobility of $N_{a,k}$, where:

$$e_c(\tau_{Move}(N_{a,k})) = (|N_{i,k}N_{a,k}| - |N_{i,k}SuccN_{i,k}|/2) \times e_{Mob}$$

where e_{Mob} is the energy consumed by $N_{a,k}$ to move one meter. Therefore, Ag_k and $N_{a,k}$ must execute the following tasks:

$$\tau_{Mob}(Ag_k) = ApplyMobility(N_{a,k})$$
$$\tau_{Move}(N_{a,k}) = MoveTo(NewPosition)$$
$$\tau_{Org}(Ag_k) = OrganizeNodes()$$

case 2: $if\ (isFree(N_{a,k}) = 0)\ ||\ C(N_{a,k}) \leq [\int_{t_x}^{t_y}(e_c(\tau_{Move}(N_{a,k}))dt + \alpha_{N_{a,k}} + \epsilon)])\ then\ Ag_k$ decides to apply the mobility of $SN_{m,k}$ according to **Cdt 1** without considering its conditions.

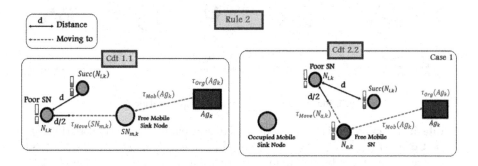

Fig. 5. Illustration diagram of examples of **Rule 2**.

- **Rule 3:** Application of the resizing of zones (Fig. 6).
  - **Cdt 1:** $if\ (Nb_{Act}(N_{i,k}, Z_k) \leq \lambda)\ then\ Ag_{Ctrl}$ decides to apply the resizing of zones of Z_k and its neighbor zone Z_a which contains the minimum number of

active SNs and/or active MSNs. As a result, Ag_{Ctrl} and Ag_k must execute the following tasks:

$$\tau_{Res}(Ag_{Ctrl}) = Resizing(Z_k, Z_a)$$
$$\tau_{Deact}(Ag_k) = Deactivate(Ag_k)$$
$$\tau_{Org}(Ag_a) = OrganizeNodes()$$

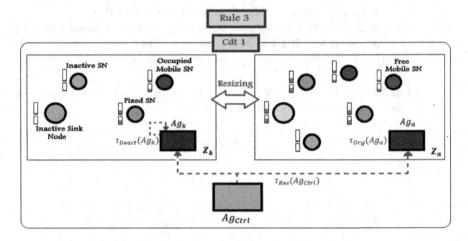

Fig. 6. Illustration diagram of an example of **Rule 3**.

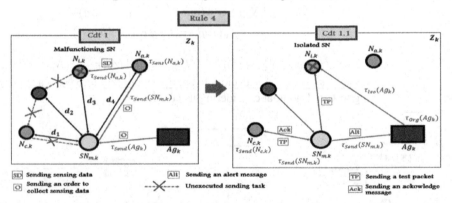

Fig. 7. Illustration diagram of an example of **Rule 4**.

- **Rule 4:** Detection and isolation of malfunctioning entities in the network (Fig. 7).
  - **Cdt 1:** $if\ (t_{rep_1}(N_{i,k}) > dl_1(N_{c,k}, SN_{m,k}))\ then\ SN_{m,k}$ sends test packets to the sensor nodes belonging to the cluster whose head is $N_{c,k}$ from closest to farthest until finding the malfunctioning one.
    - * **Cdt 1.1:** $if\ (t_{rep_2}(N_{i,k}) > dl_2(N_{i,k}, SN_{m,k}))\ then\ SN_{m,k}$ sends an alert message to Ag_k to inform it that $N_{i,k}$ is a malfunctioning sensor node. As a result, Ag_k isolates $N_{i,k}$. Therefore, Ag_k must execute the following tasks:

$$\tau_{Iso}(Ag_k) = Isolate(N_{i,k})$$
$$\tau_{Org}(Ag_k) = OrganizeNodes()$$

- **Cdt 2:** $if\,(t_{rep_1}(SN_{m,k}) > dl_1(SN_{m,k}, Ag_k))\,then\ Ag_k$ sends a test packet to $SN_{m,k}$ to detect if it is a malfunctioning sink node.
  - * **Cdt 2.1:** $if\,(t_{rep_2}(SN_{m,k}) > dl_2(SN_{m,k}, Ag_k))\,then\ Ag_k$ isolates $SN_{m,k}$. As a result, Ag_k must execute the following tasks:

$$\tau_{Iso}(Ag_k) = Isolate(SN_{m,k})$$
$$\tau_{Org}(Ag_k) = OrganizeNodes()$$

- **Cdt 3:** $if\,(t_{rep_1}(Ag_k) > dl_1(Ag_k, Ag_{Ctrl}))\,then\ Ag_{Ctrl}$ sends a test packet to Ag_k to detect if it is a malfunctioning zone agent.
  - * **Cdt 3.1:** $if\,(t_{rep_2}(Ag_k) > dl_2(Ag_k, Ag_{Ctrl}))\,then\ Ag_{Ctrl}$ isolates Ag_k and applies the resizing of zones (**Rule 3**). As a result, Ag_{Ctrl} must execute the following tasks:

$$\tau_{Iso}(Ag_{Ctrl}) = Isolate(Ag_k)$$
$$\tau_{Res}(Ag_{Ctrl}) = Resizing(Z_k, Z_a)$$

Note: **Rule 4** is used in time-driven routing protocols. While, in event-driven routing protocols, test packets are sent periodically from Ag_{Ctrl} to all SNs, passing through zone agents and MSNs taking into consideration **Cdt 1.1, Cdt 2.1,** and **Cdt 3.1** to detect and isolate the malfunctioning entities without stopping when detecting a malfunctioning entity.

- **Rule 5:** Resolve the hardware & software failure problem by calling human intervention (Fig. 8).
  - **Cdt 1:** $if\,(Nb_{flrN}(Z_k) \geq flrN \ || \ Nb_{flrSN}(Z_k) \geq flrSN)\,then\ Ag_k$ sends an alert message to Ag_{Ctrl} which transmits it to BS which calls human intervention.
  - **Cdt 2:** $if\,(Nb_{flrAg}(R) \geq flrAg)\,then\ Ag_{Ctrl}$ sends an alert message to BS which calls human intervention.

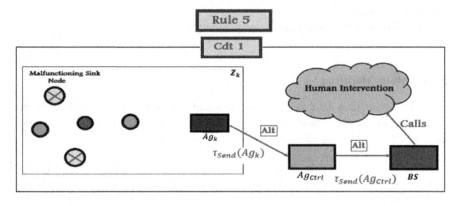

Fig. 8. Illustration diagram of an example of **Rule 5**.

5   RWSNSim: Reconfigurable Wireless Sensor Networks Simulator

In this section, we describe the suggested simulation tool and present its provided services. Furthermore, we model the used databases to store the information of sensor networks using entity relationship diagrams [39]. Finally, we present the used algorithms to apply the proposed methodology and to develop the suggested simulation tool [38].

5.1   Description

The proposed simulator *RWSNSim* is a discrete-event simulation tool designed for WSNs and RWSNs. It is developed using Java for research and educational use. It is a free, open-source, extensible, and reusable simulation tool. *RWSNSim* supports several operating systems such as Windows and UNIX. It is capable of simulating sensor networks that contain hundreds of entities. It is a desktop simulator that allows constructing WSNs and RWSNs and simulating them using two routing protocols (LEACH and WBM-TEEN) with and without the proposed methodology.

The suggested simulation tool provides several services during the simulation process, including the following:

- Create new WSNs and RWSNs with two manners: manual & regular and automatic & random.
- Save the created sensor networks in a database using *MySQL* or *hsqldb* according to the user's choice.
- Provide two routing protocols: LEACH and WBM-TEEN.
- Display the simulation graph of each simulation using *jgraph*, *jgraphx*, and *jgrapht* libraries.
- Show the execution report for each monitoring time during the simulation.
- Extract the simulation results and display them in form of line charts using *jfreechart* library.
- Comparison of different networks and simulations.

5.2   Database Modeling

Indeed, *RWSNSim* uses databases to store information related to the created sensor networks. To make these databases, we use entity relationship diagrams (ERDs) to model them. In fact, we have two ERDs that are explained as follows:

- *ERD for WSNs:* Fig. 9 displays the ERD of created WSNs in *RWSNSim* which is used to generate the databases used to store information related to the created WSNs that can be entered by the user (manual & regular manner) or generated automatically (automatic & random manner). Indeed, this ERD contains the following databases:

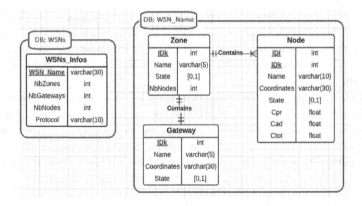

Fig. 9. Entity relationship diagram for WSNs [39].

- **[DB:WSNs]:** is a database that includes a single weak entity named *WSN_Infos* which contains the general and common information related to each WSN such as its name (*WSN_Name*) which is the key attribute, the number of sensor nodes (*NbNodes*), and the used routing protocol (*protocol*).
- **[DB:WSN_Name]:** For each constructed WSN with *RWSNSim*, a database with the same name is created to store its information. It contains three strong entities that are summarized as follows:
  - ***Zone:*** includes the common information of each zone in the network such as its state (*State*), and the number of SNs that belong to it (*NbNodes*).
  - ***Gateway:*** includes the general information of each gateway in the network like its name (*Name*) and the coordinates of its position in the network (*Coordinates*).
  - ***Node:*** comprises the main information of each sensor node in the network such as two identifiers (*IDi, IDk*) which are the key attributes of the entity and its initial total charge (*Ctot*).

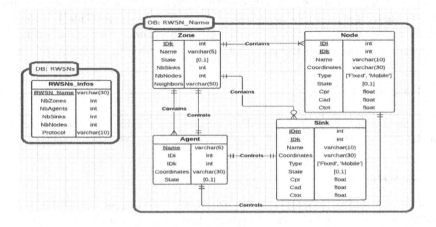

Fig. 10. Entity relationship diagram for RWSNs [39].

- *ERD for RWSNs:* Fig. 10 displays the ERD of created RWSNs in *RWSNSim* which is used to generate the databases used to store information related to the created RWSNs that can be entered by the user (manual & regular manner) or generated automatically (automatic & random manner). In fact, this ERD contains the following databases:
  - **[DB:RWSNs]:** is a database that includes a single weak entity named $RWSN\_Infos$ which contains the general and common information that related to each created RWSN such as the number of zones (*NbZones*), the number of agents (*NbAgents*), and the number of MSNs (*NbSinks*).
  - **[DB:RWSN_Name]:** For each constructed RWSN with *RWSNSim*, a database with the same name is created to store its information. It contains four strong entities that are defined as follows:
    * **Agent:** includes the general information of each agent in the network such as its identifiers (*IDi, IDk*), the coordinates of its initial position in the network (*Coordinates*), and its state (*State*).
    * **Zone:** comprises the common information of the network zones like the number of MSNs that belong to it (*NbSinks*), the number of SNs that belong to it (*NbNodes*), and the list of its neighbor zones (*Neighbors*).
    * **Sink:** contains the general information of each sink node in the network such as its type which can be fixed or mobile (*Type*), the coordinates of its initial position in the network (*Coordinates*), and its initial total charge (*Ctot*).
    * **Node:** comprises the common information of SNs in the network like two identifiers (*IDi, IDk*) which are the key attributes, its type which can be fixed or mobile (*Type*), its initial charge of the principal battery (*Cpr*), and its initial charge of the additional battery (*Cad*).

5.3 Algorithms

In order to develop *RWSNSim*, we use many algorithms to apply the suggested methodology. The zone agent Ag_k must execute **Algorithm 1** to apply the mobility in Z_k taking into consideration the **Rule 2** conditions. Moreover, the controller agent Ag_{Ctrl} must execute **Algorithm 2** to apply the resizing of zones according to the **Rule 3** conditions. Finally, the controller agent Ag_{Ctrl} must execute **Algorithm 3** to detect and isolate the malfunctioning zone agents (for time-driven routing protocols (*Ex:* LEACH)).

6   Case Study

In this section, we present a case study, simulate it using *RWSNSim*, and describe the simulation steps. Then, we evaluate the performance of the proposed methodology.

6.1 Presentation

As a case study, we propose a WSN named *WSN_Forest* and an RWSN named *RWSN_Forest* which are designed to protect the forests against fires to preserve the animals' and humans' lives.

Algorithm 1. Apply the mobility in Z_k [38].

Require: Set of SNs and MSNs.
Ensure: Minimize the distance between SNs and MSNs.
for $i = 0$ *to* $VSZ.size()$ **do**
    for $j = 0$ *to* $VSZ.get(i).vnactive.size()$ **do**
        $N \leftarrow VSZ.get(i).vnactive.get(j)$;
        if *(Rule 1.Cdt 1.Cdt 1.1)* || *(Rule 1.Cdt 2.Cdt 2.1.case 1)* || *(Rule 1.Cdt 2.Cdt 2.2.case 2)* & *(Rule 1.!(Cdt 1.Cdt 1.1))* **then**
            $S \leftarrow VSZ.get(i).getSink()$ $S.moveascloseTo(N)$;
        end
        if *((Rule 1.Cdt 2.Cdt 2.1.case 2)* & *(Rule 1.Cdt 2.!(Cdt 2.2).case 1))* || *(Rule 1.Cdt 2.Cdt 2.2.case 1)* **then**
            $M \leftarrow N.getclosestMN()$ $M.moveascloseTo(N)$
        end
    end
end

Algorithm 2. Resizing of zones in R [38].

Require: Set of active zones.
Ensure: Cover the possible largest zones in R.
for $i = 0$ *to* NbZ **do**
    $Z \leftarrow VZ.get(i)$;
    if *Rule 2.Cdt 1* **then**
        $Z1 \leftarrow findAppropriateNeigh()$;
    end
    if $Z \neq null$ AND $Z1 \neq null$ **then**
        $Z.Ag.deactivate()$;
        for $j = 0$ *to* $Z.Ag.NbNAct$ **do**
            $Z1.Ag.VN.add(Z.Ag.VNAct.get(j))$;
            for $k = 0$ *to* $Z.NbSink$ **do**
                $S \leftarrow Z.Ag.VSZ.get(k).getSink()$;
                if $S.state = 1$ **then**
                    $Z1.Ag.VSZ.add(Z.Ag.VSZ.get(k))$;
                end
            end
        end
        $findNeigh(Z1)$;
    end
end

In fact, *WSN_Forest* consists of a base station BS, 4 zones formalized by $S_Z = \{Z_1, Z_2, Z_3, Z_4\}$ where each zone is composed of a gateway denoted by G_k, and 20 sensor nodes defined by $S_N(Z_k) = \{N_{i,k} \mid i \in [1..20] \ and \ k \in [0..4]\}$. Otherwise, *RWSN_Forest* is composed of a base station BS, a controller agent Ag_{Ctrl}, 4 zones formalized by $S_Z = \{Z_1, Z_2, Z_3, Z_4\}$ where each zone is composed of a zone agent formalized by $Ag_k | k \in [1..4]$, 3 MSNs denoted by $S_{SN}(Z_k) = \{SN_{j,k} \mid j \in$

Algorithm 3. Detect the malfunctioning zone agents by Ag_{Ctrl}.

Require: Set of active zone agents.
Ensure: Detect the malfunctioning zone agents.
$sendTstPck \leftarrow false;$ $VAgTstPck \leftarrow null;$
$AllAgVerif \leftarrow false;$ $startTime \leftarrow currentTime();$
while $AllAgVerif = false$ **do**
$\quad$ $endTime \leftarrow currentTime(); waitTime \leftarrow endTime - startTime;$
$\quad$ **for** $i = 0$ *to* $VZ.size()$ **do**
$\quad\quad$ **if** $waitTime > dl1(VZ.get(i).Ag, controller)$ **then**
$\quad\quad\quad$ $VAgTstPck.add(VZ.get(i).Ag);$
$\quad\quad\quad$ $sendTstPckTo(VZ.get(i).Ag);$
$\quad\quad\quad$ $endTime \leftarrow currentTime();$
$\quad\quad\quad$ $waitTime \leftarrow endTime - startTime;$
$\quad\quad\quad$ **if** $waitTime > dl2(Ag, controller)$ **then**
$\quad\quad\quad\quad$ $isolate(Ag);$
$\quad\quad\quad$ **end**
$\quad\quad$ **end**
$\quad$ **end**
end
end

$[1..3]$ $\mid$ *and* $k \in [1..4]$}, and 20 sensor nodes (12 fixed and 8 mobile ones) defined by $S_N(Z_k) = \{N_{i,k}$ $i \in [1..20]$ *and* $k \in [1..4]\}$.

Each sensor node $N_{i,k}$ in *WSN_Forest* and *RWSN_Forest* has two sensors: a temperature sensor and a CO_2 sensor.

6.2 Simulation of Case Study

To evaluate the performance of the suggested methodology, we simulate *WSN_Forest* and *RWSN_Forest*. In the following, we show all provided services and simulation steps by *RWSNSim* during the simulation of *RWSN_Forest*.

Step 01 - Choosing the Appropriate Routing Protocol. Before creating a new sensor network with *RWSNSim*, the user has to choose an appropriate routing protocol between LEACH and WBM-TEEN. In this case study, we choose to simulate *RWSN_Forest* using WBM-TEEN protocol.

Step 02 - Creating the *RWSN_Forest* Network. Indeed, *RWSNSim* provides two manners to create a new sensor network and save it in a database. They are explained as follows:

1. *Manual & Regular:* this manner allows the user to enter manually all information related to each entity in the network, except for the identifiers. In this case study, we use this manner to create *RWSN_Forest*.
2. *Automatic & Random:* this manner allows the user to automatically generate automatically all information related to each entity in the target sensor network such as the coordinates, the state, and the batteries' charge of each entity. The system randomly selects the related information according to some inputs such as the total

number of zones and the total number of SNs and MSNs in each zone. The user can also modify each generated information in the created database, except for the identifiers of network entities.

Figure 11 displays the creation manners in the suggested simulation tool.

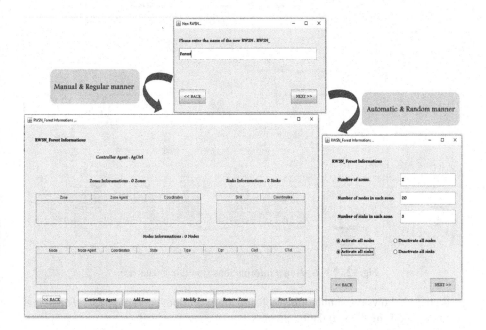

Fig. 11. The two creation manners of *RWSN_Forest*.

In fact, *RWSNSim* stores all information entered by the user or generated automatically in a database after the creation of the target sensor network. Figure 12 shows the *RWSN_Forest* information that is stored in the database used by *RWSNSim*.

Step 03 - Execution of *RWSN_Forest* Network. Before starting the network execution, *RWSNSim* demands a set of parameters and thresholds. After that, two windows appear: the simulation graph window and the execution report window. They are defined as follows:

– **Simulation Graph Window:** this window plots the different network entities and their distribution in the network. It displays also the communication between them in real-time.
– **Execution Report Window:** this window provides a comprehensive report of monitoring times and sensing data sent by sensor nodes.

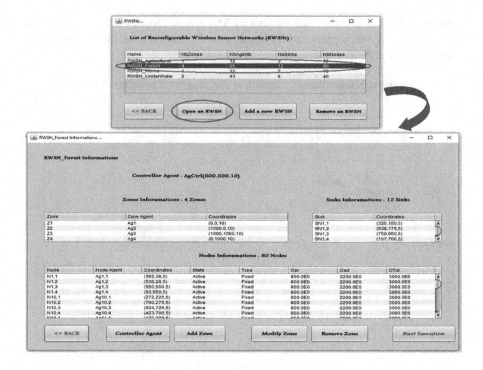

Fig. 12. *RWSN_Forest* informations stored in a database.

Figure 13 shows the simulation graph and the execution report of *RWSN_Forest* that are captured during the simulation process. .

Step 04 - Notifications & Alerts. The suggested simulation tool provides also many notification and alert windows which appear synchronized with various events that occur during the simulation process. Indeed, there are four types of notification and alert windows: Deactivation notification window, mobility notification window, Resizing notification window, and alert window. Figure 14 displays these windows.

Step 05 - Draw the Obtained Line Chart of *RWSN_Forest*: After the simulation process of the target sensor network, the suggested simulation tool provides the obtained results in the form of line charts. Figure 15 illustrates the obtained line chart of *RWSN_Forest*.

Through the mentioned provided services and steps of the simulation process, we note that the proposed simulator is not a specific simulator developed to implement a specific methodology, but rather tends to be more generalized. Indeed, it can simulate

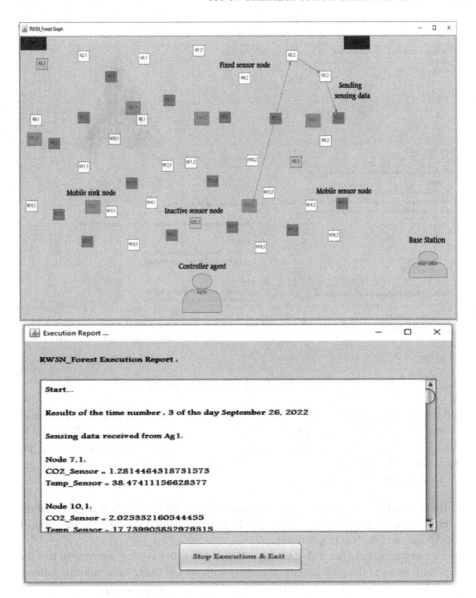

Fig. 13. *RWSN_Forest* simulation graph and execution report.

sensor networks without applying the suggested methodology. It has also the scalability to include new solutions, techniques and routing protocols.

6.3 Evaluation of Performance

In order to figure out the performance of the proposed methodology, we simulate *WSN_Forest* and *RWSN_Forest* using LEACH and WBM-TEEN routing protocols.

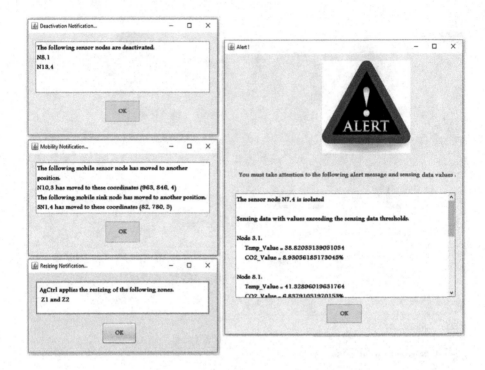

Fig. 14. *RWSN_Forest* notifications and alert windows.

In the following, we present the obtained results in the worst case, which means during the months when the energy production by each entity E is negligible ($EP_{[\rho]}(E) \approx 0$) and the consumed energy is high ($EC_{[\rho]}(E) > 0$). Figure 16 shows the obtained line charts using *RWSNSim*.

Through Fig. 16, we remark that:

- By comparing case (b) with case (a) and case (d) with case (c), we remark that the effectiveness of the use of WBM-TEEN protocol achieves a success rate approx 35.82% and 38.36%, respectively.
- By comparing case (c) with case (a) and case (d) with case (b), we remark that the effectiveness of the proposed methodology with the use of the same routing protocol achieves a success rate approx 355,22% and 363.74%, respectively.
- By comparing case (d) with case (a), we remark that the effectiveness of the proposed methodology using WBM-TEEN protocol achieves a success rate approx 529.85% compared to the case when we use LEACH protocol without the proposed methodology.

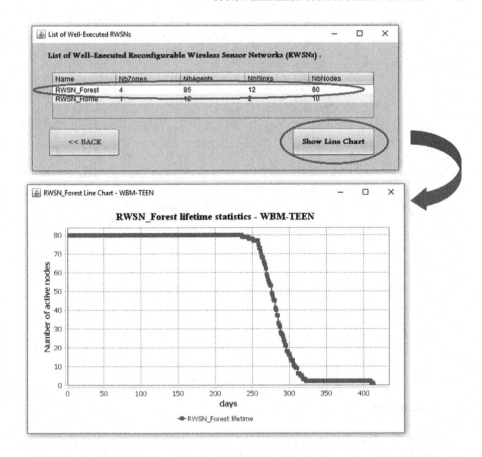

Fig. 15. *RWSN_Forest* obtained line chart.

On the other hand, when a software/hardware failure is committed in an entity E in *WSN_Forest* in case (a) or case (b), the packet dropping problem will occur which may lead to a complete network shutdown. While in case (c) or case (d), the failure will be detected and isolated when it occurs. Thus, eliminating the packet dropping problem and *RWSN_Forest* will still work without problems.

According to the obtained results, we can come up with an important inference with the choose of the appropriate routing protocol. Indeed, it is better to choose LEACH protocol as an appropriate routing protocol in the case that the network needs periodic monitoring and the sensor nodes are required to send the sensing data periodically. While it is better to choose WBM-TEEN protocol as an appropriate routing protocol in the case that the network doesn't need periodic monitoring and the sensor nodes are required to send the sensing data only when their values exceed the thresholds.

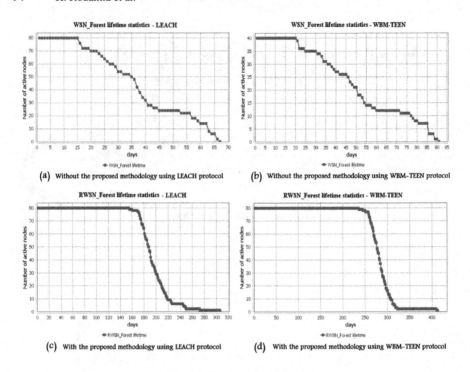

Fig. 16. Obtained line charts.

7   Conclusion

In this work, we described the architecture of sensor networks, formalized the energy model and the energy problem, and explained the hardware & software failures in sensor networks. Moreover, we propose a new methodology to resolve the energy, real-time, and hardware/software failure problems in RWSNs to keep the network alive as long as possible without human intervention. Furthermore, we developed a new simulation tool named *RWSNSim* which is a discrete-event simulator designed for wireless networks. The suggested simulator permits simulating WSNs & RWSNs with and without the proposed methodology using two routing protocol LEACH & WBM-TEEN. Indeed, we simulated an experimentation with *RWSNSim* with and without the proposed methodology. The results prove the effectiveness of the suggested methodology and the high performance of the developed simulation tool. In the future, we will strive to improve the proposed simulator by adding new routing protocols, new solutions and techniques to resolve more problems in sensor networks, new features, and new types of charts.

References

1. Agrawal, D.P.: Sensor Nodes (SNs), Camera Sensor Nodes (C-SNs), and Remote Sensor Nodes (RSNs), pp. 181–194. Springer, Singapore (2017). https://doi.org/10.1007/978-981-10-3038-3_8, ISBN 978-981-10-3037-6

2. Allouch, A., Cheikhrouhou, O., Koubâa, A., Khalgui, M., Abbes, T.: Mavsec: securing the mavlink protocol for ardupilot/px4 unmanned aerial systems. In: 2019 15th International Wireless Communications Mobile Computing Conference (IWCMC), pp. 621–628 (2019)
3. Ap, P., S., P.: Zone-based sink mobility in wireless sensor networks. Sens. Rev. **39**(6), 874–880 (09 2019). https://doi.org/10.1108/SR-11-2018-0310
4. Ara, T., Shah, P.: Light weight network security protocol for wireless sensor network (06 2014)
5. Bakhtiar, Q.A., Makki, K., Pissinou, N.: Data reduction in low powered wireless sensor networks. In: Matin, M. (ed.) Wireless Sensor Networks - Technology and Applications, chap. 8. IntechOpen, Rijeka (07 2012). https://doi.org/10.5772/50178, ISBN 978-953-51-0676-0
6. Chao, F., He, Z., Pang, A., Zhou, H., Ge, J., Baños, R.: Path optimization of mobile sink node in wireless sensor network water monitoring system. Complexity 2019, 1–10 (11 2019). https://doi.org/10.1155/2019/5781620, ISSN 1076-2787
7. Duche, R.N., Sarwade, N.P.: Sensor node failure detection based on round trip delay and paths in WSNs. IEEE Sens. J. **14**(2), 455–464 (2014). https://doi.org/10.1109/JSEN.2013.2284796
8. Elsayed, W., Elhoseny, M., Riad, A.M., Hassanien, A.E.: Autonomic self-healing approach to eliminate hardware faults in wireless sensor networks. In: Hassanien, A.E., Shaalan, K., Gaber, T., Tolba, M.F. (eds.) AISI 2017. AISC, vol. 639, pp. 151–160. Springer, Cham (2018). https://doi.org/10.1007/978-3-319-64861-3_14
9. Erman, A.T., Dilo, A., Havinga, P.: A virtual infrastructure based on honeycomb tessellation for data dissemination in multi-sink mobile wireless sensor networks. EURASIP J. Wireless Commun. Netw. **2012**(1), 17 (2012). https://doi.org/10.1186/1687-1499-2012-17
10. Gasmi, M., Mosbahi, O., Khalgui, M., Gomes, L., Li, Z.: R-node: new pipelined approach for an effective reconfigurable wireless sensor node. IEEE Trans. Syst. Man, Cybernet.: Syst. **48**(6), 892–905 (12 2016). https://doi.org/10.1109/TSMC.2016.2625817
11. Ghribi, I., Abdallah, R.B., Khalgui, M., Li, Z., Alnowibet, K.A., Platzner, M.: R-codesign: codesign methodology for real-time reconfigurable embedded systems under energy constraints. IEEE Access **6**, 14078–14092 (2018)
12. GloMoSim: GloMoSim simulator projects: online network simulator: network simulation tools. https://networksimulationtools.com/glomosim-simulator-projects/ (2020). Accessed 27 Mar 2022
13. Grichi, H., Mosbahi, O., Khalgui, M.: A development tool chain for reconfigurable WSNs. In: Fujita, H., Papadopoulos, G.A. (eds.) New Trends in Software Methodologies, Tools and Techniques - Proceedings of the Fifteenth SoMeT_16, Larnaca, Cyprus, 12–14 September 2016. Frontiers in Artificial Intelligence and Applications, vol. 286, pp. 101–114. IOS Press (2016). https://doi.org/10.3233/978-1-61499-674-3-101
14. Grichi, H., Mosbahi, O., Khalgui, M., Li, Z.: RWiN: new methodology for the development of reconfigurable WSN. IEEE Trans. Autom. Sci. Eng. **14**(1), 109–125 (2017). https://doi.org/10.1109/TASE.2016.2608918
15. Grichi, H., Mosbahi, O., Khalgui, M., Li, Z.: New power-oriented methodology for dynamic resizing and mobility of reconfigurable wireless sensor networks. IEEE Trans. Syst., Man Cybernet.: Syst. **48**(7), 1120–1130 (2018). https://doi.org/10.1109/TSMC.2016.2645401
16. Hafidi, Y., Kahloul, L., Khalgui, M., Li, Z., Alnowibet, K., Qu, T.: On methodology for the verification of reconfigurable timed net condition/event systems. IEEE Trans. Syst. Man, Cybernet. Syst. **50**(10), 3577–3591 (2020)
17. Housseyni, W., Mosbahi, O., Khalgui, M., Li, Z., Yin, L., Chetto, M.: Multiagent architecture for distributed adaptive scheduling of reconfigurable real-time tasks with energy harvesting constraints. IEEE Access **6**, 2068–2084 (2018). https://doi.org/10.1109/ACCESS.2017.2781459

18. Ji, S., Beyah, R., Cai, Z.: Snapshot and continuous data collection in probabilistic wireless sensor networks. IEEE Trans. Mobile Comput. **13**(3), 626–637 (2014). https://doi.org/10.1109/TMC.2013.30, ISSN 1536-1233

19. JSim: GitHub - nmcl/JavaSim: JavaSim simulation classes and examples (2022). https://github.com/nmcl/JavaSim. Accessed 27 Mar 2022

20. Khediri, S.E., Nasri, N., Khan, R.U., Kachouri, A.: An improved energy efficient clustering protocol for increasing the life time of wireless sensor networks. Wirel. Pers. Commun. **116**(1), 539–558 (2021)

21. Khriji, S., Houssaini, D., Kammoun, I., Kanoun, O.: Energy-efficient techniques in wireless sensor networks: technology, components and system design, pp. 287–304 (11 2018). https://doi.org/10.1515/9783110445053-017, ISBN 978-311-044-505-3

22. Khriji, S., Houssaini, D.E., Kammoun, I., Kanoun, O.: Energy-efficient techniques in wireless sensor networks: technology, components and system design, pp. 287–304. De Gruyter (11 2018). https://doi.org/10.1515/9783110445053-017, ISBN 978-311-044-505-3

23. Moridi, E., Haghparast, M., Hosseinzadeh, M., Jafarali Jassbi, S.: Novel fault-tolerant clustering-based multipath algorithm (FTCM) for wireless sensor networks. Telecommun. Syst. **74**(4), 411–424 (2020). https://doi.org/10.1007/s11235-020-00663-z

24. Moussa, N., Alaoui, A.E.B.E., Chaudet, C.: A novel approach of WSN routing protocols comparison for forest fire detection. Wireless Netw. **26**(3), 1857–1867 (2020)

25. Moussa, N., El Belrhiti El Alaoui, A.: A cluster-based fault-tolerant routing protocol for wireless sensor networks. Int. J. Commun. Syst. **32**(16), e4131 (2019). https://doi.org/10.1002/dac.4131, https://onlinelibrary.wiley.com/doi/abs/10.1002/dac.4131, e4131 dac.4131

26. Nakas, C., Kandris, D., Visvardis, G.: Energy efficient routing in wireless sensor networks: a comprehensive survey. Algorithms **13**(3) (2020). https://doi.org/10.3390/a13030072, ISSN 1999-4893, https://www.mdpi.com/1999-4893/13/3/72

27. Nayyar, A., Singh, R.: A comprehensive review of simulation tools for wireless sensor networks (WSNs). Wireless Netw. Commun. **5**(1), 19–47 (01 2015). https://doi.org/10.5923/j.jwnc.20150501.03

28. Nguyen, L., Nguyen, H.T.: Mobility based network lifetime in wireless sensor networks: a review. Comput. Netw. **174**, 107236 (06 2020). https://doi.org/10.1016/j.comnet.2020.107236, ISSN 1389-1286, https://www.sciencedirect.com/science/article/pii/S1389128619315865

29. NS3: ns-3: a discrete-event network simulator for internet systems (2022). https://www.nsnam.org/. Accessed 26 Mar 2022

30. OMNeTPP: OMNeT++ Discrete Event Simulator (2019). https://omnetpp.org/. Accessed 27 Mar 2022

31. Peijun, Z., Feng, R.: An energy efficient multiple mobile sinks based routing algorithm for wireless sensor networks. IOP Conf. Ser.: Mater. Sci. Eng. **323**, 012029 (03 2018). https://doi.org/10.1088/1757-899x/323/1/012029

32. Priya, M., C, S., k.a, S.: Proactive fault tolerant routing protocol for mobile WSN. **9**, 1892–1896 (11 2019). https://doi.org/10.35940/ijitee.L3656.119119

33. Raj, S.N.M., Bhattacharyya, D., Midhunchakkaravarthy, D., Kim, T.: Multi-hop in clustering with mobility protocol to save the energy utilization in wireless sensor networks. Wireless Pers. Commun. **117**(4), 3381–3395 (2021). https://doi.org/10.1007/s11277-021-08078-y

34. Rajan, C., Geetha, K., Priya, C.R., Geetha, S., Manikandan, A.: A simple analysis on novel based open source network simulation tools for mobile ad hoc networks. Int. J. Adv. Res. Comput. Sci. Softw. Eng. **5**(3), 716–721 (2015)

35. Ramasamy, V.: Mobile wireless sensor networks: an overview. In: Sallis, P. (ed.) Wireless Sensor Networks - Insights and Innovations, chap. 1, pp. 1–12. IntechOpen, Rijeka (10 2017). https://doi.org/10.5772/intechopen.70592, ISBN 978-953-51-3562-3; 978-953-51-3561-6

36. Robinson, H., Julie, G., Balaji, S.: Bandwidth and delay aware routing protocol with scheduling algorithm for multi hop mobile ad hoc networks. Int. J. Comput. Electr. Autom. Control Inf. Eng. **10**(8), 1512–1521 (2017)

37. Rouainia, H., Grichi, H., Kahloul, L., Khalgui, M.: 3D mobility, resizing and mobile sink nodes in reconfigurable wireless sensor networks based on multi-agent architecture under energy harvesting constraints. In: Proceedings of the 15th International Conference on Software Technologies - ICSOFT, pp. 394–406. INSTICC, SciTePress (01 2020). https://doi.org/10.5220/0009971503940406, ISBN 978-989-758-443-5; ISSN 2184-2833

38. Rouainia, H., Grichi, H., Kahloul, L., Khalgui, M.: New energy efficient and fault tolerant methodology based on a multi-agent architecture in reconfigurable wireless sensor networks. In: Kaindl, H., Mannion, M., Maciaszek, L.A. (eds.) Proceedings of the 17th International Conference on Evaluation of Novel Approaches to Software Engineering, ENASE 2022, Online Streaming, April 25–26, 2022, pp. 405–416. SCITEPRESS (2022). https://doi.org/10.5220/0011061300003176

39. Rouainia, H., Grichi, H., Kahloul, L., Khalgui, M.: Reconfigurable wireless sensor networks simulator (rwsnsim): a new discrete-event simulator. In: Fill, H., van Sinderen, M., Maciaszek, L.A. (eds.) Proceedings of the 17th International Conference on Software Technologies, Lisbon, Portugal, July 11–13, 2022. pp. 349–361. SCITEPRESS (2022). https://doi.org/10.5220/0011318300003266, ISBN 978-989-758-588-3; ISSN 2184-2833

40. RWiN: RWiN-Project: new solutions for reconfigurable wireless sensor networks. https://lisi-lab.wix.com/rwinproject (2016). Accessed 26 Mar 2022

41. RWSNSim: RWSNSim: reconfigurable wireless sensor networks simulator. https://hanenerouainia.wixsite.com/rwsnsim (2022). Accessed 20 Apr 2022

42. Salem, M.O.B.: BROMETH: methodology to develop safe reconfigurable medical robotic systems: application on pediatric supracondylar humeral fracture. Ph.D. thesis, Saarland University, Saarbrücken, Germany (2017)

43. Shalini, V.B., Vasudevan, V.: e-NL BEENISH: extended-network lifetime balanced energy efficient network integrated super heterogeneous protocol for a wireless sensor network. Int. J. Comput. Aided Eng. Technol. **15**(2–3), 317–327 (2021)

44. Thomas, S., Mathew, T.: Intelligent path discovery for a mobile sink in wireless sensor network. Procedia Comput. Sci. **143**, 749–756 (2018). https://doi.org/10.1016/j.procs.2018.10.430, ISSN 1877-0509, http://www.sciencedirect.com/science/article/pii/S1877050918321288, 8th International Conference on Advances in Computing and Communications (ICACC-2018)

45. Tzounis, A., Katsoulas, N., Bartzanas, T., Kittas, C.: Internet of things in agriculture, recent advances and future challenges. Biosyst. Eng. **164**, 31–48 (12 2017). https://doi.org/10.1016/j.biosystemseng.2017.09.007

46. Verma, S., Sood, N., Sharma, A.K.: A novelistic approach for energy efficient routing using single and multiple data sinks in heterogeneous wireless sensor network. Peer-to-Peer Netw. Appl. **12**(5), 1110–1136 (2019). https://doi.org/10.1007/s12083-019-00777-5

47. Vijayalakshmi, S., Muruganand, S.: Wireless sensor network: architecture - applications - Advancements (05 2018)

48. Wang, J., Gao, Y., Liu, W., Kumar, A., Kim, H.J.: Energy efficient routing algorithm with mobile sink support for wireless sensor networks. Sensors **19**(7), 1494 (03 2019). https://doi.org/10.3390/s19071494

49. Zagrouba, R., Kardi, A.: Comparative study of energy efficient routing techniques in wireless sensor networks. Information **12**(1), 42 (01 2021). https://doi.org/10.3390/info12010042

50. Zidi, S., Moulahi, T., Alaya, B.: Fault detection in wireless sensor networks through SVM classifier. IEEE Sens. J. **18**(1), 340–347 (2018). https://doi.org/10.1109/JSEN.2017.2771226

Adapting Cyber-Risk Assessment for the Planning of Cyber-Physical Smart Grids Based on Industrial Needs

Gencer Erdogan[1]([✉])[iD], Iver Bakken Sperstad[2][iD], Michele Garau[2][iD],
Oddbjørn Gjerde[2][iD], Inger Anne Tøndel[3][iD], Shukun Tokas[1][iD],
and Martin Gilje Jaatun[3][iD]

[1] Sustainable Communication Technologies, SINTEF Digital, Oslo, Norway
{gencer.erdogan,shukun.tokas}@sintef.no
[2] Energy Systems, SINTEF Energy Research, Trondheim, Norway
{iver.bakken.sperstad,michele.garau,oddbjorn.gjerde}@sintef.no
[3] Software Engineering, Safety and Security, SINTEF Digital, Trondheim, Norway
{ingeranne.tondel,martin.g.jaatun}@sintef.no

Abstract. During the grid planning process, electric power grid companies evaluate different options for the long-term grid development to address the expected future demands. The options can be passive measures, e.g., traditional reinforcement or building new lines, or active measures, e.g., support from ICT-solutions during operation to increase the power transfer capability. The ongoing digitalization of the electric power grid inevitably push the grid companies to assess potential cyber risks as part of the grid planning process. This applies especially for active measures which to a greater extent rely on support from ICT-solutions to operate the system closer to its limits. However, current grid planning approaches do not adequately provide the support needed in practice, and the industry is struggling to adopt and execute cyber-risk assessments. The contribution of this paper is threefold. First, we interview six companies from the energy sector, and based on the interviews we identify seven success criteria that cyber-risk assessment methods for the electric power sector need to fulfil to provide adequate support. Second, we present four risk assessment methods and evaluate the extent to which they fulfil the identified success criteria. Third, we address the specific need for approaches that are easy to use and comprehend, especially for grid planning purposes, and propose a low-threshold approach to support high-level cyber-risk assessment in an electric power grid planning process. Based on our findings, we provide lessons learned in terms of gaps that need to be addressed to improve cyber-risk assessment in the context of smart grids.

Keywords: Cyber risk · Cybersecurity · Cyber physical · Smart grid ·
Cyber-risk assessment · Grid planning · Challenges · Success criteria

1 Introduction

Grid planning is a process that electric power grid companies carry out to change power transfer capability through decisions about the construction, upgrading, replacement,

H.-G. Fill et al. (Eds.): ICSOFT 2022, CCIS 1859, pp. 98–121, 2023.
https://doi.org/10.1007/978-3-031-37231-5_5

retrofitting or decommissioning of assets [16]. Long-term grid planning is typically carried out on a time horizon of decades, and aims to develop the system optimally to meet future demands. Grid planning can rely on passive measures such as traditional reinforcement or building new lines, or active measures such as support from ICT-solutions during operation to increase the power transfer capability or facilitate other kinds of optimizations. The ongoing digitalization of the electric power grid is resulting in complex cyber-physical smart grid systems that may be highly exposed to cyber risks. Electric power grid companies are therefore pushed to assess potential cyber risks as part of the grid planning process. This is difficult because most available information about the target power grid at the planning stage is at a conceptual level.

Cyber-risk assessment is the de facto approach used by large organizations to manage cybersecurity risks, but current standards, methods and tools do not adequately provide the support needed in practice for smart grid systems. Widely used cyber-risk assessment approaches such as ISO 27005 [25] and NIST 800-39 [37] are not easily aligned with risk assessment approaches that are specific for power systems [26,31]. Although risk assessment approaches from the cybersecurity and the power domains share some overall characteristics, the industry is struggling to adopt and carry out risk assessments considering cyber-risks, and has limited knowledge on how to best use existing approaches to carry out a holistic cyber-risk assessment. This is becoming increasingly important when considering the merged cyber-physical aspect of the future power grid systems. Moreover, there is a lack of knowledge for combining an assessment of specific types of threats (e.g., cyber) with an overarching assessment to obtain a more concrete picture of the overall risk.

This paper explores the industry's challenges and needs for carrying out cyber-risk assessment in complex and integrated cyber-physical power systems and smart grids. Moreover, it explores strategies for moving towards integrated risk assessment that includes both cybersecurity and power system threats, ICT dependability issues, as well as the consideration of cyber risks in the grid planning process. Thus, the contribution of this paper is threefold. First, we carry out interviews with representatives from the industry to better understand the current and envisioned needs when it comes to cyber-risk assessment of smart grids. These interviews lead to the identification of success criteria for risk assessment methods in the context of smart grids. Second, we describe four different methods for risk assessment we have used in previous work to assess cyber-risks in smart grids. For each of these methods, we provide a description and evaluate the extent to which they meet the success criteria identified from the interviews. Based on the evaluation, we map the four methods to a qualitative scale representing the level of fulfillment of criteria. Third, we address the need for approaches that are easy to use and comprehend, especially for grid planning purposes, and propose a low-threshold approach to support high-level cyber-risk assessment. We also provide lessons learned in terms of identified gaps that need to be addressed to improve cyber-risk assessment in the context of smart grids.

The rest of the paper is organized as follows. Section 2 describes the background, while Sect. 3 describes related work. Section 4 describes our research method. Section 5 describes the findings from the interviews and the identified success criteria. Section 6 describes the four risk assessment methods used in previous work, while Sect. 7

evaluates the extent to which the methods fulfill the identified success criteria. In Sect. 8, we turn our focus on adapting a low-threshold cyber-risk assessment method for a grid planning process. Finally, Sect. 9 concludes the paper and summarizes lessons learned in terms of identified gaps. This paper is an extended version of the paper by Erdogan et al. [13]. The new content in this extended version is related to cyber-risk assessment for grid planning based on industrial needs we identified in the first version of the paper. This extension led to updated contents in Sects. 1, 2, 3, 4, and 9. Moreover, most of the contents in Sects. 2 and 3 are new, while Sect. 8 is completely new considering the adaptation of cyber-risk assessment for grid planning.

2   Background

According to ISO 27005, "a risk is a combination of the consequences that would follow from the occurrence of an unwanted event and the likelihood of the occurrence of the event" [25]. In the context of smart grids, risk assessment is the process of identifying, estimating and prioritizing risks to the grid's operations and assets. The aforementioned steps are part of the standard risk assessment processes [25,38]. The technological trends underlying the smart grid suggests a broad spectrum of the ICT being deployed for more effective grid operations. This integrated digital-power grid shift also brings increasing attack risks to the smart grid. The energy industry faces significant challenges in managing such risks.

Assessment of traditional, physical risks is an important part of grid companies' activities on all time horizons, from operation to long-term planning. Cyber risks, on the other hand, are typically assessed based on existing cyber-physical systems; they are usually not considered as part of planning activities for the long-term development of the system, which should be in place to promote security-by-design. Grid planning, or grid development, is traditionally dealing with "decisions that change power transfer capability through decisions about the construction, upgrading, replacement, retrofitting or decommissioning of assets" [16]. A simple example of such a decision is whether the grid company should a) upgrade a distribution line to meet the expected increase in electricity demand in an area, or b) defer the investment and take the risk of operational challenges in case it turns out that the existing system becomes insufficient to ensure the security of electricity supply. For such decisions, cyber-risk assessments are unlikely to influence the grid company's choice between the alternatives (a and b).

However, smart grids introduce the option of implementing so-called active grid planning measures that involve active utilization of resources in the grid during grid operation. A general framework for the planning of active distribution grids was proposed in [47]. Figure 1 gives a high-level illustration of a grid planning process according to this framework.

Figure 1 illustrates how active measures are considered on equal footing as traditional (passive) measures when generating the set of grid planning alternatives to choose from. Passive measures involve installing physical power grid infrastructure in the system. Active measures to a much larger extent also involves ICT infrastructure. For example, alternative (b) in the example above could involve installing dynamic grid reconfiguration and self-healing functionality and plan for utilizing these new resources

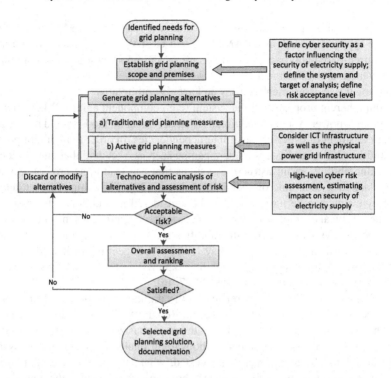

Fig. 1. Framework for planning of active distribution grids, adapted from [47]. Text boxes on the right indicates the adaptations needed to consider cyber risk.

to manage potential operational risks during the operational phase. Since this alternative (b) to a much larger extent than alternative (a) relies on ICT for operating with these active distribution grid functionalities, it is important to also consider cyber risks in the planning phase. This should be defined as a part of the grid planning study already in the initial step ("Establish grid planning scope and premises"). The remainder of this paper will however focus on assessment of cyber risk as part of the step for techno-economic analysis that includes assessment of risk in general.

3   Related Work

As indicated in Sect. 1, there are many standards and specialized approaches for cyber-risk assessment. The most widely used standards are developed by ISO and NIST. The literature offers a wide variety of modelling techniques for risk identification and assessment. Fault tree analysis (FTA) [24], event tree analysis (ETA) [23] and attack trees [43] are examples of tree-based approaches and provide support for reasoning about the sources and consequences of unwanted incidents, as well as their likelihoods. Cause-consequence analysis (CCA) [36] and Bayesian networks [4] are examples of graph-based notations. Cause-consequence analysis employs diagrams that combine the features of both fault trees and event trees, whereas the latter two serves as mathematical models for probabilistic and statistical calculations, respectively. Moreover, whereas alternative approaches such as CRAMM [3] and OCTAVE [1] rely on text and tables, graph and tree-based approaches use diagrams as an important means for communication, evaluation, and assessment.

Traditional risk assessment focuses on hazards with relatively high probability that come from inherent properties of the system (e.g., component aging). When analyzing risks in today's power systems, traditional risk assessment methods should be integrated with an assessment of cyber-physical interdependencies, in order to highlight potential vulnerabilities. Vulnerability assessment can be seen as a method that aims to identify hidden vulnerabilities in infrastructure systems that can lead to severe consequences, such as blackouts, economic or social turmoil, etc. [28]. These high-impact and low-probability events can be too complex to be considered in traditional risk-assessment approaches. Typical examples of cases where risk-based approaches may be insufficient for a proper analysis of hidden vulnerabilities are the cases of emergent behaviors, intricate rules of interaction, system of systems, broad spectrum of hazard and threats [28]. A framework for studying vulnerabilities and risk in the electricity supply, based on the bow-tie model, is proposed in [19,20,27,46].

A fundamental work on risks related to the digitalization process in power systems has been proposed by the Task Force on Reliability Consideration for Emerging Cyber-Physical Energy Systems [2]. The authors emphasize the necessity of modernizing the reliability and risk assessment methods traditionally adopted in power systems. A multi-layer modelling approach is suggested, where the power layer, communication and coupling layer and decision layer interact in order to enable the power system operation. Each of these layers are characterized by vulnerabilities that should be singularly addressed. Conventional risk assessment techniques are primarily focused on the power layer, and can be primarily classified into two categories: analytical methods and simulation methods (e.g., Monte Carlo simulation) [5]. In order to include in the power system risk assessment possible failure states in the ICT infrastructures, novel approaches have been introduced, which adopt complex network theory [58], cyber-physical interface matrix [29], co-simulation [15], and traditional event trees [33] and reliability block diagrams [10]. These works adopt approaches that are strongly related with the concept of probability of failure occurrence, therefore they find a difficult application to scenarios where the threat is deliberate and there are few statistics available to be included in probabilistic approaches. As a consequence, in order to model the effect of successful exploitation of vulnerabilities, risk modelling is performed using high-level conceptual models, such as ISO/IEC Common Criteria standard [2], stochastic Petri net models [49], Markov processes [57] and Bayesian attack graphs [56].

The above presented works propose approaches that address the problem of assessing cyber-risk in the operation of the smart grid that, despite being a relatively young research area, is converging towards a consensus regarding approaches and standards. On the other side, cyber-risk assessment in the context of smart grid planning, or in the more general context of cyber-physical critical infrastructures, represents a novel research field that is mostly unexplored. For this reason, the scientific literature presents just a few works in this research field, that only border on the main research problem of finding the optimal planning solution properly taking into account cyber-risks (see Sect. 2). Wang et al. in [51] propose an optimisation model for distributed generation and grid expansion planning taking into account substations failures due to cyber failures. The authors model the cyber failures events with random parameters characterized by a constant failure rate, and aim at minimizing the investments taking into account the costs of energy not supplied due to cyber failures. A more accurate mathematical description of human dynamics for cyber attacks is proposed in [52], which proposes the adoption of power law distribution instead of the Poisson distribution to simulate the cyber attack occurrence pattern in the reliability evaluation of electric power grid considering cyber vulnerabilities.

Instead of considering the probability of occurrence of cyber attacks to critical infrastructures, other works focus more on the resilience properties of the infrastructure, which can be defined as the ability of the system to mitigate any residual risk, as well as address unknown or emerging threats [32,53]. Huang et al. in [22] propose an optimal planning policy to enhance resilience and security of interdependent critical infrastructures (ICI), represented by communication networks, power grid and subway networks. The interdependencies between infrastructure components are modelled through holistic probabilistic networks, where the failure and recovery dynamics are modelled through Markov decision processes (MDP). An agent-based modelling approach is presented by Foglietta et al. [14], aiming at simulating interdependences between cyber-physical layers in critical infrastructures, and cascading effects in fault propagation.

4 Research Method

Figure 2 illustrates our research method, which consists of eight steps. In Step 1, we conducted four interviews with four companies in the energy sector and two interviews with two sectorial organizations. The two sectorial organizations are the Computer Emergency Response Team for the electric power sector (KraftCERT) and the Norwegian Water Resources and Energy Directorate (NVE). The energy companies are not named due to confidentiality. Thus, we carried out in total six interviews. Table 1 lists the interviews we carried out, including date, duration, participants, and the type of company/organization interviewed. The interview team consisted of two participants; one taking the role as interviewer and one taking the role as secretary. The interviews were semi-structured, covering the following topics:

– Current practice in cybersecurity and risk management in the energy sector.
– Risk management and cybersecurity approaches that work well based on the interviewee's experience.
– Needs and challenges within risk management and cybersecurity in the energy sector.

The main task of the secretary was to note the questions asked by the interviewer, as well as the answers provided by the interviewee. However, we did allow for the secretary to also come with questions sporadically, in which case the interviewer would take notes. In addition to the time spent on conducting the interviews, the interviewer and the secretary spent approximately 1 h after each interview to tidy up the transcribed interview draft.

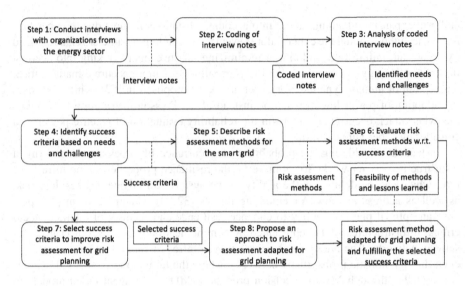

Fig. 2. Research method.

All interviewed companies/organizations are Norwegian. We recruited the interviewees through our own network, but also asking companies and organizations from the CINELDI (Centre for Intelligent Electricity Distribution) project [7], which is the project in which this work was carried out. The interviewees were people with different roles, including Chief Information Security Officer (CISO), Cybersecurity expert, and Senior Project Manager.

The output of Step 1 was a set of interview notes. The interview notes were used as input to Step 2, in which the interview team coded the collected data using the MAXQDA tool. The coding was mainly inductive, but with some high level organizing codes to structure the material (current practice; works well; challenges; needs). In Step 3, the interview team went through all the codes and highlighted the notes that indicated a need or a challenge the energy sector was experiencing with respect to risk assessment. For this, we used memos in MAXQDA that were linked to the coded segments.

In Step 4, we identified a set of success criteria based on the needs and challenges indicated by the interviews. The success criteria represent criteria for risk assessment approaches to successfully assess cyber risks in (the future) cyber-physical smart grids (according to the needs indicated by the interviewees). In Step 5, we described four risk assessment approaches we have used in industrial cases within the energy sector to assess risks in smart grids. The approaches we describe are CORAS, the Vulnerability Analysis Framework, Threat Modeling with STRIDE, and Stochastic Activity Network. These approaches were selected because of two main reasons: 1) the authors have years of experience in applying these methods in the energy sector as well as other industrial context, and 2) these approaches support risk assessment from different yet complementary perspectives, and we wanted to assess the feasibility of the approaches with respect to the identified success criteria.

Table 1. Interviews conducted. CISO = Chief Information Security Officer. PM = Project Manager. Table adapted from [13].

No.	Date	Duration	Interview team	interviewee	Organization
1	28.09.2021	1 h	1 Interviewer 1 Secretary	1 Cybersecurity Expert	KraftCERT
2	15.10.2021	1 h	1 Interviewer 1 Secretary	1 CISO	Energy company
3	19.10.2021	1 h	1 Interviewer 1 Secretary	1 CISO	Energy company
4	04.11.2021	1 h	1 Interviewer 1 Secretary	1 CISO 1 Senior PM	Energy company
5	05.11.2021	1 h	1 Interviewer 1 Secretary	1 CISO	Energy company
6	22.11.2021	1 h	1 Interviewer 1 Secretary	1 Cybersecurity Expert	NVE

In Step 6, we evaluate the four risk assessment approaches with respect to the identified success criteria; we discuss the extent to which the risk assessment approaches fulfill the success criteria and the gaps that need to be addressed. This evaluation also acts as a basis for lessons learned, summarized in Sect. 9.

Based on the identified success criteria and lessons learned, we selected, in Step 7, one success criterion to focus on in order to adapt risk assessment for grid planning. The selected success criterion is related to ease of comprehension and use by people who are not experts in cyber-risk assessment (Criterion SC1 in Sect. 5).

Finally, in Step 8 we propose an approach to risk assessment, based on existing methods, adapted for grid planning and fulfilling the selected success criterion in Step 7 (SC1).

5   Identified Success Criteria

This section describes the success criteria identified based on the interviews, as explained in Sect. 4. In total, we identified seven success criteria (SC) for risk assessment approaches, addressing needs and challenges in the industry pointed out by the interviewees. In the following, we present each success criterion and describe their motivation based on the interviews.

SC1 Be Easy to Comprehend and Use by People Who Are Not Experts in Risk Assessment. Interviewees state that it is essential that risk assessments are easy to do also by people who are not experts in cybersecurity and risk assessment. Several interviewees express that quantitative methods are not currently an option for them, and that there is a need to start with very easy methods. One interviewee even states that it is more important that a method is easy to use than the quality of the results of the analysis, because if the method is too complex and requires too much effort it will meet resistance and the risk assessment will probably not be carried out. Currently, many of the companies seem to opt for using the same methods for cyber risk as for other risks. In the companies, there is a limited number of people that have the competence to do risk assessments related to cyber risk, and information security experts become a bottleneck if they have to be involved in all such assessments. Thus, there is a push towards system owners taking on more responsibility for assessing risk, and at least one of the companies are training project managers in performing risk assessments that include information security. Note also that we talked with relatively large companies within this sector. However, one interviewee explains that more than half of the distribution grid companies are small companies with less than 50 employees. And such companies are unlikely to have dedicated in-house cybersecurity experts. If the risk analyst does not have the necessary competence, support, or training, interviewees explain that one risk is that the analyst just ticks that a risk assessment has been performed without the risks being properly assessed.

SC2 Provide Support to Determine Whether the Method Is a Good Match for a Given Context. There is a large variety in current practice and current ability to perform cybersecurity risk assessments among the companies in the electric power distribution sector. A method that is suitable for a larger company with dedicated information security experts may not be suitable for a smaller company without such experts. Based on the interviews, it seems that especially for those with limited competence, it is difficult to know how to start analyzing cyber risk and what questions to consider in the assessment. Further, there are different types of risk assessments that are performed in the companies, ranging from yearly risk assessments to smaller assessments as part of procurement or changes. There is a clearly stated need to start with simple assessment approaches, but at the same time the complexity of the target of analysis may point to a need to move towards more complex assessment approaches in some cases, including when companies have become more mature in their approach to cybersecurity risk assessments.

SC3 Support Preparation for Risk Assessment, Including Establishing a Common Understanding of Concepts and Build Necessary Knowledge of Participants from IT and OT. When cybersecurity is considered in the more traditional risk assessments, it is experienced as being abstract. Interviewees tell of experiences where cybersecurity is represented with only one scenario in combination with other types of threats, e.g., technical failures, extreme weather conditions. In many of the companies there seem to be a division between IT and OT, though some explain that understanding across IT and OT has improved, e.g., through participating in workshops. One of the interviewees explains that there commonly is a lack of training of people that become involved in a risk assessment. One example pointed out is that individuals from OT are involved (which is encouraged) in risk assessments without any prior understanding of cyber risk and the risk assessment process, thus leading to misunderstandings and challenges during assessment. IT and OT people may, e.g., disagree on the interpretation of key concepts such as likelihood and consequence and have a different understanding of criticality. In the sector, there is some support material available from sectorial organizations. However, there is a need for more support – concrete examples and lists of scenarios are highlighted in the interviews – to motivate for risk assessments, help understand what may happen, and improve quality. It is difficult to contribute meaning-fully to a risk assessment without some basic understanding of a potential attack, what techniques can be used, and how such attacks can be mitigated. Furthermore, though people from OT are experts in their domain they might not have the knowledge needed to evaluate cyber risk, e.g., know the architecture of the OT systems.

SC4 Manage Complexity in the Risk Assessment, Considering the Target of Analysis. The analysis target is complex, and the complexity is increasing, which makes it difficult to do good risk assessments. There are several reasons for these challenges. There are ongoing changes in work processes and in systems and their use, and some of these changes happen gradually. Often, manual systems are seen as backups, but eventually the organization looses experience in using these manual backup systems, and thus they lose much of their value. This gradual change can be difficult to capture in risk assessments. For example, if an assessment uses a previous analysis as a start-ing point, it is easy to become influenced of the previous conclusions and not see what has changed and the assumptions that may no longer be valid. Furthermore, there are connections and dependencies between systems that may be difficult to capture in an assessment. Interviewees provide examples that though OT systems are clearly mission-critical, other systems like Advanced Metering Infrastructure (AMI) may also be critical as they are necessary for other key functions, such as being able to bill customers. How-ever, these other systems may not get enough attention. It is challenging to understand how one risk affects other risks. Assessments are often done for single systems or for single types of incidents, but it is challenging to understand any relations between these and combine analysis results to get a more holistic view of the risk.

SC5 Support Risk Estimation, e.g., Likelihood and Consequence Estimation, as Well as Ranking of Assets Considered in the Risk Assessment. There is a need to know what are the most critical assets and work processes to protect. Risk estimation is often done through estimation of the likelihood and consequence of certain incidents. However, the criteria that are used to estimate likelihood and consequence in assess-ments of other types of risk may not be relevant when assessing cyber risk. Moreover, interviewees tell that disagreements between different professions often happen related to likelihood and consequence estimation. When it comes to consequence, the main challenges are related to estimation of indirect consequences (e.g., reputation). One interviewee points to security economy as important moving forward, to make the eco-nomic costs of security incidents clearer to the decision makers. When it comes to likeli-hood estimation, this is considered particularly difficult as one is dealing with malicious threats. Several interviewees consider replacing likelihood estimates with evaluations of threat actors and their capacity and intention, and the vulnerabilities present. However, changing the method into something that is different from what is used for assess-ments of other types of risks in the company is not without challenges. For example, this makes it difficult to aggregate results from different analysis to support decision-making. Furthermore, interviewees explain that there is not enough data to use for esti-mating likelihood, and point to the risk of underestimating the likelihood for things that have not yet happened. One interviewee explains that support for reuse of likelihood estimates would be highly useful. Support for reuse would reduce the need to involve key experts in every analysis. Many of the assessments are of objects that have similar characteristics. Moreover, many aspects about the threats are similar for other companies of the same type.

SC6 Provide Support for Increasing Trustworthiness of the Risk Assessment Results, as Well as Manage and Represent Uncertainty. Criticism of current risk assessments is that they are subjective and that they are not able to identify all important issues to consider, to improve cybersecurity. Due to challenges related to risk estimation (SC5), a few interviewees point to the need to consider uncertainty in the risk estimates. Trustworthiness in risk estimation is important, to be confident in what to report to management, and in providing arguments for how security investments are important for the business. Several of the interviewees move towards more pentesting and system monitoring, as these are considered more effective than risk assessments in identifying vulnerabilities. Thus, this brings up possibilities for combining risk assessments with pentesting and monitoring, in ways that increase trustworthiness in assessment and effectiveness in testing and monitoring. Some interviewees envision a future with more real time risk assessments, and wish for more tool support that can help them in the risk assessments and that are able to bring in data as support, e.g., to identify relevant threat scenarios.

SC7 Facilitate Risk Management through Documentation, Maintenance of Assessments, and expression of Risk Treatments. As pointed out by one interviewee, risk assessment does not necessarily imply risk management. Though an analysis identify many risks, it may not be straight forward to know what to do about these risks. Another interviewee points out that the more traditional way of thinking within this sector, that everything should be secure, may not work moving forward, and that there will be a need to build resilience into the system so that they can tolerate some cyber-incidents taking place. Regarding documentation, one interviewee explained about a lack of culture for documenting risk analysis. Moreover, interviewees point to the importance of having updated risk assessments. However, it is challenging to ensure such updates are made whenever there are changes made in the systems. Furthermore, with increasing number of systems, scalability of the assessment approach is also an issue, especially if information security experts need to be involved or even responsible for such assessments. Another challenge is communicating the results of the risk assessment in a way that is comprehensible to management and that puts the cyber-risk topic on their agenda. On the positive side, one interviewee tells about regular reporting of cyber risk to the board, and another tells about using high-level threat modeling in the management group, to discuss why attacks are possible and what can be done. On the other hand, one interviewee points to the risk assessment as difficult to communicate to the management.

6   Risk Assessment Methods

This section describes the four risk assessment approaches we have used in industrial cases within the energy sector: CORAS, the Vulnerability Analysis Framework (VAF), Threat Modeling with STRIDE (TM-STRIDE), and Dependability analysis with Stochastic Activity Network (SAN). It is beyond this paper to describe each method in detail, we therefore provide a brief description of each approach and refer to other sources for further details.

6.1 CORAS

CORAS is a method for conducting security risk assessment [34]. In the CORAS method, a security risk assessment is conducted in eight steps: 1) preparations for the analysis, 2) customer presentation of the target, 3) refining the target description using asset diagrams, 4) approval of the target description, 5) risk identification using threat diagrams, 6) risk estimation using threat diagrams, 7) risk evaluation using risk diagrams, and 8) risk treatment using treatment diagrams.

CORAS provides a customized language for threat and risk modelling, and comes with detailed guidelines explaining how the language should be used to capture and model relevant information during the various steps of security risk assessment. The CORAS method provides a web-based tool [8] designed to support documenting, maintaining and reporting assessment results through risk modelling. CORAS is a general approach to cybersecurity risk assessment and has been applied to a large variety of risk assessment targets and concerns within numerous domains, including security, safety, law, civil protection, emergency planning, defense, health, and energy [34, 39, 40].

6.2 The Vulnerability Analysis Framework (VAF)

The Vulnerability Analysis Framework (VAF) [17, 20, 46] is an analysis approach aimed at identifying and analyzing vulnerabilities related to extraordinary events with respect to the security of electricity supply. The key concepts in VAF are *susceptibility* (i.e., the extent to which a system is susceptible to a threat), and *coping capacity* (i.e., the extent to which a system is able to cope with the negative consequences of a potential threat). These are concepts used in bow-tie diagrams, and VAF can utilize bow-tie diagrams for some of its six analysis steps: 1) identify critical consequences, 2) identify component outages leading to critical consequences, 3) identify threats that can cause the critical outages, 4) identify vulnerabilities associated with the power system's susceptibility and coping capacity, 5) identify factors influencing coping capacity, and 6) vulnerability evaluation, identify existing and missing barriers against critical outages.

The VAF has been used for analysis focusing on the more traditional threats experienced in power systems, such as meteorological events and technical failures. However, it has also been successfully used for analysis of a cyber-physical power system where cyber threats were included in the analysis [50]. This resulted in the recommendation that interdependencies were identified and documented from Step 3 and onwards, e.g., using the interdependence types identified by Rinaldi et al. [41]; physical, cyber, geographical, and logical.

6.3 Threat Modeling with STRIDE (TM-STRIDE)

Threat modeling is a process that reviews the security of any connected system, identifies problem areas, and determines the risk associated with each area. We refer to the result as a threat model, even though it might not necessarily satisfy the formal requirements of a "model". Incidentally, threat modelling is part of what McGraw refers to as Architectural Risk Analysis [35].

The STRIDE mnemonic (Spoofing, Tampering, Repudiation, Information disclosure, Denial of service, Elevation of privilege) was introduced by Microsoft, and gained prominence through Swidersky & Snyder's [48] book on threat modeling and Howard & Lipner's [21] book on the Microsoft Security Development Lifecycle. A later book by Shostack [44] also covers a number of compatible software tools, including the Microsoft Threat Modeling tool [6], which conforms to the methodology presented by Swidersky & Snyder.

The first step in this threat modeling approach is to draw a data flow diagram [9] which helps to understand the system's attack surface by providing an overview of entities, processes and data stores, identifying trust boundaries and sketching how data flows in the system. The resulting threat model is thus a visual representation of four main elements: the assets within a system, the system's attack surface, a description of how the components and assets interact, and threat actors who could attack the system and how the attack could occur.

6.4 Dependability Analysis with SAN (DA-SAN)

A novel approach for dependability analysis of power systems is proposed by Zerihun, Garau, and Helvik [55] based on Stochastic Activity Network (SAN) modelling. SAN is a variant of Petri Nets [42] and provides a flexible formalism which is particularly suitable for complex interacting entities, through the input and output ports that allow representing interaction with simple conditional statements. The approach provides an efficient method to analyze the impact of ICT vulnerabilities on power system operation.

Major events such as failure and repair within power system and ICT systems are modelled along with the ICT infrastructure management (MANO system, VM redundancy, etc.) with the SAN formalism. The power flow and power system operation calculations are performed with numerical solvers, included in the SAN model with external C++ libraries purposely developed. The tool implemented exploits and enhances the inherent advantages of the SAN formalism: efficient computation simulation, structured modelling, and modularity and flexibility.

In [55], the SAN method is evaluated on a test distribution network, where the impact of ICT internal and external vulnerabilities on the performances of a state estimation calculation is quantitatively analysed. Among internal vulnerabilities, radio link failures, server failures, measuring devices, etc. have been considered. Among external vulnerabilities, the impact of signal fading due to rain precipitation has been inspected.

7 Evaluation of Risk Assessment Methods

Figure 3 illustrates a comparison of the risk assessment methods CORAS, the Vulnerability Analysis Framework (VAF), Threat Modeling with STRIDE (TM-STRIDE), and Dependability Analysis with SAN (DA-SAN) in a scale reflecting their fulfillment of the success criteria described in Sect. 5. The placement of each method in the scale in Fig. 3 is based on the authors' expert knowledge and experience in using the methods as outlined in Sect. 6.

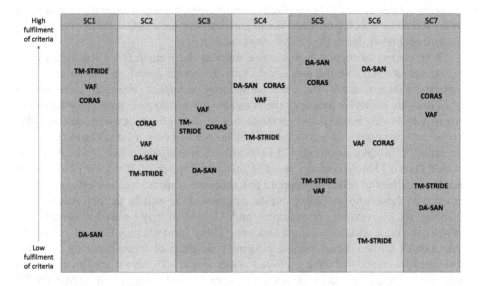

Fig. 3. Comparison of methods with respect to fulfillment of the success criteria described in Sect. 5. Figure adapted from [13].

Companies within the electric power sector need risk assessment approaches that are easy to comprehend and use (SC1). The methods VAF and CORAS have empirically been shown to be easy to comprehend and use by people with different backgrounds [30, 45]. However, we believe VAF is slightly easier to comprehend by personnel of the electric power sector companies because VAF uses concepts and constructs that are commonly used in the power sector. CORAS has also been used in many industrial risk assessments for the power sector [39,40]. Threat modelling using Data Flow Diagrams is a widely used approach, and it is therefore reasonable to argue that it is easy to use, in particular considering cyber risks. The approach DA-SAN needs specialized expertise and may not be easy to use unless one has the specific competence and skills. Although VAF, CORAS, and TM-STRIDE may be easier to comprehend and use compared to DA-SAN, none of the methods fully meet the SC1 criterion. Based on the interviews and our experiences, we argue that not many of the existing risk assessment approaches are easy to comprehend and use for non-experts in the electric power sector because most approaches do not have domain-specific support for the electric power sector (see Sect. 2).

Considering the criterion SC1, and the fact that all the identified criteria described in Sect. 5 points out the need for some kind of support to more easily carry out risk assessment, comprehensibility and ease of use seems to be the most important success criterion. One way of addressing this challenge would be to make the existing approaches more light-weight, but this would come at the cost of expressiveness and the methods' ability to handle complexity. Thus, to successfully achieve criterion SC1, it is necessary to develop risk assessment methods that are easy for the electric power sector to use, as well as providing guidelines to select from a variety of approaches that balances between ease of use and the need for assessing complex scenarios. According to the interviews, such guidelines would pave the way for a faster uptake of cyber-risk assessment knowledge in the electric power sector.

With respect to support to determine whether the method is a good match for a given context (SC2), all the methods do provide general guidelines for the analyst to understand the context in which the method may be applied. However, these general guidelines are meant for security experts and are not an adequate support for non security experts in the electric power sector as they are struggling to answer questions like: "how can I carry out a simple high-level risk assessment even if I don't have cyber-risk expertise?", "what questions should I consider when assessing risks?", "which method should I use if I have a complex target of analysis?", and so on. Thus, the power sector needs guidelines to select appropriate risk assessment methods considering the competence of those who will carry out the assessment, as well as the objectives of the planned risk assessment. For example, the VAF method may be used to identify and explore the most critical unwanted incidents. These incidents may be used as input to the CORAS method, which may help identify the chain of events that may cause the unwanted incidents, including exploited vulnerabilities. The threat scenarios and vulnerabilities identified using CORAS may in turn be used as input to the TM-STRIDE method to analyze how the vulnerabilities are exploited from a data-flow perspective. Finally, the DA-SAN method may be used to identify the consequences of the identified vulnerabilities and unwanted incidents on a power-grid system using simulation techniques.

Regarding SC3, among the methods we have considered, CORAS and TM-STRIDE have thorough steps to prepare a risk assessment in terms of establishing the context and making sure that all involved stakeholders have a common understanding of the context, concepts, and objectives of the risk assessment. The VAF method also has the necessary steps to prepare an assessment, but is slightly easier to use in the context of the electric power sector because it does not require any vocabulary specific to power system security or cybersecurity. The DA-SAN method has preparation steps in terms of modelling the target. Though it is important to obtain a common understanding of the context, concepts, and objectives, the power sector needs support in terms of domain-specific cyber-risk example scenarios as well as training material about cyber-risk assessment to properly prepare participants of risk assessment and help contribute meaningfully during an assessment. These aspects may be included as part of a method, for example during the preparation of an assessment participants can be introduced to risk assessment with example scenarios specific to the electric power sector. However, a proper educational support would be to train the relevant people using facilities such as cyber ranges that are capable of simulating cyber-attacks on energy infrastructure. Our previous work shows that cyber-risk training using cyber ranges are effective for a variety of domains such as electric power distribution, railroad transport, and education (university) [11, 12].

The infrastructure of electric energy systems is becoming increasingly complex, and it is therefore necessary to manage the complexity of the target of analysis (SC4). The methods we consider in this paper have mechanisms in place to address complexity. However, while the methods DA-SAN and TM-STRIDE lack the capability to express risks the target of analysis is exposed to as part of the target models, the methods VAF and CORAS lack the expressiveness to represent the target of analysis as part of the risk models. Each aforementioned method have of course been developed for their specific purpose, but it is reasonable to argue that a method capable of capturing both the target of analysis and risks could be beneficial when assessing risks in the context of the electric power sector because of its cyber-physical aspects. According to the interviews, one aspect that is especially important to consider in the context of complexity, is the ability to maintain risk assessments over time. With the digitalization of the power systems, changes (both from a cyber perspective and from a physical perspective) may happen frequently. Whenever an update is introduced in the power systems, then it is important to consider this change in the risk assessment as well. The CORAS method has explicit support to consider a risk picture before a change is introduced, and after a change is introduced in the target system.

The success criterion SC5 points out the need for support for risk estimation and ranking of assets. The methods VAF and TM-STRIDE do not provide support in estimating risks, but rather rely on external methods to estimate risks. DA-SAN supports risk estimation in terms of quantification of the consequence of failure states in the Cyber Physical Power System (CPPS), while CORAS mainly supports likelihood estimation using the CORAS calculus. Ideally, according to the interviews, a risk assessment method should provide guidelines for both likelihood and consequence estimation. One possible approach is to combine different methods to fully achieve SC5. For example, DA-SAN can support CORAS with consequence estimates, while CORAS can support DA-SAN with likelihood estimates. Another option is to develop method-independent support for risk estimation for the electric power sector to support risk estimation in a broader set of methods.

For all risk assessments, it is important that the assessments are trustworthy and that the uncertainty of the results are considered as part of the assessment (SC6). The methods CORAS and VAF actively involve people with different backgrounds in the risk assessment process to obtain information from relevant experts, and thereby increase the trustworthiness of the risk assessment. TM-STRIDE offers no direct support in relation to trustworthiness and uncertainty assessment. Among the four methods considered in this paper, DA-SAN is the only method that provides mechanisms (and tools) to quantitatively assess the uncertainty of the risk assessment to increase the trustworthiness. DA-SAN does this as part of the simulation. Trustworthiness and uncertainty are in general very important factors for decision support when evaluating whether to invest in new security mechanisms, either for physical security or software security.

Regarding SC7, the methods CORAS and VAF use the diagrams produced in the risk assessment as a basis for documentation and communication with the stakeholders. These methods also support the identification of risk treatments and may therefore help decision makers to identify and select appropriate risk treatments. CORAS also supports change management of assessment results, as described above related to maintenance of risk assessments. The methods TM-STRIDE and DA-SAN mainly create and use models to identify risks, but also to document the findings. Maintenance of risk assessment results and treatment identification are not supported by TM-STRIDE and DA-SAN. One important challenge none of the methods are able to support is continuous updated risk assessments. Based on our experience, we believe this challenge is not supported by current risk assessment methods for the electric power sector in general, but it is something that must eventually be supported to cope with the tsunami of data produced by the IoT devices that will be integrated in the power systems. Dynamic and real-time risk assessment must inevitably be addressed and properly supported, but the current state of risk assessment in the power sector shows that basic needs and challenges (as described in this section) must be addressed before the dynamic/real-time aspects can be supported.

8   Adaptation of Cyber-Risk Assessment for Grid Planning

In the context of grid planning, the target of analysis is a system that has not yet been implemented. Because the goal of planning is to identify and select a grid planning solution to implement (see Fig. 1), most available information about the target of analysis is at a conceptual level. There is therefore little certain information about the final system in the planning phase. Moreover, as the planning phase may produce several alternatives of grid solutions to implement, there may be multiple potential future systems to assess. Even though the planning phase may span weeks to years (depending on the grid level), there is too little time to assess all alternatives in detail with respect to cyber risks. Thus, there is a need for high-level cyber-risk assessment methods in the planning phase that are easy to comprehend and use without having the need to go into technical details or having risk assessment expertise (SC1).

As explained in Sect. 7, VAF, CORAS, and TM-STRIDE are to some extent easy to comprehend, but none of the methods fully meet the Success Criterion SC1. According to the interviews (see Sect. 5), we see that there is a need for easier methods that do not consider quantitative aspects as a required input to the risk assessment, and that are sufficiently high-level so it is easy to carry out by people who are not experts in cyber-risk assessment. Based on these points, we propose to adopt a low-threshold approach specifically developed to facilitate ease of use for people who are not necessarily experts in cyber-risk assessment. Moreover, we propose an approach to be used in the step "Techno-economic analysis of alternatives and assessment of risk" of the grid planning framework illustrated in Fig. 1. The approach we propose is named Human and Organizational Risk Modelling (HORM), co-developed by one of the authors of this paper, and it is based on Customer Journey Modelling Language (CJML) [18]. Moreover, the main target group of HORM is SMEs, which means that the approach is also suitable for grid companies since more than half of the distribution grid companies are small companies with less than 50 people who typically do not have dedicated in-house cybersecurity experts.

In the following we briefly explain HORM, and then we provide an example in context of self-healing grids based on our previous work [39]. As mentioned, HORM is based on CJML. Figure 4 illustrates the basic elements of CJML. All actors in a scenario have their own swimlane as illustrated by the three actors in Fig. 4. An actor can perform an action, or there may be a communication point between two actors. An action element is used for non-communicating events, while a communication point has a sender and a receiver that must be positioned in the corresponding swimlanes of the actors. The arrow on a communication point illustrates that the information flows from the sender to the receiver of that information. A communication happens via communication channels, for example email, chat, or SMS. All actions and communication points have textual descriptions in the diagrams. Finally, all actions and communication points follow a timeline, as illustrated in Fig. 4.

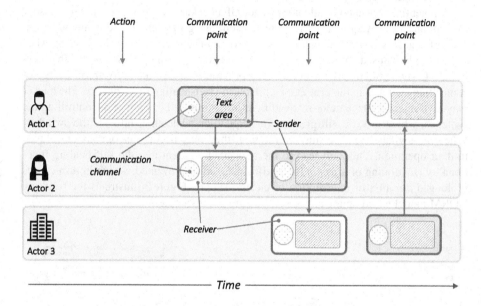

Fig. 4. The basic elements in Customer Journey Modelling Language (CJML).

HORM is based on CJML and is freely available[1]. HORM provides a method, an extension of the graphical modelling language of CJML with cyber-risk concepts and notations, and supporting tools. With respect to cyber-risk concepts, HORM includes malicious actors (such as hackers), threat scenarios, and unwanted incidents. HORM may be used to identify and analyze potential cyber risks, but it is intentionally not developed to estimate risks as this requires domain expertise and detailed information about the target of analysis, which is scarce in the context of grid planning, as pointed out above. We refer to the sources of HORM and CJML for further detailed explanation [18].

Having covered the basics of HORM and CJML, let us consider a self-healing grid example we will use as a basis to identify potential cyber risks as part of grid planning. Self-healing grids are electric power grids where sensing, control, and communication technology is used for automatic reconfiguration and power restoration [39]. Assume

---

[1] https://cjml.no/horm/.

the following context: a grid company is considering to implement a self-healing grid with centralized control as one of several alternatives during the grid planning phase. Although a self-healing grid functionality introduces benefits, it does come with potential cyber-risks. The grid company is especially worried about protecting the reliability of electric supply (security of supply) and wants to investigate potential threat scenarios that may cause prolonged duration of interruption of electric supply. Thus, as part of the planning process, the grid company wants to carry out a high-level cyber-risk assessment to identify potential threat scenarios that may cause the unwanted incident of interruption of electric supply.

A potential unwanted incident may occur if a hacker tries to access the Supervisory Control and Data Acquisition (SCADA) system using the default username and passwords for access control, which is a fairly common vulnerability in most of SCADA systems [54]. Thus, a hacker may exploit this security misconfiguration and gain access to the SCADA system, which in turn may provide access to the software in charge of controlling switches in the grid that facilitates the self-healing functionality. The hacker may then inject inadequate or misleading information into the software controlling the switches, which in turn will produce inadequate or misleading info for the switches. When the switches receive this information, they may become erroneous or delayed in their operation. This will lead to the unwanted incident that the self healing functionality (sectioning of areas in the grid) is delayed or prevented, which in turn causes prolonged duration of interruption of electric supply. Figure 5 illustrates the resulting HORM model based on the above self-healing grid example.

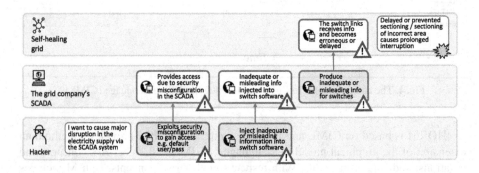

Fig. 5. Hacker causes prolonged duration of interruption of electric supply.

The above example illustrates that it is possible to create high-level cyber-risk model with little information about the context of the planned grid. Given the level of abstraction of HORM models, it is reasonable to argue that models such as Fig. 5 is a good starting point to support decision making in the grid planning, and to decide whether detailed cyber-risk assessment is needed.

9   Conclusions and Lessons Learned

The electric power sector is struggling to adopt and carry out risk assessments considering cyber risks in the context of smart grids, and in particular in context of grid planning. In this paper, we have interviewed representatives from the power sector to better understand the current and envisioned needs and challenges of risk assessment methods for smart grids. Based on the needs and challenges, we identify a set of success criteria that should be fulfilled for the electric power sector to successfully carry out cyber-risk assessment. Then we evaluate the methods CORAS, TM-STRIDE, VAF, and DA-SAN with respect to the identified success criteria. The methods CORAS, TM-STRIDE, VAF, and DA-SAN are methods the authors have used in previous work to carry out risk assessment of energy systems and smart grids. Based on the evaluation, we discuss the extent to which the aforementioned methods fulfill the success criteria and discuss gaps that need to be addressed in general. Finally, we turned our focus on a process used for grid planning and proposed a high-level cyber-risk assessment approach that may be used within the grid planning process.

We interviewed six companies from the energy sector to better understand their needs and challenges for cyber-risk assessment. Based on the needs and challenges described by the interviewees, we identified seven success criteria cyber-risk assessment methods for the electric power sector need to fulfill. In short, these are related to: ease of use and comprehensible methods (SC1), support to determine whether a method is a good match for a given context (SC2), adequate preparation to conduct cyber-risk assessment (SC3), manage complexity (SC4), adequate support for risk estimation (SC5), adequate support for trustworthiness and uncertainty handling (SC6), and support for documenting and maintaining risk assessments and identifying appropriate risk treatments (SC7).

The methods we evaluated in this paper (CORAS, TM-STRIDE, VAF and DA-SAN) fulfill the above success criteria to a certain extent, but none of the methods fulfill all the success criteria. The reader is referred to Sect. 7 for a detailed discussion about the gaps that need to be addressed.

With respect to electric power grid planning and the adoption of cyber-risk assessment for the grid planning process, we argued why there is a need for methods that are easy to use and comprehensible by non-experts (SC1), and proposed to use the Human and Organizational Risk Modelling (HORM) approach to carry our high-level cyber-risk assessment in the grid planning step "techno-economic analysis of alternatives and assessment of risk" (see Fig. 1). In summary, we conclude with the following lessons learned.

1. Considering the fact that all success criteria (SC1-SC7) point to the need for some kind of support to more easily carry out risk assessment, we see that there is especially a need to improve the comprehensibility and ease of use of risk assessment methods for the electric power sector in general.
2. There is a need for support in helping risk analysts in the power sector, including people both from IT and OT, in selecting the right risk assessment method for the right context. There is also a need for domain-specific training material and example scenarios to help participants contribute meaningfully during an assessment (SC2 and SC3).

3. There is a need for improving comprehensibility and ease of use of methods, but on the other hand, there is also a need for managing complexity of risk assessments to consider complex target of analyses. These may be two conflicting needs, but they indicate that risk assessment methods for the electric power sector need to be easy to comprehend and use, but also able to sufficiently consider a complex target of analysis (SC4).
4. Risk assessment methods for the power sector need to support risk quantification, trustworthiness and uncertainty handling (SC5 and SC6).
5. The risk assessment needs to be easy to maintain, and the risk assessment results need to provide better decision support (SC7).
6. There is especially a need for high-level cyber-risk assessment methods in the planning phase that are easy to comprehend and use without having the need to go into technical details or having risk assessment expertise (SC1). To this end, we propose in this paper to adopt HORM for cyber-risk assessment in the planning phase, as mentioned above.

The proposal of using HORM in grid planning is our initial step towards addressing the needs of the industry for cyber-risk assessment in context of smart-grid. We believe HORM is a reasonable approach to address SC1. However, in future work, we will try out HORM in a real-world grid planning case and investigate its feasibility.

Acknowledgements. This work has been carried out as part of the CINELDI project (257626/E20) funded by the Research Council of Norway, as well as the CyberKit4SME project (883188) funded by the European Union's Horizon 2020 Research and Innovation Programme.

References

1. Alberts, C., Dorofee, A., Stevens, J., Woody, C.: Introduction to the octave approach. Carnegie-Mellon University, Tech. rep. (2003)
2. Aravinthan, V., et al.: Reliability modeling considerations for emerging cyber-physical power systems. In: Proceedings of the 2018 IEEE International Conference on Probabilistic Methods Applied to Power Systems (PMAPS'18), pp. 1–7. IEEE (2018)
3. Barber, B., Davey, J.: The use of the CCTA risk analysis and management methodology CRAMM in health information systems. Medinfo **92**, 1589–1593 (1992)
4. Ben-Gal, I.: Bayesian networks. Encyclopedia of Statistics in Quality and Reliability 1 (2008)
5. Billinton, R., Allan, R.N.: Reliability Evaluation of Power Systems, 2nd edn. Plenum Press, New York (1996)
6. Bygdås, E., Jaatun, L.A., Antonsen, S.B., Ringen, A., Eiring, E.: Evaluating threat modeling tools: Microsoft TMT versus OWASP Threat Dragon. In: Proceedings of the 2021 International Conference on Cyber Situational Awareness, Data Analytics and Assessment (CyberSA'21), pp. 1–7. IEEE (2021)
7. Centre for Intelligent Electricity Distribution (CINELDI) (2022). https://www.sintef.no/projectweb/cineldi/. Accessed 2 Nov 2022
8. CORAS Risk Modelling Tool (2022). https://coras.tools/. Accessed 2 Nov 2022
9. DeMarco, T.: Structure analysis and system specification. In: Pioneers and Their Contributions to Software Engineering, pp. 255–288. Springer (1979). https://doi.org/10.1007/978-3-642-48354-7_9

10. Ding, Z., Xiang, Y., Wang, L.: Incorporating unidentifiable cyberattacks into power system reliability assessment. In: Proceedings of the 2018 IEEE Power Energy Society General Meeting (PESGM'18), pp. 1–5. IEEE (2018)
11. Erdogan, G., Hugo, Å., Romero, A., Varano, D., Zazzeri, N., Žitnik, A.: An approach to train and evaluate the cybersecurity skills of participants in cyber ranges based on cyber-risk models. In: Proceedings of the 15th International Conference on Software Technologies (ICSOFT'20), pp. 509–520. SciTePress (2020)
12. Erdogan, G., et al.: Developing cyber-risk centric courses and training material for cyber ranges: a systematic approach. In: Proceedings of the 7th International Conference on Information Systems Security and Privacy (ICISSP'21), pp. 702–713. SciTePress (2021)
13. Erdogan, G., Tøndel, I.A., Tokas, S., Garau, M., Jaatun, M.G.: Needs and challenges concerning cyber-risk assessment in the cyber-physical smart grid. In: Proceedings of the 17th International Conference on Software Technologies (ICSOFT'22), pp. 21–32. SciTePress (2022)
14. Foglietta, C., Panzieri, S.: Resilience in critical infrastructures: the role of modelling and simulation. In: Issues on Risk Analysis for Critical Infrastructure Protection. IntechOpen (2020)
15. Garau, M., Celli, G., Ghiani, E., Soma, G.G., Pilo, F., Corti, S.: ICT reliability modelling in co-simulation of smart distribution networks. In: Proceedings of the 1st International Forum on Research and Technologies for Society and Industry Leveraging a better tomorrow (RTSI'15), pp. 365–370. IEEE (2015)
16. GARPUR Consortium: D3.1: Quantification method in the absence of market response and with market response taken into account. Tech. rep., GARPUR (2016). Accessed 2 Nov 2022
17. Gjerde, O., Kjølle, G.H., Detlefsen, N.K., Brønmo, G.: Risk and vulnerability analysis of power systems including extraordinary events. In: Proceedings of the 2011 IEEE Trondheim PowerTech, pp. 1–5. IEEE (2011)
18. Halvorsrud, R., Boletsis, C., Garcia-Ceja, E.: Designing a modeling language for customer journeys: lessons learned from user involvement. In: 2021 ACM/IEEE 24th International Conference on Model Driven Engineering Languages and Systems (MODELS'21), pp. 239–249 (2021)
19. Hofmann, M., Kjølle, G.H., Gjerde, O.: Development of indicators to monitor vulnerabilities in power systems. In: Proceedings of the 11th International Probabilistic Safety Assessment and Management Conference (PSAM'11), pp. 1–10. Curran Associates, Inc. (2012)
20. Hofmann, M., Kjølle, G.H., Gjerde, O.: Vulnerability analysis related to extraordinary events in power systems. In: Proceedings of the 2015 IEEE Eindhoven PowerTech, pp. 1–6. IEEE (2015)
21. Howard, M., Lipner, S.: The Security Development Lifecycle. Microsoft Press, Redmond, WA (2006)
22. Huang, L., Chen, J., Zhu, Q.: Distributed and optimal resilient planning of large-scale independent critical infrastructures. In: 2018 Winter Simulation Conference (WSC'18), pp. 1096–1107. IEEE (2018)
23. IEC: Dependability management-part 3: application guide-section 9: risk analysis of technological systems (1995)
24. IEC: IEC 61025:2006 Fault tree analysis (FTA). Standard, IEC (2006)
25. ISO: ISO/IEC 27005:2018 - Information technology - Security techniques - Information security risk management. Standard, ISO (2018)
26. Jakobsen, S.H., Garau, M., Mo, O.: An open-source tool for reliability analysis in radial distribution grids. In: Proceedings of the 2021 International Conference on Smart Energy Systems and Technologies (SEST'21), pp. 1–6. IEEE (2021)
27. Kjølle, G.H., Utne, I.B., Gjerde, O.: Risk analysis of critical infrastructures emphasizing electricity supply and interdependencies. Reliab. Eng. Syst. Safety **105**, 80–89 (2012)

28. Kröger, W., Zio, E., Schläpfer, M.: Vulnerable systems. Springer (2011). https://doi.org/10.1007/978-0-85729-655-9
29. Lei, H., Singh, C., Sprintson, A.: Reliability analysis of modern substations considering cyber link failures. In: Proceedings of the 2015 IEEE Innovative Smart Grid Technologies - Asia (ISGT'15), pp. 1–5. IEEE (2015)
30. Lewis, S., Smith, K.: Lessons learned from real world application of the bow-tie method. In: Proceedings of the 6th Global Congress on Process Safety, pp. 22–24. OnePetro (2010)
31. Li, W.: Risk Assessment of Power Systems: Models, Methods, and Applications. John Wiley & Sons (2014)
32. Linkov, I., Kott, A.: Fundamental concepts of cyber resilience: introduction and overview. In: Kott, A., Linkov, I. (eds.) Cyber Resilience of Systems and Networks. RSD, pp. 1–25. Springer, Cham (2019). https://doi.org/10.1007/978-3-319-77492-3_1
33. Liu, Y., Deng, L., Gao, N., Sun, X.: A reliability assessment method of cyber physical distribution system. Energy Procedia 158, 2915–2921 (2019)
34. Lund, M., Solhaug, B., Stølen, K.: Model-Driven Risk Analysis: The CORAS Approach. Springer (2011). https://doi.org/10.1007/978-3-642-12323-8
35. McGraw, G.: Software Security: Building Security in. Addison-Wesley (2006)
36. Nielsen, D.S.: The cause/consequence diagram method as a basis for quantitative accident analysis. Risø National Laboratory (1971)
37. NIST: Nist special publication 800–39 - managing information security risk organization, mission, and information system view. Standard, NIST (2011)
38. NIST: Special publication 800–30 guide for conducting risk assessments. Standard, NIST (2012)
39. Omerovic, A., Vefsnmo, H., Erdogan, G., Gjerde, O., Gramme, E., Simonsen, S.: A feasibility study of a method for identification and modelling of cybersecurity risks in the context of smart power grid. In: Proceedings of the 4th International Conference on Complexity, Future Information Systems and Risk (COMPLEXIS'19), pp. 39–51. SciTePress (2019)
40. Omerovic, A., Vefsnmo, H., Gjerde, O., Ravndal, S.T., Kvinnesland, A.: An industrial trial of an approach to identification and modelling of cybersecurity risks in the context of digital secondary substations. In: Kallel, S., Cuppens, F., Cuppens-Boulahia, N., Hadj Kacem, A. (eds.) CRiSIS 2019. LNCS, vol. 12026, pp. 17–33. Springer, Cham (2020). https://doi.org/10.1007/978-3-030-41568-6_2
41. Rinaldi, S.M., Peerenboom, J.P., Kelly, T.K.: Identifying, understanding, and analyzing critical infrastructure interdependencies. IEEE Control Syst. Mag. 21(6), 11–25 (2001)
42. Sanders, W.H., Meyer, J.F.: Stochastic activity networks: formal definitions and concepts∗. In: Brinksma, E., Hermanns, H., Katoen, J.-P. (eds.) EEF School 2000. LNCS, vol. 2090, pp. 315–343. Springer, Heidelberg (2001). https://doi.org/10.1007/3-540-44667-2_9
43. Schneier, B.: Modeling security threats. Dr. Dobb's J. 24(12) (1999)
44. Shostack, A.: Threat Modeling: Designing for security. John Wiley & Sons, Hoboken (2014)
45. Solhaug, B., Stølen, K.: The coras language - why it is designed the way it is. In: Proceedings of the 11th International Conference on Structural Safety and Reliability (ICOSSAR'13), pp. 3155–3162. Citeseer (2013)
46. Sperstad, I.B., Kjølle, G.H., Gjerde, O.: A comprehensive framework for vulnerability analysis of extraordinary events in power systems. Reliab. Eng. Syst. Safety 196, 106788 (2020)
47. Sperstad, I.B., Solvang, E., Gjerde, O.: Framework and methodology for active distribution grid planning in Norway. In: Proceedings of the 2020 International Conference on Probabilistic Methods Applied to Power Systems (PMAPS'20), pp. 1–6. IEEE (2020)
48. Swiderski, F., Snyder, W.: Threat Modeling. Microsoft Press (2004)
49. Ten, C.W., Liu, C.C., Manimaran, G.: Vulnerability assessment of cybersecurity for SCADA systems. IEEE Trans. Power Syst. 23(4), 1836–1846 (2008)

50. Tøndel, I.A., Vefsnmo, H., Gjerde, O., Johannessen, F., Frøystad, C.: Hunting dependencies: using bow-tie for combined analysis of power and cyber security. In: Proceedings of the 2020 2nd International Conference on Societal Automation (SA'20), pp. 1–8. IEEE (2021)
51. Wang, H.H., Shi, L., Ni, Y.: Distribution system planning incorporating distributed generation and cyber system vulnerability. J. Eng. **2017**(13), 2198–2202 (2017)
52. Xiang, Y., Wang, L., Zhang, Y.: Adequacy evaluation of electric power grids considering substation cyber vulnerabilities. Int. J. Electrical Power Energy Syst. **96**, 368–379 (2018)
53. Xu, L., Guo, Q., Sheng, Y., Muyeen, S.M., Sun, H.: On the resilience of modern power systems: a comprehensive review from the cyber-physical perspective. Renew. Sustain. Ener. Rev. **152**, 111642 (2021)
54. Yadav, G., Paul, K.: Assessment of SCADA system vulnerabilities. In: Proceedings of the 2019 24th IEEE International Conference on Emerging Technologies and Factory Automation (ETFA'19), pp. 1737–1744. IEEE (2019)
55. Zerihun, T.A., Garau, M., Helvik, B.E.: Effect of communication failures on state estimation of 5G-enabled smart grid. IEEE Access **8**, 112642–112658 (2020)
56. Zhang, Y., Wang, L., Xiang, Y., Ten, C.W.: Power system reliability evaluation with SCADA cybersecurity considerations. IEEE Trans. Smart Grid **6**(4), 1707–1721 (2015)
57. Zhang, Y., Wang, L., Xiang, Y., Ten, C.W.: Inclusion of SCADA cyber vulnerability in power system reliability assessment considering optimal resources allocation. IEEE Trans. Power Syst. **31**(6), 4379–4394 (2016)
58. Zhu, W., Panteli, M., Milanović, J.V.: Reliability and vulnerability assessment of interconnected ICT and power networks using complex network theory. In: Proceedings of the 2018 IEEE Power Energy Society General Meeting (PESGM'18), pp. 1–5. IEEE (2018)

Three Forms of Mutant Subsumption: Basic, Strict and Broad

Samia AlBlwi[1], Imen Marsit[2], Besma Khaireddine[3], Amani Ayad[4], JiMeng Loh[1], and Ali Mili[1(✉)] [iD]

[1] NJIT, Newark, NJ, USA
{sma225,mili}@njit.edu
[2] University of Sousse, Sousse, Tunisia
[3] University of Tunis, Tunis, Tunisia
[4] Kean University, Union, NJ, USA
amanayad@kean.edu

Abstract. Mutant subsumption is the property of a mutant to be more stubborn than another, i.e. to be harder to distinguish from the base program. The traditional definition of mutant subsumption distinguishes between three forms of subsumption, namely: *true subsumption*, *static subsumption*, and *dynamic subsumption*. Also, the traditional definition of mutant subsumption appears to assume that programs and their mutants converge for all test data, but in practice this is not the case: executions may lead to infinite loops or attempt illegal operations of all kinds. In this paper we revisit the definition of mutant subsumption by taking into consideration the possibility that executions may diverge, and we propose an orthogonal classification of subsumption.

Keywords: Mutation testing · Mutant subsumption · Basic subsumption · Strict subsumption · Broad subsumption

1 Three Forms of Subsumption: It's Not What You Think

In [15,16] Kurtz et al. introduce the concept of mutant subsumption, whereby a mutant M of program P is said to *subsume* a mutant M' of P if and only if M produces a different outcome from P for at least one input, and any input for which M produces a different outcome from P causes M' to produce a different outcome from P as well. This concept has given rise to much research aiming to minimize mutant sets using the criterion of subsumption [9,17,25,27,28]: if a mutant set μ includes M and M' such that M subsumes M', we can remove M' from μ without affecting the effectivenes of μ, provided we do keep M.

While it is defined in terms of execution outcomes, the concept of subsumption remains vague as to the exact definition of an execution outcome; also, while the definition is based on whether two executions are identical or distinct, it remains to determine when two outcomes are comparable, and when two comparable outcomes can be considered correct. We discuss these questions below:

This research is partially supported by NSF under grant DGE 1565478.

– *What is the Outcome of a Terminating Program?*. We argue that even when two programs terminate normally, it is not always clear whether they have the same outcome: Consider the following two programs whose purpose is to swap two integer variables x and y:

```
P1: {int x, y, z; z=x; x=y; y=z;}
P2: {int x, y, z; z=y; y=x; x=z;}
```

Wehther we consider these two programs to have the same outcome or two different outcomes depends on what we consider to be the outcome of each program: If we consider the final value of x and y to be the outcome of these programs, then they do have the same outcome; if we consider the final state of these programs to be the outcome of their executions, then they have different outcomes, as the final value of z is not the same for P1 and P2.

– *Is Non-Termination an Outcome or the Absence of Outcome?* When we execute a program on some input (or starting at some initial state), then the program may terminate after a finite number of steps in some final state; we then say that the execution *converges*. But the execution may also lead to an exception such as: entering an infinite loop; attempting a division by zero; attempting to reference a nil pointer; attempting to access an array outside of its bounds; applying the log function to a negative number, etc. We then say that the execution *diverges*; the question that this situation raises is whether we consider divergence to be an execution outcome, or do we consider that when a program diverges, it has no outcome (in which case we cannot compare its outcome to that of another program)?

The discussion of divergence may sound like a mundane academic question, but it is in fact very relevant to mutation: indeed, several mutation operators are prone to cause mutants to diverge, even when the base program converges. For example,

- If we consider the following loop that indexes an array `A[0..N-1]` using some index variable `i` in the base program P

  ```
  P: while (i<N) {a[i]=0; ... i=i+1;}
  ```
  and a mutation operator changes condition `(i<N)` onto `(i<=N)`, then the mutant will diverge, due to an array reference out of bounds.
- If the base program P has a variable x of type integer and a variable y of type float, and includes the following guarded assignment

  ```
  P: if ((x!=0) && (x!=1)) {y=1.0/(x*(x-1));... }
  ```
  and a mutation operator changes the conjunction into a disjunction then the resulting mutant will diverge for $x = 0$ and $x = 1$, due to a division by zero.
- If the base program has an integer variable x and includes a loop of the form

  ```
  P: while (x>0) {x=x-2; ..;}
  ```
  a mutation operator changes the condition `(x>0)` into `(x!=0)` then the resulting mutant will diverge whenever the initial value of x is odd, due to an infinite loop.

Not only do we need to make provisions for cases where mutants diverge, we must also consider the possibility that the base program itself may diverge for some inputs: indeed, test data is not determined by the domain of the program, but rather by the domain of the specification that the program is supposed to satisfy. For all these reasons, it is important to (re)define subsumption in a way that makes provisions for cases where the base program and/ or its mutants fail to converge.

– *Comparing Execution Outcomes.* Now that we recognize that not all executions converge, and not all converging executions have well-defined outcomes, we must decide two questions:
  • When are two outcomes comparable?
  • When are two comparable outcomes identical?
In this paper, we will present three distinct definitions of mutant subsumption, which depend on how we answer these two questions.

Interestingly, we find that once we admit the possibility that the base program and its mutants may diverge, there is no difference between *true subsumption* and *dynamic subsumption*, as defined originally: dynamic subsumption with respect to program P for some test suite T is the same as true subsumption with respect to program P', the pre-restriction of P to T. Also, we argue that there is no difference between *true subsumption* and *static subsumption*, since *static subsumption* refers to a static method to establish true subsumption, rather than to a different property between the base program and its mutants.

Hence rather than the distinction between *true subsumption*, *static subsumption* and *dynamic subsumption*, we present an orthogonal classification: *basic subsumption*, *strict subsumption*, and *broad subsumption*; this classification is based on what one considers to be execution outcomes, what one considers to be comparable outcomes, and what one considers to be distinct execution outcomes. We also show, in passing, that the property of mutant subsumption is very similar to the property of *relative correctness*, which orders candidate programs for correctness with respect to a specification, and was introduced to define program faults [19]. Given the ongoing discussions about the relationships between faults and mutations [2,3,12,24], it is hardly surprising that similar concepts are introduced to model mutations [15,16] and faults [19]; but it is noteworthy nevertheless.

In Sect. 2, we briefly introduce some mathematics that we need to carry out our discussions, and we use these mathematics to introduce some background material on program semantics. In Sect. 3 we introduce three definitions of differentiator sets, where a differentiator set between two programs is the set of inputs for which the programs return different outcomes; there are three different forms of differentiator sets, depending on how we interpret program outcomes and how we compare program outcomes. In Sect. 4 we use the three forms of differentiator sets to introduce three different forms of mutant subsumption. In Sect. 5 we use the definitions presented in Sect. 4 to derive a statistical model that predicts the shape of subsumption graphs; specifically, we estimate the likelihood of subsumption between any two mutants, the estimated number of subsumption relations between any two mutants (i.e. the number of arcs in a subsumption graph), and the number of maximal nodes in a subsumption graph. In Sect. 6 we consider a benchmark program, generate its mutants, weed out its equivalent mutants, then compute the three differentiator sets of each mutant with the base program; using these differentiator sets, we derive the subsumption relations between the mutants and draw the three subsumption graphs between the mutants; the fact that these subsumption graphs are different from each other proves that the three forms of subsumption are indeed meaningful. In Sect. 7 we summarize our findings, critique them, then discuss venues for further research.

This paper extends the paper titled *Generalized Mutant Subsumption*, which was published in the proceedings of ICSOFT 2022 [1].

2 Mathematical Background

2.1 Sets

Because we use sets to represent program spaces, we represent sets by C-like variable declarations. If we declare a set S by the variable declarations:

```
xType x; yType y;
```

then S is the cartesian product of the sets of values that the types xType and yType take; elements of S are denoted by lower case s, and are referred to as *states*. Given an element s of S, we may refer to the x-component (resp. y-component) of s as $x(s)$ (resp. $y(s)$). But we may, for the sake of convenience, refer to the x component of states s, s', s'' (e.g.) simply as x, x', x''.

2.2 Operations on Relations

A relation on set S is a subset of the cartesian product $S \times S$; special relations on set S include the *universal relation* $L = S \times S$, the *identity relation* $I = \{(s, s')|s' = s\}$ and the *empty relation* $\phi = \{\}$. Operations on relations include the set theoretic operations of union ($\cup$), intersection ($\cap$), difference($\backslash$) and complement ($\overline{R} = L \backslash R$). They also include the *product* of two relations, denoted by $R \circ R'$ (or RR', for short) and defined by

$$R \circ R' = \{(s, s')|\exists s'' : (s, s'') \in R \wedge (s'', s') \in R'\}.$$

The *converse* of relation R is the relation denoted by $\widehat{R}$ and defined by $\widehat{R} = \{(s, s')|(s', s) \in R\}$. The *domain* of relation R is denoted by $dom(R)$ and defined by $dom(R) = \{s|\exists s' : (s, s') \in R\}$. The *pre-restriction* of relation R to set T is the relation denoted by ${}_{T\backslash}R = \{(s, s')|s \in T \wedge (s, s') \in R\}$.

2.3 Properties of Relations

A relation R is said to be *reflexive* if and only if $I \subseteq R$; relation R is said to be *symmetric* if and only if $R = \widehat{R}$; relation R is said to be *transitive* if and only if $RR \subseteq R$; relation R is said to be *asymmetric* if and only if $R \cap \widehat{R} = \phi$; relation R is said to be antisymmetric if and only if $R \cap \widehat{R} \subseteq I$. A relation R is said to be an *equivalence relation* if and only if it is reflexive, symmetric and transitive. A relation R is said to be a *partial ordering* if and only if it is reflexive, transitive and antisymmetric. A relation R is said to be a *strict partial ordering* if and only if it is transitive and asymmetric.

A relation R is said to be *deterministic* (or: to be a *function*) if and only if $\widehat{R}R \subseteq I$. A relation R is said to be *total* if and only if $RL = L$. A relation R is said to be a *vector* if and only if $RL = R$; a vector V on set S is a relation of the form $V = A \times S$ for some non-empty subset A of S. We may use vectors to define pre-restrictions and post-restrictions: Given a relation R and a vector $V = A \times S$, the pre-restriction of R to A can be written as $V \cap R$ and the post-restriction of R to A can be written $R \cap \widehat{V}$.

A relation R' is said to *refine* a relation R if and only if $RL \cap R'L \cap (R \cup R') = R$; this is denoted by $R' \sqsupseteq R$ or $R \sqsubseteq R'$. When relations are used as specifications, refinement simply means that R' represents a stronger specification than R; in terms of pre/post specifications, this is equivalent to having weaker preconditions and stronger postconditions [6,8,10,23].

2.4   Absolute Correctness

2.4.1   Total Correctness

We can capture the semantics of a program either by a function from some input space to some output space, or by a homogeneous deterministic relation on some state space S; for the sake of simplicity, and without significant loss of generality, we adopt the latter option; hence we will talk about *initial states* and *final states* of a program, rather than about *inputs* and *outputs*. A consequence of this resolution is that we define the execution of a program in terms of the initial state on which it is executed; also, the outcome of an execution is therefore defined by the final state of the execution, whenever the execution converges.

Given a program P on space S, we let the *function* of P be the set of pairs of states (s, s') such that if execution of P starts in state s it terminates normally (i.e. converges) in state s'. As a result of this definition, the domain of P is the set of initial states for which program P converges. For the sake of convenience, we usually equate a program with its function, and use the same symbol (e.g. P) to refer to both.

A specification on space S is a relation on S. For the sake of our discussions herein, we consider that programs are deterministic, but specifications may be non-deterministic. The following definition introduces (absolute) correctness.

Definition 1. *Given a specification R on space S and a program P on S, we say that P is* correct *with respect to R if and only if P refines R.*

This definition is equivalent, modulo differences of notation, to traditional definitions of (total) correctness [6,8,18]. The following Proposition, due to [22], provides a simple necessary and sufficient condition of correctness.

Proposition 1. *Program P on space S is correct with respect to specification R on S if and only if:*

$$dom(R \cap P) = dom(R).$$

The domain of $(R \cap P)$ is called the *competence domain* of P with respect to R; it is the set of initial states for which P behaves according to R. Figure 1 shows a simple example of a (non-deterministic) specification R and two programs P and P' such that P is correct with respect to R and P' is not; the competence domains of P and P' are shown by the ovals.

Program P is correct with respect to specification R if and only if for any initial state s in $dom(R)$, execution of program P on state s terminates normally in a state $s' = P(S)$ such that the pair (s, s') is in R. There are situations where it is difficult or unnecessary to prove that program P terminates normally for all initial states in $dom(S)$, but we are interested to prove that if it does terminate normally in a final state s' then (s, s') is in R; this is the subject of the next section.

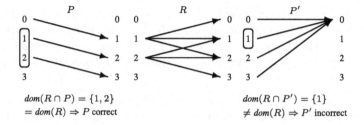

$dom(R \cap P) = \{1, 2\}$
$= dom(R) \Rightarrow P$ correct

$dom(R \cap P') = \{1\}$
$\neq dom(R) \Rightarrow P'$ incorrect

Fig. 1. Due to [1]: Total Correctness.

2.4.2 Partial Correctness

The following definition, due to [21], is equivalent, modulo differences of notation, to traditional definitions of partial correctness, given in [6,8,11,18].

Definition 2. *We say that P is partially correct with respect to R if and only if P refines* $R \cap PL$.

To contrast correctness with partial correctness, we may refer to the former as *total correctness*. The following proposition, due to [21], gives a characterization of partial correctness that parallels the characterization of total correctness given in proposition 1.

Proposition 2. *Program P on space S is partially correct with respect to specification R on S if and only if:*

$$dom(R \cap P) = dom(R) \cap dom(P).$$

See Fig. 2, due to [1]: Program Q is partially correct with respect to R because for any initial state of $dom(R)$ for which it terminates, program Q delivers a final state that satisfies specification R; by contrast, program Q' is not partially correct with respect to R, even though it terminates normally for all initial states in $dom(R)$, because it does not satisfy specification R; neither Q nor Q' is totally correct with respect to R. We admit without proof that if P is totally correct with respect to R then it is necessarily partially correct with respect to R; the proof stems readily from Propositions 1 and 2.

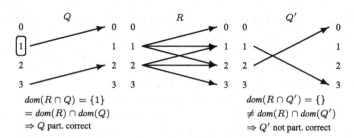

$dom(R \cap Q) = \{1\}$
$= dom(R) \cap dom(Q)$
$\Rightarrow Q$ part. correct

$dom(R \cap Q') = \{\}$
$\neq dom(R) \cap dom(Q')$
$\Rightarrow Q'$ not part. correct

Fig. 2. Due to [1]: Partial Correctness.

2.5 Relative Correctness

Whereas absolute correctness is a property that involves a specification and a program, relative correctness involves a specification, say R, and two candidate programs, say P and P', and ranks P and P' according to how close they are to being correct. The following definition, due to Diallo et al. [5], introduces the concept of relative correctness.

Definition 3. *Given a specification R on space S and two programs P and P', we say that P' is more-correct than P with respect to R if and only if the competence domain of P' with respect to R is a superset of that of P; if the competence domain of P' is a proper superset of that of P, we say that P' is strictly more-correct than P with respect to R.*

If we want to contrast correctness (Definition 1) with relative correctness, we may refer to the former as *absolute correctness*. Figure 3 illustrates relative correctness by showing a specification (R) and two sets of programs: Q' is strictly more-correct than Q with respect to R by virtue of imitating the correct behavior of Q; P' is strictly more-correct than P with respect to R by virtue of a different correct behavior. It is clear from Definitions 1 and 3 that relative correctness culminates in absolute correctness in the following sense: an absolutely correct program is more-correct than any candidate program; indeed, the competence domain of any program P with respect to specification R is by construction a subset of $dom(R)$; P is absolutely correct when its competence domain reaches its maximum.

Relative correctness is used to define program faults [14]: a syntactic feature f of an incorrect program P is said to be a *fault* in P with respect to R if and only if it can be replaced by a feature f' so that the program P' that stems from this substitution is strictly more-correct than P with respect to R.

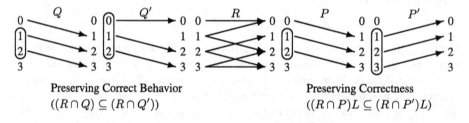

Preserving Correct Behavior   Preserving Correctness
$((R \cap Q) \subseteq (R \cap Q'))$ $((R \cap P)L \subseteq (R \cap P')L)$

Fig. 3. Due to [1]: Relative Correctness: $(Q' \sqsupseteq_R Q) (P' \sqsupseteq_R P)$.

To illustrate the partial ordering properties of relative correctness, we consider the following specification on space S of integers, defined by

$$R = \{(s, s') | 1 \le s \le 3 \land s' = s^3 + 3\}.$$

We consider twelve candidate programs, listed in Table 1.

Figure 4 shows how these candidate programs are ordered by relative correctness; this ordering stems readily from the inclusion relations between the competence domains of the candidate programs with respect to R; the competence domains are given in Table 2, to allow interested readers to check Fig. 4; the competence domain of a program p_i with respect to R can be derived by solving the equation $(s, P_i(s)) \in R$. The green oval shows those candidates that are absolutely correct, and the orange oval shows candidate programs that are incorrect; the red oval shows the candidate programs that are least correct (they violate specification R for every initial state in the domain of R). This example is clearly artificial, but we choose it for its illustrative nature.

Table 3 summarizes and organizes the definitions of correctness to help contrast them. For each entry, we present the definition then a set-theoretic characterization.

Table 1. Candidate Programs for Specification R.

p0: {s=s*s*s+4;}	**p6:** {s=s*s*s+s*s-5*s+9;}
p1: {s=s*s*s+5;}	**p7:** {s=s*s*s+s*s-3*s+5;}
p2: {s=s*s*s+6;}	**p8:** {s=s*s*s+s*s-4*s+8;}
p3: {s=s*s*s+s+2;}	**p9:** {s=2*s*s*s-6*s*s+11*s-3;}
p4: {s=s*s*s+s+1;}	**p10:** {s=3*s*s*s-12*s*s+22*s-9;}
p5: {s=s*s*s+s;}	**p11:** {s=4*s*s*s-18*s*s+33*s-15;}

Table 2. Competence Domains of Candidate Programs.

p0	{}	p1	{}	p2	{}
p3	{1}	p4	{2}	p5	{3}
p6	{2, 3}	p7	{1, 2}	p8	{1, 3}
p9	{1, 2, 3}	p10	{1, 2, 3}	p11	{1, 2, 3}

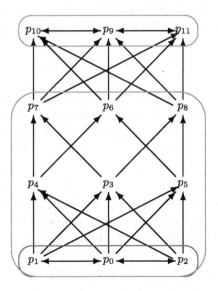

Fig. 4. Due to [1]: Ordering Candidate Programs by Relative Correctness with Respect to R. (Color figure online)

3 Three Forms of Differentiator Sets

3.1 Divergence and Differentiator Sets

In Sect. 1, we had argued that while the definitions of mutant subsumption refer to program outcomes and to the condition under which two program outcomes are identical, they are not perfectly clear about what constitutes the outcome of a program, when two program outcomes are comparable, and if they are when can we consider them to be identical. In this section, we address this ambiguity by introducing several definitions of *differentiator sets*, which reflect different interpretations to the questions above.

Table 3. Definitions of Correctness.

	Partial Correctness	Total Correctness
Absolute Correctness	$P \sqsupseteq (R \cap PL) \Leftrightarrow$ $dom(R) \cap dom(P)$ $= dom(R \cap P)$	$P \sqsupseteq R$ $\Leftrightarrow$ $dom(R) = dom(R \cap P)$
Relative Correctness		$P' \sqsupseteq_R P$ $\Leftrightarrow$ $dom(R \cap P') \supseteq dom(R \cap P)$

Given two programs, say P and Q, the *differentiator set* of P and Q is the set of initial states for which execution of P and Q yield different outcomes. For the purposes of this paper, we adopt the three definitions of differentiator sets proposed by Mili in [20]:

– *Basic Differentiator Set.* The basic differentiator set of two programs P and Q on space S is defined only if P and Q converge for all s in S; it is the set of states s such that $P(s) \neq Q(s)$. This set is denoted by $\delta_B(P, Q)$ and defined by:

$$\delta_B(P, Q) = \overline{dom(P \cap Q)}.$$

– *Strict Differentiator Set.* The strict differentiator set of two programs P and Q on space S is defined regardless of whether P and Q converge for all initial states. It includes all the states for which executions of P and Q both converge and yield distinct outcomes. This set is denoted by $\delta_S(P, Q)$ and defined by:

$$\delta_S(P, Q) = dom(P) \cap dom(Q) \cap \overline{dom(P \cap Q)}.$$

– *Loose (or Broad) Differentiator Set.* The loose (broad) differentiator set of two programs P and Q on space S is defined regardless of whether P and Q converge for all initial states. It includes all the states for which executions of P and Q both converge and yield distinct outcomes, as well as the states for which only one of the programs converges and the other diverges. This set is denoted by $\delta_L(P, Q)$ and defined by:

$$\delta_L(P, Q) = (dom(P) \cup dom(Q)) \cap \overline{dom(P \cap Q)}.$$

Figure 5 illustrates the three definitions of differentiator sets (represented in red in each case). To gain an intuitive understanding of these definitions, it suffices to note the following details:

– The domain of program P ($dom(P)$) is the set of initial states on which execution of P converges (i.e. terminates normally after a finite number of steps without raising any exception or attempting any illegal operation). We assume that when a program enters an infinite loop, it gets timed out by the run-time environment, so that non-termination is an observable outcome.

- The domain of $(P \cap Q)$ is the set of inputs for which programs P and Q converge and return the same outcome.
- The complement of the domain of $(P \cap Q)$ is the set of inputs for which program P and Q converge and return distinct outcomes. In other words,

$$\overline{dom(P \cap P)} = \{s : s \in dom(P) \wedge s \in dom(Q) \wedge P(s) \neq Q(s)\}.$$

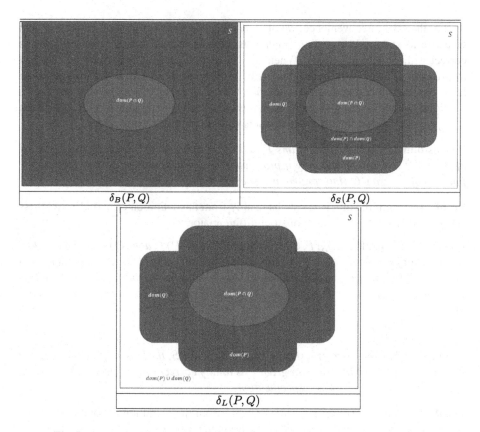

Fig. 5. Due to [1]: Three Definitions of Differentiator Sets. (Color figure online)

3.2 Correctness and Differentiator Sets

Given that differentiator sets reflect the extent of behavior difference between two programs, we expect that when a differentiator set is empty, the programs have some measure of identity/ similarity. This is discussed in the following Propositions; first, we briefly introduce a lemma from relational algebra [4,26].

Lemma 1. *If two functions F and G satisfy the conditions $F \subseteq G$ and $dom(G) \subseteq dom(F)$ then $F = G$.*

Proposition 3. *Given two programs P and Q on space S such that $dom(P) = S$ and $dom(Q) = S$. The basic differentiator set of P and Q is empty if and only if $P = Q$.*

Proof. The proof of sufficiency is trivial.

Proof of Necessity: If $\delta_B(P,Q) = \emptyset$ then $dom(P \cap Q) = S$. By hypothesis, $dom(P) = S$. By set theory, we have $(P \cap Q) \subseteq P$. By the lemma above, we infer $(P \cap Q) = P$, whence by set theory we infer $P \subseteq Q$. By permuting P and Q in the argument above, we find $Q \subseteq P$.   **qed**

For the sake of convenience, we often equate a program with its function; this may give rise to some odd-sounding statements such as the claim that some program is correct with respect to another. When we say that program P is correct with respect to program Q, we really mean that P, as a program written in some programming language, is correct with respect to the *function* of program Q, which we interpret as a relational specification on space S. With this qualification in mind, we proceed with the next propositions linking differentiator sets with properties of correctness.

Proposition 4. *Given two programs P and Q on space S, the strict differentiator set of P and Q is empty if and only if program P is partially correct with respect to the function of program Q (interpreted as a specification).*

Proof. The proof of sufficiency stems readily from the definition of partial correctness (Definition 2) and the definition of strict differentiator sets.

Proof of Necessity. From $\delta_S(P,Q) = \emptyset$ we infer $dom(P) \cap dom(Q) \subseteq dom(P \cap Q)$. By set theory (and monotonicity of the $dom()$) we infer $dom(P \cap Q) \subseteq dom(P)$ and $dom(P \cap Q) \subseteq dom(Q)$, whence $dom(P \cap Q) \subseteq dom(P) \cap dom(Q)$. From $dom(P \cap Q) = dom(P) \cap dom(Q)$ we infer that P is partially correct with respect to the function of Q.   **qed**

Proposition 5. *Given two programs P and Q on space S, the loose differentiator set of P and Q is empty if and only if program P is totally correct with respect to the function of program Q (interpreted as a specification).*

Proof. The proof of sufficiency stems readily from the definition of total correctness (Definition 1) and the definition of loose differentiator sets.

Proof of Necessity. From $\delta_L(P,Q) = \emptyset$ we infer $dom(P) \cup dom(Q) \subseteq dom(P \cap Q)$. From which we infer, a fortiori: $dom(P) \subseteq dom(P \cap Q)$. The reverse inclusion is a tautology. From Definition 1 we infer that P is totally correct with respect to the function of Q.   **qed**

In Propositions 4 and 5, the roles of P and Q can be permuted: each is (partially/ totally) correct with respect to the function of the other; in the context of mutation testing, we use these propositions asymmetrically (if and only if the differentiator set of a mutant with respect to the base program is empty then the mutant is partially or totally correct, depending on which differentiator set is involved, with respect to the function of the base program).

4   Three Forms of Subsumption

4.1   Definitions and Properties

In [15, 16], Kurtz et al define the concept of *true subsumption* as follows:

Definition 4. *Given a program P on S and two mutants M and M', we say that M subsumes M' with respect to P if and only if:*

P1 There exists an initial state s for which P and M produce different outcomes.
P2 For all s in S such that P and M produce different outcomes, so do P and M'.

Since this definition makes no mention of P, M or M' failing to converge, we assume that P, M and M' are considered to converge for all initial states. The following Proposition formulates subsumption by means of basic differentiator sets.

Proposition 6. *Given a program P on space S and two mutants M and M' of P, M subsumes M' if and only if:*

$$\emptyset \subset \delta_B(P, M) \subseteq \delta_B(P, M').$$

Proof. We consider the first condition
$\emptyset \subset \delta_B(P, M)$
$\Leftrightarrow$ {definition of $\delta_B(P, M)$}
$\exists s : s \in \overline{dom(P \cap Q)}$
$\Leftrightarrow$ {interpreting the complement}
$\exists s : \neg(s \in dom(P \cap Q))$
$\Leftrightarrow$ {interpreting $dom(P \cap Q)$}
$\exists s : \neg(P(s) = Q(s)))$
$\Leftrightarrow$ {definition 4}
Condition P1.
As for the second conditions,
$\delta_B(P, M) \subseteq \delta_B(P, M')$
$\Leftrightarrow$ {definition of $\delta_B(,)$}
$\forall s : s \in \overline{dom(P \cap M)} \Rightarrow s \in \overline{dom(P \cap M')}$
$\Leftrightarrow$ {interpreting the complement}
$\forall s : \neg(s \in dom(P \cap M)) \Rightarrow \neg(s \in dom(P \cap M'))$
$\Leftrightarrow$ {interpreting the domain}
$\forall s : \neg(P(s) = M(s)) \Rightarrow \neg(P(s) = M'(s))$
$\Leftrightarrow$ {Applying the negation}
$\forall s : P(s) \neq M(s) \Rightarrow P(s) \neq M'(s)$
$\Leftrightarrow$ {definition 4, interpreting outcomes}
Condition P2.   **qed**

Proposition 6 provides an alternative formula to define mutant subsumption in the case where we assume that all programs and mutants terminate for all initial states. This Proposition is formulated in terms of basic differentiator sets, which are defined when the program and its mutants are assumed to converge for all initial states; but in Sect. 3, we have introduced two more definitions of differentiator sets, which do not assume universal convergence of programs and mutants, and take a liberal interpretation of program outcomes and when to consider outcomes as identical or distinct. The following definitions generalize the concept of subsumption to the case when programs and their mutants do not necessarily converge for all initial states.

Definition 5. Strict Subsumption. *Given a program P on space S and two mutants M and M' of P, we say that M strictly subsumes M' if and only if:*

$$\emptyset \subset \delta_S(P, M) \subseteq \delta_S(P, M').$$

Definition 6. Loose Subsumption. *Given a program P on space S and two mutants M and M' of P, we say that M loosely subsumes M' if and only if:*

$$\emptyset \subset \delta_L(P, M) \subseteq \delta_L(P, M').$$

In Sect. 6, we see that the distinction between the basic definition of subsumption (Definition 4, [15, 16]), strict subsumption, and loose subsumption is not a mere academic exercise. These definitions yield vastly different subsumption graphs.

4.2   Subsumption and Relative Correctness

Mutant subsumption was introduced in 2014 as an ordering relation between mutants of a given base program to reflect the property of a mutant to be more stubborn, i.e. harder to distinguish from the base program [15, 16]. Relative correctness was introduced the same year as an ordering relation between candidate programs of the same specification, to reflect the property of a program to be more-correct than another with respect to a given specification [19]. The following Proposition provides that these two properties are virtually equivalent.

Proposition 7. *Given a program P on space S and two mutants M and M' of P, M subsumes M' if and only if M is not equivalent to P and it is more-correct than M' with respect to (the function of) P.*

Proof. According to Proposition 3, condition P1 is equivalent to: P and M are not equivalent.

On the other hand, we have shown above that condition P2 is equivalent to:

$\delta_B(P, M) \subseteq \delta_B(P, M')$

$\Leftrightarrow$ $\underline{\{\text{definition of } \delta_B(,)\}}$

$\forall s : s \in \overline{dom(P \cap M)} \Rightarrow s \in \overline{dom(P \cap M')}$

$\Leftrightarrow$ $\{\text{Boolean identity}\}$

$\forall s : s \in dom(P \cap M') \Rightarrow s \in dom(P \cap M)$

$\Leftrightarrow$ $\{\text{set theory}\}$

$dom(P \cap M') \subseteq dom(P \cap M)$

$\Leftrightarrow$ $\{\text{Definition 3}\}$

$M \sqsupseteq_P M'$.   **qed**

4.3 Subsumption and Dynamic Subsumption

The following definition is due to Kurtz et al [15, 16].

Definition 7. *Given a program P, a test suite T and two mutants of P, say M and M′, we say that M dynamically subsumes M′ with respect to P for test suite T if and only if:*

D1 There exists a test $t \in T$ such that P and M compute different outcomes on t.
D2 For every possible test $t \in T$, if M computes a different outcome from P, then so does M′.

From Definitions 4 and 7, it is easy to see that true subsumption is a special case of dynamic subsumption, namely the case when T is the set of all possible tests. In the following Proposition, we show that dynamic subsumption is also a special case of true subsumption.

Proposition 8. *Given a program P, a test suite T and two mutants of P, say M and M′, M dynamically subsumes M′ with respect to P for test suite T if and only if M subsumes M′ (in the sense of true subsumption) with respect to $P' =_{T\backslash} P$, where $_{T\backslash} P$ is the pre-restriction of P to T.*

The program that computes function $_{T\backslash} P$ can be written as:
```
p': {if (s in T) {p;} else {abort();}}
```

Proof. From clause D1 of Definition 7, we infer that there exists a test t in T such that:
$t \in T : t \in dom(P) \land t \notin dom(P \cap M)$.
From $t \in T$ and $t \in dom(P)$ we infer: $t \in dom(_{T\backslash} P)$. Also, from $t \notin dom(P \cap M)$ we infer, a fortiori: $t \notin T \cap dom(P \cap M)$ since $T \cap dom(P \cap M) \subseteq dom(P \cap M)$. Given that $T \cap dom(P \cap M)$ can be rewritten as $dom(_{T\backslash} P \cap M)$, condition D1 (of Definition 7) is the same as condition P1 (of Definition 4) where the reference program is $P' =_{T\backslash} P$.
    As for condition D2, it can be written as:
$\forall t \in T : t \notin dom(P \cap M) \Rightarrow t \notin dom(P \cap M')$.
$\Leftrightarrow$ {logic}
$\forall t \in T : t \in dom(P \cap M') \Rightarrow t \in dom(P \cap M)$.
$\Leftrightarrow$ {factoring}
$\forall t \in T : t \in T \cap dom(P \cap M') \Rightarrow t \in T \cap dom(P \cap M)$.
By virtue of the identities $T \cap dom(R) = dom(_{T\backslash} R)$ and $(_{T\backslash} (R \cap Q)) = (_{T\backslash} R \cap Q)$, we write condition D2 as:
$\forall t \in T : t \in dom(_{T\backslash} P \cap M') \Rightarrow t \in dom(_{T\backslash} P \cap M)$.
This condition is equivalent to condition P2 of Proposition 4 for the program $P' =_{T\backslash} P$.
                                                                            qed

Dynamic subsumption of M over M' for base program P with respect to test suite T is the same as true subsumption of M over M' for base program $_{T\backslash} P$.

5 Statistical Modeling

5.1 Probability of Subsumption

In [7], Gazzola et al present a comprehensive survey of program repair; this survey high-lights the predominance of search space size as the most critical concern in program repair. At its core, program repair is the act of making a program more-correct than it is [13]; when the program has only one fault (which is what many program repair exper-iments assume), then making the program absolutely correct is indistinguisahble from making it relatively correct (i.e. more-correct than it is). Most program repair methods rely on common mutation operators to generate repair candidates, essentially the same kind of mutation operators that are used in mutation experiments; on the other hand, according to Proposition 7, the search for candidate repairs is based on the same crite-rion (relative correctness) as the determination of subsumption relations. This raises the following question:

- *If mutants are generated by the same operators, and pairs of mutants are compared using the same criterion (relative correctness ⇔ subsumption), why is it so difficult to find program repairs (i.e. to reveal relative correctness relationships) yet so easy to reveal subsumption relations, as most subsumption graphs published in the lit-erature are very dense (in terms of number of arcs over number of nodes)? Is this perhaps the result of loss of recall in program repair, or loss of precision in mtant subsumption?*

We are not going to answer this question in this paper (as that requires an empirical study well beyond the scope of this paper), but we will discuss the mathematics that enable us to analyze this matter.

Relative correctness is determined by checking an inclusion relationship between competence domains, and subsumption is determined by checking an inclusion rela-tionship between differentiator sets. Hence both criteria can be modeled statistically by considering the following question: If we choose K **non-empty** subsets of a set of size T, what is the probability that any two subsets be in an inclusion relationship? Once we estimate this probability, we can answer two related questions:

- What is the expected number of inclusion relationships between these K subsets? This would be the expected number of arcs in a subsumption graph of K nodes.
- What is the expected number of maximal subsets among the K subsets? This would be the size of the minimal set of mutants, as determined by subsumption.

These two questions are addressed in the next two subsections. It is important to note that by modeling subsumption and relative correctness with set inclusion, we are assum-ing that the competence domains of two mutants with respect to a specification are statistically independent. Our statistical analysis is sound only to the extent that this assumption is valid.

5.2 Graph Density

By abuse of notation, we use the same symbol to denote a set and its cardinality. Given a set T and K non-empty subsets thereof, we ponder the question: what is the probability that any two subsets among K are in an inclusion relationship? Let D be the random variable that takes its values in subsets of T. The probability that D takes any particular value E is given by the inverse of the number of non-empty subsets of T:

$$prob(D = E) = \frac{1}{2^T - 1}.$$

The probability that D takes the value of a subset of size n is:

$$prob(|D| = n) = \frac{\binom{T}{n}}{2^T - 1}.$$

Given a subset E of size n, the probability that another subset E' is a subset of E is:

$$prob(E' \subseteq E) = \frac{2^n - 1}{2^T - 1},$$

where the numerator is the number of subsets of E and the denominator is the total number of subsets of T. The probability that two subsets E and E' of T are in a subset relation is:

$prob(E' \subseteq E)$
$=$ {conditional probability}
$\sum_{n=1}^{T} prob(E' \subseteq E |\, |E| = n) \times prob(|E| = n)$
$=$ {substitutions}
$\sum_{n=1}^{T} \frac{2^n - 1}{2^T - 1} \times \frac{\binom{T}{n}}{2^T - 1}.$
$=$ {simplification}
$\sum_{n=1}^{T} \frac{2^n - 1}{(2^T - 1)^2} \times \binom{T}{n}.$
$=$ {factorization}
$\frac{1}{(2^T - 1)^2} \times \sum_{n=1}^{T} 2^n \binom{T}{n}$
$-\frac{1}{(2^T - 1)^2} \times \sum_{n=1}^{T} \binom{T}{n}.$
$=$ {highlighting the binomial formula}
$\frac{1}{(2^T - 1)^2} \times \sum_{n=1}^{T} 2^n \times 1^{T-n} \binom{T}{n}$
$-\frac{1}{(2^T - 1)^2} \times \sum_{n=1}^{T} \binom{T}{n}.$
$=$ {simplifying}
$\frac{3^T}{(2^T - 1)^2} - \frac{2^T}{(2^T - 1)^2}.$

For large (or even moderate) values of T, this can be approximated by $(\frac{3}{4})^T$. Under the assumption of statistical independence cited above, the expected number of arcs in a subsumption graph of K nodes can be approximated by:

$$(\frac{3}{4})^T \times K(K - 1).$$

In practice, even with moderate values of T, this expected number is very small.

5.3   Number of Maximal Nodes

Using the probability estimate $p = \frac{3}{4}^T$, we can estimate the probability that any subset of T is maximal: A given subset is maximal if and only if all $(K - 1)$ other subsets are not supersets there of; hence,

$$prob(maximality) = (1 - (\frac{3}{4})^T)^{K-1}.$$

Whence we derive the expected number of maximal mutants in a subsumption (/ relative correctness) graph that stems from K mutants and a test suite of size T:

$$K \times (1 - (\frac{3}{4})^T)^{K-1}.$$

6   Illustration: Three Subsumption Graphs

We consider the Java benchmark program of *jTerminal* (available online at http://www.grahamedgecombe.com/projects/jterminal), an open-source software product routinely used in mutation testing experiments [25]. We apply the mutant generation tool *LittleDarwin* in conjunction with a test generation and deployment class that includes 35 test cases [25]; we augmented the benchmark test suite with two additional tests, intended specifically to *trip* the base program *jTerminal*, by causing it to diverge. We let T designate the augmented test suite codified in this test class; all our analysis of mutant equivalence, mutant redundancy, mutant survival, etc. is based on the outcomes of programs and mutants on this test suite (and carefully selected subsets thereof). Execution of LittleDarwin on jTerminal yields 94 mutants, numbered m1 to m94; the test of these mutants against the original using the selected test suite kills 48 mutants; for the sake of documentation, we list them below:

m1, m2, m7, m8, m9, m10, m11, m12, m13,
m14, m15, m16, m17, m18, m19, m21, m22,
m23, m24, m25, m26, m27, m28, m44, m45,
m46, m48, m49, m50, m51, m52, m53, m54,
m55, m56, m57, m58, m59, m60, m61, m62,
m63, m83, m88, m89, m90, m92, m93.

The remaining 46 mutants are semantically equivalent to the pre-restriction of jTerminal to T. The first order of business is to partition these 48 mutants into equivalence classes modulo semantic equivalence; we find that these 48 mutants are partitioned into 31 equivalence classes, and we select a member from each class; we let μ be the set of selected mutants: $\mu =$

m1, m2, m7, m11, m13, m15, m19, m21, m22,
m23, m24, m25, m27, m28, m44, m45, m46, m48,
m49, m50, m51, m52, m53, m55, m56, m57, m60,
m63, m92, m93.

We resolve to draw the subsumption graphs of these mutants according to the three definitions:

- Basic/ True Subsumption:

$$\emptyset \subset \delta_B(jTerminal, M) \subseteq \delta_B(jTerminal, M').$$

- Strict Subsumption:

$$\emptyset \subset \delta_S(jTerminal, M) \subseteq \delta_S(jTerminal, M').$$

- Loose Subsumption:

$$\emptyset \subset \delta_L(jTerminal, M) \subseteq \delta_L(jTerminal, M').$$

To this effect, we must compute the differentiator sets
$\delta_B(jTerminal, M)$,
$\delta_S(jTerminal, M)$,
$\delta_L(jTerminal, M)$
for all 31 mutants selected above, with respect to *jTerminal*. Note that this experiment is artificial in the sense that whereas the strict and loose definitions of differentiator sets can be applied to the same combination of program and test suite, the basic definition can only be applied when we know, or assume, that the base program and all the mutants converge for all the elements of the test suite. In the case of *jTerminal* and its mutants, this assumption does not hold, as virtually all of them fail to converge on at least some elements of T. We obviate this difficulty by considering that divergence is itself an execution outcome, but this is merely a convenient assumption for the sake of the experiment.

By computing the basic, strict and loose differentiator sets of all the mutants with respect to *jTerminal* and comparing them for inclusion, we derive the subsumption relations between the mutants, which we can represent by graphs; these graphs are given in, respectively, Figs. 6, 7 and 8. Nodes in these graphs represent mutants and arrows represent subsumption relations: whenever there is an arrow from mutant M to mutant M', it means that M subsumes M' (hence M' can be eliminated from the mutant set without affecting its effectiveness). When two mutants subsumes each other (for example $M27$ and $M28$ in 7), this means that though these mutants are distinct from each other (they compute functions), they have the same differentiator set with respect to *jTerminal*.

From these graphs, we derive minimal mutant sets by selecting the maximal nodes in the subsumption ordering. Once we have the minimal mutant sets, we derive minimal test suites that kill all the mutants in these sets. We verify, in each case, that the test suites that kills all the mutants of the minimal mutant sets actually kill all the 48 non-equivalent mutants derived in our experiment; this comes as no surprise, since this precisely the rationale for deleting subsumed mutants.

For strict subsumption, for example, we find the following minimal mutant set:
m22, m23, m27, m28, m44, m45, m48, m50, m51, m54, m56, m61, m83, m92, m93.

Using this mutant set, we derive minimal test suites that kill all these mutants; we find 6 minimal test suites, of size 7:
Suite 1: {t7,t16,t18,t20,t21,t22,t25}
Suite 2: {t7,t16,t18,t20,t21,t22,t26}

```
Suite 3: {t16,t18,t20,t21,t22,t23,t25}
Suite 4: {t16,t18,t20,t21,t22,t25,t27}
Suite 5: {t16,t18,t20,t21,t22,t23,t26}
Suite 6: {t16,t18,t20,t21,t22,t26,t27}
```

By virtue of subsumption, these test suites kill all 31 mutants selected above; by virtue of equivalence, they necessarily kill all 48 killable mutants of *jTerminal*.

Using the basic interpretation of subsumption, we find 96 minimal test suites, all of them of size 12; for the loose interpretation of subsumption, we find 48 minimal test suites, all of them of size 11. Due to space limitations, we do not include these test suites. Suffice it to say that their number and their size are vastly different from those found under the strict interpretation.

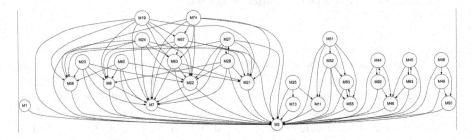

Fig. 6. Due to [1]: Basic Subsumption Graph, jTerminal Mutants.

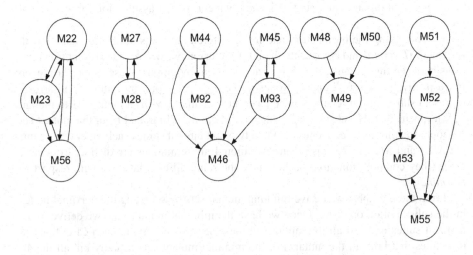

Fig. 7. Due to [1]: Strict Subsumption Graph, jTerminal Mutants.

7 Concluding Remarks

7.1 Summary

In this paper we consider the definition of mutant subsumption, and we resolve to generalize it by taking into consideration the possibility that the execution of programs or

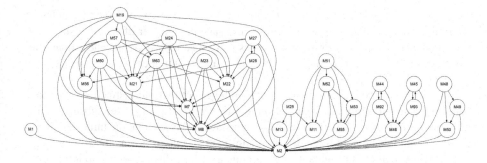

Fig. 8. Due to [1]: Loose Subsumption Graph, jTerminal Mutants.

their mutants may diverge. The possibility of divergence raises the question of what is the outcome of an execution (is divergence an outcome or the absence of outcome), under what condition can we compare two outcomes (can we compare the outcome of a program that converges with that of a program that diverges? can we compare the outcome of two programs that diverge?), and under what condition can we consider that two comparable outcomes are identical or distinct (when two programs diverge, do they have the same outcome?). We argue that the definition of subsumption varies according to how we answer these questions, and we identify three possible formulas for subsumption, based on three sensible interpretations of these questions.

We further argue that considering the possibility of divergence is not a mundane academic exercise, but an important consideration in mutation testing, as several mutation operators are prone to trigger divergence, even when the base program makes careful provisions to avoid it. Also, we find that once we admit the possibility that programs may define a partial function (i.e. that they may diverge for some initial states), then there is no difference between true subsumption and dynamic subsumption: dynamic subsumption with respect to a program P and test suite T is the equivalent to true subsumption with respect to the pre-restriction of P to T.

We also find, interestingly, that the property of mutant subsumption with respect to a base program P is equivalent to the property of relative correctness with respect to the function of program P interpreted as a specification. The main difference is that relative correctness culminates in absolute correctness, which characterizes the candidate programs at the top of the relative correctness graph; these are the absolutely correct programs. By contrast, due to condition P1, mutant subsumption culminates at the layer immediately below the top of the graph; these are the maximally stubborn mutants (whose differentiator sets are singletons).

We generalize the definition of mutant subsumption by modeling the subsumption of mutant M over mutant M' with respect to program P by an equation of the form:

$$\emptyset \subset \delta(P, M) \subseteq \delta(P, M'),$$

where $\delta(,)$ is the differentiator set function, for three possible definitions of $\delta(,)$. Both $\delta(P, M)$ and $\delta(P, M')$ are subsets of T. This model enables us to reason about the probability of occurrence of subsumption relations: Given that differentiator sets are subsets of T, there are $2^{|T|} - 1$ possible non-empty differentiator sets; using combinatorial formulas, we can estimate the probability that two random subsets of T have an inclusion relation; then we can use this probability to estimate the number of arcs in a subsumption graph and the number of maximal nodes in a subsumption graph. These quantities can be estimated in terms of the cardinality of T and the number of mutants; this is the subject of Sect. 5.

In Sect. 6 we show empirical evidence to the effect that the distinctions we make between basic subsumption, strict subsumption and broad (aka loose) subsumption is meaningful: In the benchmark example we consider in this section, the three definitions of differentiator sets yield three distinct definitions of what it means to kill a mutants, three distinct definition of mutant subsumption, and three distinct subsumption graphs.

7.2   Critique

It is important to acknowledge that when we talk about execution outcomes, we leave much room for interpretation: not only does divergence raise a host of issues about what constitutes the outcome of an execution, but even when an execution converges, it is not always clear what constitutes the outcome of the execution. To clarify this matter, it helps to adopt a homogeneous model, based on state spaces and a mapping from initial states to final states, or a heterogeneous model, based on a mapping from an input stream to an output stream. It is also important to specify which definition of differentiator set one adopts, as that determines many important parameters of the analysis.

The analogy between mutant subsumption and relative correctness is interesting, but to ensure that it is useful beyond academic curiosity we need to explore how advances in each branch can benefit the other branch.

The statistical study of Sect. 5 is interesting but it raises a paradox: intuitively, if we take two random subsets of a set T, the probability that one of them is a subset of the other decreases very quickly with the cardinality of T. This seems to suggest that subsumption graphs ought to have very few arcs between mutants, but most published subsumption graphs are very dense, i.e. have many arcs for the number of nodes they have [9, 15–17, 25, 27, 28]. The only possible explanation of this discrepancy is that the differentiator sets of mutants generated from a base program are not random; but it is difficult to imagine what statistical relation may hold between the differentiator sets of two mutants of the same program.

7.3   Prospects

We envision to explore the practical implications of the classification of subsumption relations, the possible synergies between the study of mutant subsumption and the study of relative correctness, and the empirical validation of the statistical model of subsumption relations.

References

1. AlBlwi, S., Marsit, I., Khaireddine, B., Ayad, A., Loh, J., Mili, A.: Generalized mutant subsumption. In: Proceedings, ICSOFT 2022. Lisbon, Portugal, July 2022

2. Andrews, J.H., Briand, L.C., Labiche, Y., Namin, A.S.: Using mutation analysis for assessing and comparing testing coverage criteria. IEEE Trans. Softw. Eng. **32**(8), 608–624 (2006)
3. Andrews, J., Briand, L., Labiche, Y.: Is mutation an appropriate tool for testing experiments? In: Proceedings, ICSE (2005)
4. Brink, C., Kahl, W., Schmidt, G.: Relational Methods in Computer Science. Advances in Computer Science. Springer, Heidelberg (1997). https://doi.org/10.1007/3-540-36280-0
5. Diallo, N., Ghardallou, W., Mili, A.: Correctness and relative correctness. In: Proceedings, 37th International Conference on Software Engineering, NIER track. Firenze, Italy, 20–22 May 2015. https://doi.org/10.1109/ICSE.2015.200
6. Dijkstra, E.: A Discipline of Programming. Prentice Hall (1976)
7. Gazzola, L., Micucci, D., Mariani, L.: Automatic software repair: a survey. IEEE Trans. Softw. Eng. **45**(1) (2019)
8. Gries, D.: The Science of Programming. Springer, New York (1981). https://doi.org/10.1007/978-1-4612-5983-1
9. Guimaraes, M.A., Fernandes, L., Riberio, M., d'Amorim, M., Gheyi, R.: Optimizing mutation testing by discovering dynamic mutant subsumption relations. In: Proceedings, 13th International Conference on Software Testing, Validation and Verification (2020)
10. Hehner, E.: A Practical Theory of Programming. Springer, New York (1993). https://doi.org/10.1007/978-1-4419-8596-5
11. Hoare, C.: An axiomatic basis for computer programming. Commun. ACM **12**(10), 576–583 (1969). https://doi.org/10.1145/363235.363259
12. Just, R., Jalali, D., Inozemtseva, L., Ernst, M., Holmes, R., Fraser, G.: Are mutants a valid substitute for real faults in software testing? In: Proceedings, FSE (2014)
13. Khaireddine, B., Martinez, M., Mili, A.: Program repair at arbitrary fault depth. In: Proceedings, ICST 2019. Xi'An, China, April 2019
14. Khaireddine, B., Mili, A.: Quantifying faultiness: what does it mean to have n faults? In: Proceedings, FormaliSE 2021, ICSE 2021 Colocated Conference, May 2021
15. Kurtz, B., Amman, P., Delamaro, M., Offutt, J., Deng, L.: Mutant subsumption graphs. In: Proceedings, 7th International Conference on Software Testing, Validation and Verification Workshops (2014)
16. Kurtz, B., Ammann, P., Offutt, J.: Static analysis of mutant subsumption. In: Proceedings, IEEE 8th International Conference on Software Testing, Verification and Validation Workshops (2015)
17. Li, X., Wang, Y., Lin, H.: Coverage based dynamic mutant subsumption graph. In: Proceedings, International Conference on Mathematics, Modeling and Simulation Technologies and Applications (2017)
18. Manna, Z.: A Mathematical Theory of Computation. McGraw-Hill (1974)
19. Mili, A., Frias, M.F., Jaoua, A.: On faults and faulty programs. In: Höfner, P., Jipsen, P., Kahl, W., Müller, M.E. (eds.) RAMICS 2014. LNCS, vol. 8428, pp. 191–207. Springer, Cham (2014). https://doi.org/10.1007/978-3-319-06251-8_12
20. Mili, A.: Differentiators and detectors. Inf. Process. Lett. **169** (2021)
21. Mili, A., Tchier, F.: Software Testing: Operations and Concepts. Wiley (2015)
22. Mills, H.D., Basili, V.R., Gannon, J.D., Hamlet, D.R.: Structured Programming: A Mathematical Approach. Allyn and Bacon, Boston (1986)
23. Morgan, C.C.: Programming from Specifications. International Series in Computer Sciences, 2nd edn. Prentice Hall, London (1998)
24. Namin, A.S., Kakarla, S.: The use of mutation in testing experiments and its sensitivity to external threats. In: Proceedings, ISSTA (2011)
25. Parsai, A., Demeyer, S.: Dynamic mutant subsumption analysis using littledarwin. In: Proceedings, A-TEST 2017. Paderborn, Germany, 4–5 September 2017

26. Schmidt, G.: Relational Mathematics. No. 132 in Encyclopedia of Mathematics and its Applications, Cambridge University Press, November 2010
27. Souza, B.: Identifying mutation subsumption relations. In: Proceedings, IEEE/ACM International Conference on Automated Software Engineering, pp. 1388–1390, December 2020
28. Tenório, M.C., Lopes, R.V.V., Fechine, J., Marinho, T., Costa, E.: Subsumption in mutation testing: an automated model based on genetic algorithm. In: Latifi, S. (ed.) 16th International Conference on Information Technology-New Generations (ITNG 2019). AISC, vol. 800, pp. 169–175. Springer, Cham (2019). https://doi.org/10.1007/978-3-030-14070-0_24

On the Efficiency of Building Large Collections of Software: Modeling, Algorithms, and Experimental Results

Stephen R. Tate[(✉)] and Bo Yuan

Department of Computer Science, UNC Greensboro, Greensboro, NC 27402, USA
srtate@uncg.edu

Abstract. Building software from source code requires a build environment that meets certain requirements, such as the presence of specific compilers, libraries, or other tools. Unfortunately, requirements for different packages can conflict with each other, so it is often impossible to use a single build environment when building a large collection of software. This paper develops techniques to minimize the number of distinct build environments required, and measures the practical impact of our techniques on build time. In particular, we introduce the notion of a "conflict graph," and prove that the problem of minimizing the number of build environments is equivalent to the graph coloring problem on this graph. We explore several heuristic techniques to compute conflict graph colorings, finding solutions that result in surprisingly small sets of build environments. Using Ubuntu 20.04 as our primary experimental dataset, we computed just 4 different environments that were sufficient for building the "Top 500" most popular source packages, and 11 build environments were sufficient for building all 30,646 source packages included in Ubuntu 20.04. Finally, we experimentally evaluate the benefit of these environments by comparing the work required for building the "Top 500" with our environments to the work required using the traditional minimal environment build. We saw that the total work required for building these packages dropped from 139h36m (139 h and 36 min) to 54 h 18 m, a 61% reduction.

Keywords: Build environments · Large scale analysis

1   Introduction

In this paper, we explore the efficiency of building large collections of installable and executable software from source code, focusing on designing environments for performing source code to binary builds. We define the problem from a system independent standpoint, develop models and algorithms at that level, and then we perform experiments and evaluation in the specific setting of Ubuntu version 20.04, which is representative of large collections of system software. We use terminology that is common to Linux distributions, referring to "source packages" that are used to build "binary packages," but even in settings that don't use packages *per se*, equivalent objects exist even if by other names. To appreciate the scope of the problem in our experimental environment, Ubuntu 20.04 consists of 30,646 source packages that are used to create 62,450 binary packages that end users can install. Using a source package to build

© The Author(s), under exclusive license to Springer Nature Switzerland AG 2023
H.-G. Fill et al. (Eds.): ICSOFT 2022, CCIS 1859, pp. 145–168, 2023.
https://doi.org/10.1007/978-3-031-37231-5_7

binary packages involves certain software requirements, or dependencies, which must be installed to support the build. For example, any source package containing C code will need a C compiler to produce the binaries. Requirements extend beyond the obvious language tools though, and most packages also require certain support libraries be installed to perform the build, and can also require packaging tools and other utilities. Furthermore, dependencies can have their own dependencies, and those dependencies can have dependencies, and so on. The challenges that we address in this paper originally arose not from building binaries, but from performing large scale static analysis on open source software, which has an almost identical set of requirements — for example, running the Clang static analyzer on a source package performs static analysis as a side effect of compilation, so needs all of the build requirements to be installed to perform the analysis. While our motivation was static analysis, we use the "build environment" terminology and problem statement here, since that a more widely-understood setting.

In Debian-based Linux distributions, the build process is typically run using the pbuilder[1] tool, which creates a minimal build environment in a chroot jail and adds the necessary dependencies to that environment before starting the build. By adding only the minimal set of dependencies, issues of conflicts are avoided entirely, assuming the package maintainer defined a feasible build environment. While this provides a simple and robust method for performing an isolated build of a single package, when used for building multiple packages the cost of creating each package's minimal build environment becomes very high. Describing work to re-build an entire Debian distribution from sources, Nussbaum reported that some packages required a large amount of time to simply set up the build environment, including a requirement for 485 additional package installations before the build process could even begin for openoffice.org [11]. This problem has gotten even worse since Nussbaum's 2009 work, with the version of LibreOffice in Ubuntu 20.04 requiring *904 additional packages*, above and beyond the "build essentials" that all build environments include, and in our tests it took a little over 13 min to simply set up before the build could even begin. While pbuilder can save created build environments for future use, this is mostly useful for working on a single package that will reuse the exact same build environment on future runs. When the cost of creating package-specific environments became a limiting factor of our work, we began exploring the question of whether we could create generally-useful environments that can be used for large sets of packages. Doing so would greatly improve the efficiency of building or analyzing large sets of packages, and the results of that exploration is the subject of this paper.

When planning to build a large set of packages, it is tempting to think that the right solution is to install all dependencies required by all packages being built. Unfortunately, dependencies can conflict with one another, meaning that certain combinations of packages cannot be installed at the same time. For example, in Ubuntu 20.04, building firefox requires the package autoconf2.13 to be installed, while the source package apache2 lists autoconf2.13 as a direct conflict. Because of this conflict, it is impossible to set up a single build environment that can support building both firefox and apache2. While this is a direct and obvious conflict, some conflicts only appear with deeper digging. For example,

---

[1] https://pbuilder-team.pages.debian.net/pbuilder/.

building `firefox` requires `libcurl4-openssl-dev` and building `git` requires the `libcurl4-gnutls-dev`, and while neither source package lists any conflicts, the two dependencies, `libcurl4-openssl-dev` and `libcurl4-gnutls-dev`, conflict with each other and so induce an indirect conflict in the build environments for `firefox` and `git`. Therefore, to get a complete picture of possible build environments, all dependencies and conflicts, both direct and transitively induced, must be considered.

In this paper, we define a graph that captures the necessary information on dependencies and conflicts for a set of source packages, and show that the graph coloring problem on this graph reflects the corresponds to the design of build environments. Due to the NP-completeness of minimum graph coloring, we cannot efficiently compute optimal solutions, but we explore how well various heuristic approaches perform in practice. Finally, we put these results into practice and test the efficiency of our computed build environments. We make the following specific contributions in this paper:

- Define a "conflict graph" that captures software build dependencies and conflicts, develop efficient algorithms to construct the conflict graph, and explore the properties of this graph for various Ubuntu "Long Term Support" (LTS) releases.
- Show how finding a minimum graph coloring on this graph provides the smallest set of different build environments that need to be created to support building all packages.
- Explore how graph coloring on nested subgraphs supports the ability to analyze subsets of packages (e.g., support analyzing both "the 500 most popular packages" and "the 1000 most popular packages" with a single set of build environments).
- Present experimental results from applying heuristic graph coloring algorithms to these problems using the Ubuntu 20.04 release, and check for evidence of optimality by computing max cliques in these graphs.
- Present experimental results performing software builds, showing that our computed build environments reduce the amount of work required to build the "Top 500" packages in Ubuntu 20.04 by over half.

The problems that we explore are interesting from an abstract modeling and algorithms standpoint, and the reduction and algorithms result in direct practical gains for designing systems for large scale software build and analysis. All code and data reported on in this paper is freely available (see Sect. 4).

The modeling and coloring results from this paper were originally presented in preliminary form at the ICSOFT 2022 conference [14], and this paper updates the earlier report by adding checks for optimality by computing max cliques (Sect. 4.4), adding full experimental tests on the efficiency of using our computed build environments (Sect. 5), and updating examples throughout to use data from the newer Ubuntu 20.04 release rather than Ubuntu 18.04. The presentation has also been improved throughout and all figures have been updated.

2 Dependency and Conflict Computations

In this section we define the basic terminology and model required for representing packages, dependencies, and conflicts. We simplify some real-world issues for our model, and will discuss those issues and their impact in Sect. 2.3. *Packages* are sets of files coupled with meta-data, or attributes, that give information about the package. In our model we have a set of *source packages* S and a set of *binary packages* B, where source packages contain files and information necessary to build binary packages. Attributes for either source or binary packages can include lists of dependencies and conflicts, which for package p we denote by $D(p)$ and $C(p)$, respectively. If $p \in B$ is a binary package, then $D(p)$ is the set of all binary packages that must be installed any time p is installed in order for p to be functional, and $C(p)$ is the set of all binary packages that cannot be installed at the same time as p. If $p \in S$ is a source package, then $D(p)$ is the set of binary packages that must be installed and available in the build environment for p, and $C(p)$ is the set of all binary packages that must *not* be installed when building binaries from this source package. In all cases, the $D(p)$ and $C(p)$ definitions specify immediate dependencies and conflicts, and these can induce additional dependencies and conflicts as described in the following subsection.

2.1 Dependency Sets

Package dependencies are defined by package maintainers, and give just immediate dependencies, or what we will call first-level dependencies, which we denote $D_1(p) = D(p)$. Packages in $D_1(p)$ can have their own dependencies, which are called "second-level dependencies," which in turn define "third-level dependencies," and so on. To simplify later cases, we define "level-0 dependencies" of p to be simply the set $\{p\}$, giving the recursive definition

$$D_k(p) = \begin{cases} \{p\} & \text{if } k = 0; \\ \bigcup_{x \in D_{k-1}(p)} D(x) & \text{if } k \geq 1. \end{cases}$$

The full set of dependencies for package p is then

$$D^*(p) = \bigcup_{k \geq 0} D_k(p),$$

and while this union is unbounded in k, only a finite number of levels can add new dependencies since the set of packages is finite. If p is a source package, then all packages in $D^*(p)$ must be installed in order to build binary packages from p. Since dependencies are directed relations between packages, we can view packages and dependencies as a directed graph (the "dependency graph"). Then $D^*(p)$ is the set of vertices reachable from p in the dependency graph, or equivalently $D^*(p)$ consists of the neighbors of p in the transitive closure of the dependency graph.

While the dependency graph provides a clean abstraction of dependency relations, in our work we work directly with dependency sets. The following algorithm computes a new level of dependencies for package p, where packages in dependencies at prior levels are passed in as parameter E (the "exclusion set"). When called recursively on line 4 below, the new exclusion set E' is at least one element larger than the incoming set E (since E' contains x but E does not), and so the number of levels of recursion is limited by the number of packages (i.e., items that can be added to E). Therefore, recursion must be limited, and the algorithm always completes in a finite number of steps.

ALLDEPS(p, E)

1   $S = \{p\}$
2   $E' = E \cup D(p)$
3   **for** $x \in D(p) - E$
4      $S = S \cup$ ALLDEPS(x, E')
5   **return** S

Since ALLDEPS recurses through all levels of dependencies until no additional packages can be added, the end result is ALLDEPS$(p, \emptyset) = D^*(p)$ for any package p. The computed dependency set grows monotonically, and once a package is included in the set no additional recursive calls will be made for that package. Therefore, using an efficient set implementation, the ALLDEPS is very fast. To further improve performance when computing dependency sets of many packages, we cache results for binary packages as they are completed, so we can short-circuit the recursion with pre-computed sets. We discuss this and experimental performance results in Sect. 4.

2.2 Conflict Sets and Relation

In addition to dependencies, packages can conflict with other packages, which means that they cannot be installed simultaneously. While the Debian package management system has different types of conflicts (e.g., "Conflicts" and "Breaks" attributes in Debian packages), in our model we consider different types of conflicts as the same and refer to them generically as "conflicts." For any package p, we define $C(p)$ to be the set of packages that are listed as conflicting with it, meaning the immediate conflicts. As with $D(p)$, additional indirect conflicts can also be induced through dependencies.

Note that $C(p)$, as defined attributes listed in package p, is not necessarily a symmetric relation between packages. For example, the package maintainer for package p_1 may recognize that there is a conflict with a package p_2, so $p_2 \in C(p_1)$, but the package maintainer for p_2 may not even know that package p_1 exists, so would not list p_1 as a conflict and thus $p_1 \notin C(p_2)$. Regardless of whether or not both packages recognize the conflict, if it exists in either direction then the packages cannot be installed simultaneously. We take care of both the possible lack of symmetry and indirect conflicts from dependencies in the following definition.

$$C^*(p) = \{r \mid r \in C(d) \text{ for some } d \in D^*(p) \quad \text{or}$$
$$d \in C(r) \text{ for some } d \in D^*(p)\}. \tag{1}$$

Note that $C^*(p)$ is symmetric, meaning that $r \in C^*(p)$ if and only if $p \in C^*(r)$. The package p in this definition can be either a source package or a binary package, and if p_1 and p_2 are source packages with $p_1 \in C^*(p_2)$ that means that their build environments are incompatible (some package required to build p_1 conflicts with some package required to build p_2). Conversely, if $p_1 \notin C^*(p_2)$ then the build environments are compatible: all packages in $D^*(p_1) \cup D^*(p_2)$ can be installed together, and that environment will support building binary packages from both p_1 and p_2.

2.3   Model vs Real World

Our model captures the basic ideas of dependencies and conflicts, while avoiding some complications found in real-world package management systems. In this section we summarize the main differences between our model and the Debian package management system that inspires this work.

Disjunctions in Dependencies. While our model uses a set of packages $D(p)$ to represent a conjunction of dependencies, the Debian package manager allows each dependency to be satisfied in multiple ways – a disjunction of packages, which we call an "or-list" for that dependency. For example, in Ubuntu 20.04, the weechat package has a single dependency, which is satisfied by either of two packages: weechat-curses or weechat-headless. We keep and propagate these disjunctions up to the level of the source package when computing $C^*(p)$, and then select a set of non-conflicting packages to satisfy each disjunction in left-to-right preference order. This is the same prioritization used by the official Debian build systems, as described in the Debian Policy Manual: "To avoid inconsistency between repeated builds of a package, the auto-builders will default to selecting the first alternative, after reducing any architecture-specific restrictions for the build architecture in question" [8]. Our code first removes all disjunctions that are met by some other (possibly transitively-induced) dependency, and then performs an exhaustive backtracking search over disjunctions to satisfy dependencies, which can take exponential time in the worst case. Other authors have shown that the basic co-installability question for packages is NP-complete due to these disjunctions (see the "Related Work" section), but in our experiments we found that real-world package data resulted in quick dependency resolution in practice, with backtracking in our search being very rare.

"Provides" Pseudo-packages. Similar to explicitly providing alternatives for a dependency, Debian allows for certain package names to represent "virtual packages" which can be satisfied by a number of real packages. For example, in Ubuntu 20.04, lpr is both a binary package and a virtual package, and the virtual package is provided by not only the binary package named lpr but also by packages lprng and cups-bsd which are drop-in replacements for the lpr package. Our tools treat virtual packages as if they were disjunctions, described above, prioritizing a package with the given name over other packages which provide equivalent functionality.

Versions Requirements in Dependencies. Dependencies can include version numbers as well as package names. For example, in Ubuntu 20.04 the libfwsil requires libc6 version 2.14 or greater. While these can technically specify arbitrary version requirements, in Ubuntu 20.04 all version requirements are met with the current ("candidate") version. For example, the base libc6 package distributed in Ubuntu 20.04 is version 2.31, so the stated version requirement is clearly met. Version requirements seem to be mostly relevant for users who attempt to install newer versions of packages (with newer versions specified in dependencies) on older base systems. Since we did not find any relevant version-specific dependencies when sticking with just base distribution packages, we ignore version requirements in our study.

Recommended Packages. Dependencies and conflicts aren't the only relations between packages, and packages can also "Recommend" or "Suggest" other packages. Since these are not necessary in a build environment, our tools ignore these packages.

3   The Conflict Graph and Coloring

In this section we define the "conflict graph" and show that there is a one-to-one correspondence between valid vertex colorings of this graph and feasible sets of build environments. This provides a standard and well-understood graph theory context for understanding sets of build environments.

The conflict graph is an undirected graph that has one vertex for each source package, and each edge represents a conflict in the minimum build environments for edge's two endpoints (source packages). In particular, we define the graph $G = (V, E)$ where the vertex set $V = S$ (the set of source packages), and

$$E = \{(p_1, p_2) \mid p_1, p_2 \in S \text{ and } p_1 \in C^*(p_2)\}.$$

Since vertices are source packages, we interchangeably use the terms "vertex" and "source package" in the rest of this paper. If two vertices are connected in this graph, it means that there are incompatibilities in the build environments for the two source packages, so there is no build environment that can be used for both.

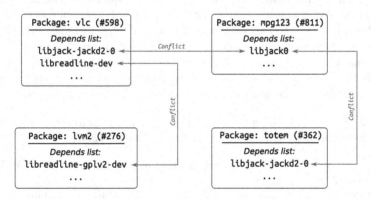

Fig. 1. Example of a conflict graph from Ubuntu 20.04 source packages.

Figure 1 illustrates a conflict graph for four source packages in Ubuntu 20.04. The graph comprises nodes and edges, and additional information about specific dependencies and conflicts is provided in the labels. Specifically, the dependencies for each package p in $D^*(p)$ are displayed, along with conflicts among packages listed as dependencies, indicating which packages are incompatible with each other.

3.1   Colorings and Build Environments

A k-coloring of a graph $G = (V, E)$ is a mapping from vertices to a set of k colors, $c : V \rightarrow \{1, \ldots, k\}$, such that every edge in G has endpoints that have been assigned different colors. In other words, for every $(u, v) \in E$, we have $c(u) \neq c(v)$. The usual goal in finding a graph coloring is to minimize the number of colors k required, and the minimum k for a graph G is called the *chromatic number* of the graph, denoted $\chi(G) = k$.

Colorings of the conflict graph have a direct correspondence with sets of build environments. Specifically, consider a k-coloring on a conflict graph: two source packages that have incompatible build environments due to a conflict correspond to two vertices that are connected by an edge, so in any valid coloring those source packages will be assigned different colors. We will associate each color with a distinct build environment, so this property ensures that two source packages with incompatible build environments in fact use different build environments. We now prove that colorings on the conflict graph have a one-to-one correspondence with sets of build environments for the source packages.

Lemma 1. *Every set of k distinct build environments that can be used to build all source packages can be used to define a k-coloring on the conflict graph.*

Proof. For every $i = 1, \cdots, k$, let P_i denote the set of binary packages included in the ith build environment, and define a coloring c that assigns color i to any vertex (source package) that uses this build environment. Since all source packages have a build environment, every vertex is assigned a color. To see that this is a valid coloring of the conflict graph, consider two vertices v_1 and v_2 that are connected by an edge (v_1, v_2) in the conflict graph, meaning that $v_1 \in C^*(v_2)$. By (1) it follows that there is a $d_1 \in D^*(v_1)$ and $d_2 \in D^*(v_2)$ such that either $d_1 \in C(d_2)$ or $d_2 \in C(d_1)$. Therefore, if v_1 uses build environment P_a and v_2 uses build environment P_b, then $d_1 \in P_a$ and $d_1 \notin P_b$ and so $P_a \neq P_b$. Since v_1 and v_2 use different build environments, they must have different colors in c. As this holds for any edge (v_1, v_2) in the conflict graph, and there are k build environments, c is a valid k-coloring of the conflict graph. ∎

Lemma 2. *Every k-coloring of the conflict graph can be used to create a set of k distinct build environments that is sufficient to build all source packages.*

Proof. Let $c : V \rightarrow \{1, \ldots, k\}$ be a k-coloring of conflict graph $G = (V, E)$. The k-coloring partitions the vertex set V, and we can define $V_i = \{v \mid c(v) = i\}$ (this is often called a "color class"). Next, for each $i = 1, \ldots, k$, define a set of binary packages $P_i = \cup_{v \in V_i} D^*(v)$. We claim that for every source package $v \in V_i$, P_i is a valid and feasible build environment for that source package. The fact that P_i is sufficient follows directly from the definition, since that requires all dependencies of any $v \in V_i$ to be included in P_i.

For feasibility, we need to show that all packages in P_i can be installed simultaneously with no conflicts. For the sake of contradiction, assume that there are conflicting packages $p_1, p_2 \in P_i$ with $p_1 \in C(p_2)$. The inclusion of p_1 and p_2 in P_i must be the result of two source packages $v_1, v_2 \in V_i$ with $p_1 \in D^*(v_1)$ and $p_2 \in D^*(v_2)$. Since $p_1 \in C(p_2)$, it follows that $v_1 \in C^*(v_2)$ by (1), and so there is an edge (v_1, v_2) in the conflict graph. However, since v_1 and v_2 are in the same V_i partition component, they must both have color i which violates the basic coloring requirement. This contradiction completes the proof. ∎

The following theorem follows directly from the two preceding lemmas.

Theorem 1. *The conflict graph has a k-coloring if and only if there is a set of k distinct build environments that is sufficient to build all source packages.*

The proofs above are constructive arguments that provide efficient algorithms for converting from a k-coloring of the conflict graph to a set of build environments, but is this the best way to solve the problem? k-coloring is NP-hard, and does not have efficient approximation algorithms (unless P=NP), so is this a useful reduction? In other words, the question remains of whether finding build environments might in fact be easier than graph coloring – is there some sort of structure to conflict graphs that would lead to efficient solutions, even though the minimum graph coloring problem on general graphs is NP-complete?

Unfortunately, the answer to this question is "no." For an arbitrary graph G we can easily create a set of source packages and conflicts for which the conflict graph is G simply by making a distinct source-to-source conflict for each edge in G. Note that we don't even need to consider binary packages and dependencies for this construction. To be precise about this, using the notation from Sect. 2 (where S is a set of source packages, B is a set of binary packages, D is a dependency function, and C is a conflict function), we define a decision problem (language) MIN-BUILDENV= $\{\langle S, B, D, C, k\rangle \mid$ there exist a set of k feasible build environments that is sufficient for building all source packages in $S\}$. The construction which was described at the beginning of this paragraph is a reduction from MIN-COLOR= $\{\langle G, k\rangle \mid$ there is a valid k-coloring of $G\}$ to MIN-BUILDENV. Since MIN-COLOR is a known NP-complete problem (problem [GT4] in Garey and Johnson [6]). This leads to the following theorem, which we state without further proof.

Theorem 2. *MIN-BUILDENV is NP-complete.*

This result is discouraging as far as worst-case complexity of MIN-BUILDENV, but instances created in the reduction are somewhat unnatural and real-world instances may very well be easy cases that are in fact tractable. We explore properties of conflict graphs derived from real-world software in Sect. 4, but leave open the question of whether typical real-world instances can be solved efficiently. Before getting to the experimental results, we define and discuss an interesting variant of our problem.

3.2   Nested Sets of Source Packages

As mentioned in Sect. 1, our work in creating a formal framework in which to study this problem arose from a project performing large-scale analysis of open source software to search for security vulnerabilities. To maximize the practical impact of our work, we concentrate primarily on the most widely used packages, which we gauge from the now defunct "Ubuntu Popularity Contest" project [15]. We develop our techniques using a small set of packages, and then test on the most popular 100 Ubuntu packages. If that shows promising results, we might devote more computational resources and analyze the most popular 500, 1000, or even 5000 packages. In this process, we work with increasingly larger nested sets of source packages, which motivates an extended version of our build environment definition problem. For example, if we set up a minimal set of build environments for the most popular 500 packages, can we use those environments (with possible extensions) for the most popular 1000 packages? Unfortunately, it is impossible to optimize for both 500 and the expanded set of 1000 simultaneously.

To understand the problem, we will revisit the example in Fig. 1. The numbers beside each package name refer to the position of the package in the Ubuntu Popularity Contest ranking, so lvm2 is the 276th most popular package, vlc is the 598th most popular package, and so on. First consider what would happen if we created build environments for the most popular 500 packages, which would include both lvm2 and totem in our example. Since there are no conflicts between these two packages, the subgraph consisting of just those two packages can be colored with a single color, meaning that a single build environment can be constructed that can be used to build both lvm2 and totem. When we expand this to the "Top 1000 packages," we end up with the full 4-vertex conflict graph shown in Fig. 1. To reuse the build environments we previously constructed, we would need to extend the existing coloring (where lvm2 and totem are given the same color) into a coloring for the entire 4-vertex graph. Unfortunately, when we retain those colors we require 3 colors (or 3 different build environments) for the 4-vertex graph. On the other hand, if we were to color the 4-vertex graph from scratch we could do so with just 2 colors. In other words, by trying to keep the same build environments from the "Top 500 packages" solution, we are forced to take a sub-optimal solution to the "Top 1000 packages" case.

Since extending from the smaller set of packages to the larger doesn't work, can we go in the other direction? Can we compute a solution to the larger problem and then restrict that solution to the smaller set? Again, referring to Fig. 1, we can see that any 2-coloring of this graph results in the two more popular packages, lvm2 and totem, being assigned different colors. This means that when we restrict our larger solution to just the two most popular packages, we are forced to use two distinct build environments when a single build environment would suffice.

Using a larger set of build environments not only increases storage requirements, but also negatively impacts time required for running a large set of builds due to caching. If we build a package using build environment A, and can reuse that same build environment for a second package, many of the files in build environment A will be cached in memory already, leading to a faster build for the second package. If the second package used a separate build environment B, as in the example in the previous paragraph, then the files in environment B would need to be loaded from disk in building the second package, giving a performance hit.

In our work, we have prioritized creating the smallest set of build environments for each of the nested sets of source packages, and do not try to reuse environments from one collection of source packages to the next. Our experiments show that the amount of extra space required to host multiple independently-computed sets of build environments is modest, and we feel that the gains while working within that collection outweigh the costs. We leave further optimization in this setting to future work.

3.3   Conflict Graph Simplification

When a conflict graph is created and examined, it quickly becomes clear that there are some simplifications that can be made to reduce the size of the graph while still maintaining the correspondence between coloring and build environments. The most obvious is that approximately two-thirds of all source packages in modern Ubuntu releases have no conflicts at all, either direct or induced indirectly, so can be built in any build environment simply by including the necessary conflict-free dependencies. In terms of the conflict graph, these source packages exist as isolated vertices in the conflict graph. Since these vertices do not affect the coloring, they can be removed from the graph and then assigned arbitrary colors at the end.

More generally, we can merge isomorphic vertices into a single vertex. If source packages p_1 and p_2 have the same set of conflicting source packages, meaning that $C^*(p_1) \cap S = C^*(p_2) \cap S$, then vertices p_1 and p_2 have the same neighbors and any color that is valid for p_1 will also work for p_2 without any other changes necessary in the graph coloring. Because of this, we merge isomorphic vertices, repeating this process until a fixed point is reached. As we'll see in the next section, this reduces the size of the graph we need to color by over 90%, which greatly improves both the speed and effectiveness of the heuristic graph coloring algorithms that we use.

This process is illustrated in Fig. 2, where we show two steps of merging isomorphic vertices. In this example, source packages A and B each conflict with all of C, D, and E, giving the conflict graph drawn on the left. In the first step, we note that vertices A and B have exactly the same set of neighbors (i.e., conflicting source packages), so are merged into a single vertex that represents both A and B. In the second step, we see that C, D, and E are similarly isomorphic, so are merged into a single vertex. It is clear that this final graph has an optimal 2-coloring, which can be translated back to the original, larger graph.

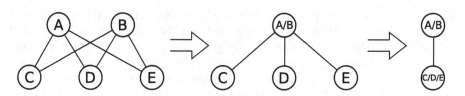

Fig. 2. Illustration of Graph Simplification.

4   Experimental Results

In this section, we present experimental results that we obtained by analyzing four recent Ubuntu LTS releases. We created virtual machines for each of the releases in that time frame, with the main, restricted, universe, and multiverse components loaded into the package database, and with updates turned off so that only versions in the original distribution were included. We next developed software to extract dependency and conflict information from package information using Python and the Python APT Library[2].

---

[2] https://apt-team.pages.debian.net/python-apt/library.

This worked well for Ubuntu releases 16.04 and later, but the version of `python-apt` included with 14.04 lacked key features that we relied on. To analyze the Ubuntu 14.04 release, we created a docker container based on Ubuntu 20.04 with all of the Python packages needed to create the conflict graph, including a sufficiently modern version of `python-apt`. We then manually removed all of the Ubuntu 20.04 package information files from that Docker container, and replaced them with files extracted from a Ubuntu 14.04 installation, and in that way successfully constructed the conflict graph for Ubuntu 14.04. Our code and results from this set of Ubuntu distributions is available in a GitHub repository under an open source license[3].

First, we examine basic properties of dependencies and conflict graphs, as well as effect graph simplification as described in Sect. 3.3, to gain insight into the size and structure of real-world data. Then in the following sections, we report on results from running heuristic graph coloring algorithms on the generated graphs, and discuss what that means for setting up build environments.

4.1 Graphs from Ubuntu LTS Releases

Table 1. Basic graph metrics for Ubuntu releases (table appeared in [14]).

Ubuntu version:	14.04	16.04	18.04	20.04
Buildable SPKGS	22,028	25,401	28,886	30,646
Full graph edges	207,894	214,982	376,028	387,175
Full graph density	0.0009	0.0007	0.0009	0.0008
Simplified graph vertices	1,646	1,943	1,476	1,770
Simplified graph edges	37,087	45,992	43,363	51,492
Simplified graph density	0.027	0.024	0.040	0.033

We first consider the basic properties of the conflict graphs constructed from four major long-term-support (LTS) releases of the Ubuntu Linux distribution, which were released at two year intervals from 2014 to 2020. To gain insight into what to expect in future releases, we evaluate some fundamental graph metrics on these releases, examining what has remained consistent and what has changed over time. Table 1 presents the results for both the complete conflict graphs and the simplified graphs, providing information on their sizes and density measures. The column labeled "Buildable SPKGS" shows the number of buildable source packages with each release. It is worth noting that both the 16.04 and 18.04 release had six source packages that were not buildable due to conflicts in their dependency attributes. These issues were resolved through updates to the LTS release, but for the sake of consistency, we excluded these unbuildable source packages from our analysis of non-updated releases.

As can be seen in the table, the number of source packages has increased with every new release, giving an overall 39% increase from 14.04 to 20.04. Our graph simplification algorithm, as described in Sect. 3.3, consistently reduces the number of vertices in the conflict graph by between 92% and 95%. This significant size reduction allows our heuristic graph coloring algorithms to run significantly faster and with higher success rates, as we will see in Sect. 4.2.

---

[3] https://github.com/srtate/BuildEnvAnalysis.

Also of interest is the structure and complexity of the dependencies and conflicts. We originally predicted that dependency chains would be relatively short, and while the vast majority of dependency chains are under 10 links long, in our work on the 20.04 release we found one dependency chain of length 18, for package node-brfs. We found, unsurprisingly, a large number of packages with mutual dependencies, although some came from the same source package, so it's unclear why separate binary packages are built if they must always be installed together (e.g., tasksel and tasksel-data depend on each other, and are both built from source package tasksel). While such mutual dependencies give cycles of length two in the dependency graph, there are simple cycles of varying lengths larger than two as well—for example, console-setup depends on console-setup-linux, which depends on kbd, which depends on console-setup.

With this understanding of release sizes and metrics, we next report our experimental results using heuristic graph coloring algorithms on the constructed conflict graphs.

4.2 Coloring Results for Ubuntu 20.04

Since graph coloring is an NP-hard problem, the graphs constructed from Ubuntu distributions, even after simplification, are far too large for any exact optimal graph coloring algorithm to be practical. Therefore, we need to rely on approximate (heuristic) graph coloring algorithms, and we utilize the suite of graph coloring algorithms created by Joseph Culberson[4]. This software supports a variety of heuristics, ranging from a simple greedy algorithm to versions that use heuristics and randomization to find better colorings. Random seeds to be provided on the command line, which enables us to script a large number of many runs with varying random seeds. This software was designed for the DIMACS challenges on graph coloring, readings graphs in the "DIMACS standard format," so our package analysis software outputs the conflict graphs in this format. Additionally, we output "translation table" that allows us to convert between a generic vertex number and its corresponding source package name.

We first considered two versions of graphs that represent all source packages: the full conflict graph and the simplified version computed as described in Sect. 3.3. Note that for the simplified graphs, the translation table mapping package names to vertices is many-to-one, so vertices are not synonymous with individual source packages. We automated the process of running the coloring algorithms with different random seeds and different heuristic options, and allowed the coloring programs to run for up to a full 24-h day on a Linux system with an Intel i7-7700 processor. For both the full and simplified graphs generated from the Ubuntu 20.04 distribution, the coloring software found colorings using as few as 11 colors, meaning that 11 distinct build environments are sufficient to build all 30,646 source packages. Since these are approximation algorithms, there's no way to tell from this software if 11 is the minimum possible number of build environments, but subsequent tests reported in Sect. 4.4 show that this is in fact an optimal solution.

Comparing the performance and success of coloring the full graph versus the simplified graph shows the value of graph simplification: the colorings found on the

---

[4] http://webdocs.cs.ualberta.ca/~joe/Coloring/.

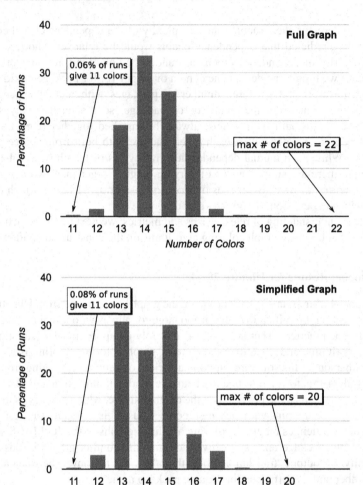

Fig. 3. Number of colors found by heuristic run, as a percentage of all runs.

simplified graph translate directly to the full graph, but the reduced size allowed the coloring software to run much faster and explore more options with more random seeds. We completed over a million (specifically, 1,050,000) runs on the simplified graph in 24 h, while we could only complete 23,835 runs on the full graph. Working with a smaller graph also increased the probability that the heuristic algorithm would find small colorings, avoiding getting stuck in parts of the graph that lead to using larger numbers of colors. Figure 3 shows histograms of the colors found over all runs, for both the simplified and the full graphs. Notice that with the simplified graph the values are skewed more to the left, meaning colorings with fewer colors. The range for the simplified graph is also lower, with the coloring software producing colorings ranging from 11 to 20 colors on the simplified graph, and 11 to 22 colors on the full graph.

While the percentage of runs finding the smallest (11 color) solution is only slightly higher for the simplified graph (0.0806% of runs) than the full graph (0.0587% of runs), that small advantage coupled with the much higher rate of testing graphs, means that the simplified graph found the smallest coloring much faster than using the full graph. More specifically, the first coloring using 11 colors was found in just under 5 min on the simplified graph, but an 11-color result on the full graph was not obtained for 99 min.

4.3 Subgraph Colorings

Table 2. Basic metrics for Ubuntu 20.04 top-X subgraphs (table appeared in [14]).

	Top 500	Top 1000	Top 2000	Top 4000	All SPKGS
Vertices	117	198	355	594	1,770
Edges	151	375	2,388	6,385	51,492
Density	0.022	0.019	0.038	0.036	0.033
Best coloring	4	4	6	7	11

Next, we construct colorings for nested subgraphs, as described in Sect. 3.2. To construct these graphs for the Ubuntu 20.04 distribution, we first used the "Ubuntu Popularity Contest" project data to find the top 500, 1000, 2000, and 4000 source packages. Note that this is not as simple as just taking the first names from the popularity contest ranking for two reasons: First, not all packages listed are standard packages in the Ubuntu release we are interested in (20.04 in this case), and second, the ranking is for binary packages, not source packages. To find our lists, we first filtered the popularity contest list to include only binary packages that are a part of the Ubuntu 20.04 release, then we mapped binary package names to the source package used to build that package, and finally we removed all but the first occurrence of each source package (since a source package can build multiple binary packages, and it is common for multiple binary packages for the same source package to be in the "Top X" lists). As a result of this pre-processing, we obtained a ranked list of source packages used in Ubuntu 20.04 from which we could extract the "Top X" lists.

Next, given the Top 500 source packages, we identified the vertices in the simplified conflict graph corresponding to those packages, removed duplicates, and then computed the subgraph induced by those vertices. We repeated this for the top 1000, 2000, and 4000 source packages. Given these graphs, we ran 105,000 iterations of the graph coloring algorithm on each to determine the smallest coloring we could find in that amount of time. The results, showing graph sizes and the best coloring we found, are in Table 2.

When we started this project, we expected that the main, most popular Ubuntu packages would share a somewhat similar mainstream build environment with few conflicts, leaving most conflicts to arise from more esoteric packages that used unusual libraries. However, we were surprised to find that even in the smallest (Top 500) list, there were over a hundred non-isomorphic conflict sets (final vertices after simplification), and a fairly consistent graph density of 0.02–0.04 in each graph. The colorings we found do reflect increasing levels of conflicts when more, less popular packages are included, growing from just 4 colors (build environments) used for the Top 500 and Top 1000 lists, up to the 11 colors required for all packages.

As a final note, this project was motivated by our experience in an earlier project in which we were performing large scale static analysis on the Top 1000 source packages in Ubuntu 18.04. When we ran into build environment conflicts, we handled this problem in an *ad hoc* way, resulting in around a dozen build environments for the Top 1000 packages. Developing a formal foundation for creating these build environments, as we report in this paper, reduces the number of build environments for that set of packages to just 4 distinct environments. This is a huge improvement in terms of managing the 1000 runs of the static analyzer, and as we will see in Sect. 5 it also resulted in a large efficiency when performing the actual builds.

4.4 Lower Bounds Using Max Clique

The graph colorings reported in the previous section were computed using heuristic algorithms, so in this section we consider the question "are the colorings found above the best possible?" Even when the chromatic number of a graph is small, determining the optimal coloring can be computationally intractable. Consider that every planar graph is 4-colorable, but determining if a planar graph is 3-colorable is NP-complete (determining if it is 2-colorable is easy) [6].

The maximum clique problem is the problem of finding the largest completely connected subgraph in an input graph. Since every vertex in a completely connected subgraph is connected to every other vertex in that subgraph, when coloring such a graph each vertex in the clique must have a different color, and so the size of a maximum clique is a lower bound for the number of colors required to color that graph. Furthermore, for inputs where the size of the maximum clique is guaranteed to be bounded by a constant k, we can find the largest clique in time $O(n^k)$. In our case, since we found a valid coloring of size 4 in the "Top 500" graph, we know that the maximum clique can be no larger than 4 vertices and so we could find a maximum clique in that graph in $O(n^4)$ time. Unfortunately, for the full graph the brute-force search for cliques of size 11 would take time $\Theta(n^{11})$, so we need a faster algorithm.

The graphs we are dealing with are quite sparse (see Table 1), and maximum clique algorithms designed for sparse graphs proved to be very successful. In particular, Pattabiraman *et al* designed a max clique algorithm for sparse graphs, specifically looking at applications with Web connectivity graphs [12]. Importantly, their algorithms provide optimal solutions, not heuristic approximations, and gain speed improvements through novel pruning techniques during the search for a clique. The authors produced software implementing their algorithm and made it publicly available, and we used this on the conflict graphs generated as part of this project.[5] The results are shown in Table 3.

Table 3. Computing coloring lower bounds using max clique.

	Top 500	Top 1000	Top 2000	Top 4000	All SPKGS
Best coloring	4	4	6	7	11
Max clique	3	4	6	6	11

As can be seen from the results, the size of the max clique matched the number of colors in our graph coloring for three of the graphs: the Top 1000, Top 2000, and

---

[5] Software available at http://cucis.ece.northwestern.edu/projects/MAXCLIQUE/.

full graphs. That means that our graph colorings are optimal in those cases, and due to the one-to-one correspondence between coloring the conflict graph and designing build environments, we can conclude, for example, that there is no set of fewer than 6 build environments that is sufficient for building all Top 2000 source packages (with the caveat that there may be better solutions with different handling of dependency disjunctions – see the open problems). For two graphs, the "Top 500" and "Top 4000" graphs, the size of the largest clique was one smaller than the number of colors in the best coloring we found. This means that there is still some uncertainty about whether 3 or 4 build environments is sufficient for the "Top 500" packages, but even in the two cases in which we can't assert optimality, we are within one of an optimal solution.

5   Build Times in Practice

The previous sections have developed a model and associated algorithms for designing build environments. In this section, we report on experiments performed to measure the practical impact of these techniques.

5.1   Build Experiment Setting

To test the efficiency of our computed build environments, we used a server with dual Intel Xeon E5-2623 v3 CPUs, each with 4 true cores with hyperthreading, bringing the total number of threads to 8 per CPU or 16 total. The system has 64 GB of RAM with a small 64 GB SSD-based filesystem for the main filesystem (storing all executables) and a larger 2.8 TB HDD-based filesystem used for holding source code and performing the builds.

We performed all experiments using the "Top 500" source packages from Ubuntu 20.04, but with a few packages removed (see "Practical Challenges" below). We compared the standard build process, using pbuilder, with the use of four pre-built environments as computed by the coloring-based algorithm of this paper (described in Sect. 4.3). While source packages with no conflicts could be assigned any color (build environment) we put them all into "build group 1" resulting in a very large build environment. The four environments we constructed had the following sizes:

	SPKGs using	BPKGs installed	Size (MB)
Environment 1	355	3,976	11,905
Environment 2	21	1,928	5,326
Environment 3	27	1,816	5,422
Environment 4	97	1,140	2,716

The pbuilder tests used a pre-constructed base environment, which included all essential and build-essential packages, but then followed the standard Debian process after that: a chroot environment is created for the base environment on top of which the dependencies are installed, then source packages are unpacked and binary packages are built after dropping privileges for the build. Building with our computed build environments is similar, except the four different build environments are pre-loaded with the union of all dependencies for the supported source packages, and so no additional build dependencies have to be installed for each build – we simply unpack the source packages and then perform the build in a chroot environment after dropping privileges.

For both techniques, we used GNU `parallel` to perform 12 builds in parallel, but restricted each individual build to a single-threaded make (i.e., "`-j 1`" provided to make). The decision to do single-threaded `make` was so that each package build used a similar set of resources, avoiding the inconsistency that results from some packages being able to make use of concurrent builds and others not. The choice of 12 parallel builds was somewhat arbitrary, but was determined to be a good trade-off between using available threads for building and leaving some excess capacity for slack and system management functions.

5.2   Practical Challenges

As we started performing the actual builds, it quickly became clear that there were packaging issues that went beyond the modeling simplifications that described in Sect. 2.3. Here are some of the issues we encountered:

Bad Package Definitions. Some source packages had errors in dependencies and conflicts, resulting in unbuildable packages under either `pbuilder` or our build environments. For example, the `gconf-editor` source package depends on binary package `gnome-doc-utils`, but `gnome-doc-utils` is not packaged for Ubuntu 20.04. This makes the `gconf-editor` package impossible to build in a pure Ubuntu 20.04 environment. Given this fact, it is unclear how the Ubuntu maintainers created the binary package for `gconf-editor`, but the binary could have been a pre-20.04 package included with 20.04, or the maintainers could have used additional package sources to provide `gnome-doc-utils`. Regardless, since it is impossible to build with a pure 20.04 system, this is a packaging bug. Earlier work by Nussbaum [11] explored using a cluster to test all source package definitions for exactly this kind of bug, but this is apparently not a part of the Ubuntu release quality assurance process.

Builds That Require Additional System Resources. Some package builds hung when using either `pbuilder` or our build environments due to use of resources beyond files. For example, `gnome-keyring` could not be built in a batch process with standard command line arguments, since some of the tests required terminal interaction. Other packages failed to access network resources, including attempts to listen on network ports that were already in use on the server when testing. Almost all of these kinds of problems failed in running tests after the binaries were built, and so one potential solution is to exclude testing from the build process. This could potentially speed up the process too, since some packages spent a significant amount of computational time performing tests.

Problems with Build Environments that are Too Large. Our original assumption was that build environments couldn't be "too large" as long as no conflicting packages were installed. However, this turned out to be a false assumption. A specific problem we encountered came from a configuration script used to set up the build, which enabled some tests based on the availability of testing tools. Since our build environment is larger than necessary, our build attempted to run tests that were not run in the minimal environment used by `pbuilder`. A minor consequence of the extra tests being run is that the build can take longer than under the `pbuilder` minimal environment. However, a much more serious problem is that some packages *failed* these additional tests, so did not produce the desired binary package. It's debatable what the actual error is in this case. Is it the failed tests, meaning the built executables have bugs that were not caught in the `pbuilder` build? Or is the problem that the testing tools should have been omitted from the build environment, as they were in the minimal `pbuilder` environment? If the latter is the case, then since these tools cause the build to fail, they should be included in the source package "Conflicts" list to ensure that they are not installed when the package is being built.

The three issues described above caused real problems, but were relatively rare, causing problems with less than 6% of source packages. Since the goal of this project is to test the efficiency of build environments, we did not manually tweak the builds to correct these individual issues, and we just omitted those packages from our test set. In the end, we were left with 472 packages in the Top 500 that built cleanly and without any manual intervention, and the results reported below are for those 472 packages.

5.3 Results

After adjusting for the issues described in the previous section, for the 472 packages in our test set we saw a substantial improvement by using our build environments, both from the standpoint of total work (sum of individual package build times) and an overall elapsed wall-clock time. When looking at the total work performed over our 12 parallel jobs, `pbuilder` required 139 h 36 s (139 h and 36 min), while using our build environments required only 54 h 18 s, a 61% improvement and saving over 85 h of CPU time. The overall elapsed time also showed improvement, but less dramatically, taking 25 h 05 m with `pbuilder` and 19 h 55 s with our build environments. The reason that the overall elapsed time did not show as dramatic an improvement as the total work was that a few packages took a *very* long time to build, with the longest being `libreoffice` which took over 19 h to build by either technique. This build process long outlasted other builds, with the final 8 h of the test builds consisting of just that one build running. Since the overall elapsed time was dominated by this one build, which only improved slightly with the pre-constructed build environments, the overall time had a more modest improvement than total work. Since our goal was to evaluate change in total work based on using the build environments constructed from our coloring algorithm, we leave exploration of scheduling improvements to future work. Some improvement could certainly be obtained by scheduling jobs in order of decreasing work (so `libreoffice` would start first), but that would require *a priori* knowledge of build times. Alternatively, we could revisit our decision to limit each package to a single-threaded make, and work on balancing parallel builds with parallelization over packages.

Improvement in Mean and Median Times. For the packages in our test set, the mean package build time using `pbuilder` was 17 m 44 s (17 min and 44 s), while the median was 8 m 23 s. Using our coloring-determined environments reduced the mean build time to 6 m 54 s (a 61% decrease) and the median to just 45 s (a 91% improvement). The difference between the mean and median, as well as the dramatic improvement in the median time, emphasizes the fact that while there are some huge packages that raise the average, most packages are quite small, taking less than 45 s to build once the environment is set up. For these small packages the vast majority of the time `pbuilder` requires is used to simply create the individualized build environments.

Package with Largest Time Improvement. In terms of improvement in absolute time, the greatest improvement was for the `gcc-10` package. This package required a little over 9 h to build using `pbuilder`, but only 7 h and 51 min to build in our environments. The 70 min decrease in time was substantially more than just the time savings from creating the build environment, since that only took approximately 21 min in the `pbuilder` trial. The reason for the additional 50 min in time savings is not clear at this time. We do know that both `pbuilder` and our build environments produced the same binary packages, which passed all tests, so everything was correctly built. The `gcc-10` build is extremely complex, with a build log that is over 200,000 lines of text, and we are currently combing through that log for additional clues.

Package with the Largest Percentage Improvement. Some packages had very dramatic speed-ups. For example, the `language-pack-gnome-en` source package doesn't really require a "build" at all—it simply packages a set of text files with the directory paths needed for the binary install, so the "build" really just consists of copying files and creating the package archives. This "build" in a pre-constructed environment takes around 2 s. However, `pbuilder` still needs to create the build environment, including the packaging tools (like `debhelper`), resulting in a total time of 316 s. Using the pre-constructed environment resulted in a 99.4% reduction in time for this package.

Slower Builds. Our original focus on dependencies led to a mistaken belief that as long as all the dependencies were present, the runtime should be mostly independent of whether other, non-required packages were installed. However, it turned out that the build process for some packages slowed down in larger environments, even if the additional packages had nothing to do with the package being built. In particular, there were two packages (`ubuntu-themes` and `gdb`) that required more time to build in our pre-constructed environments. The largest increase was for the `ubuntu-themes` package, taking 28 m 56 s using `pbuilder` and 32 m 55 s with our build environments, for a 14% slowdown. Investigating, we found that the slowdown was from the "scour" utility minimizing SVG files, and while the slowdown in each run of "scour" was small (less than 0.2 s each) the fact that it was run on over 4000 SVG files resulted in the slower package build. Digging further into the reason for the slower run, we discovered that the "scour" utility is written in Python, and our larger pre-constructed environment had 111 system-wide Python packages installed, which resulted in all 111 `PKG-INFO` files being read program startup. In contrast, the minimal `pbuilder` environment only had 3 system-wide Python packages installed, resulting in far less overhead when the Python interpreter was started at each run.

6   Related Work

The study of large software systems has been greatly facilitated by the public nature of open-source software, which provides a wealth of data to draw upon. In this paper, we focused on the specific problem of defining small sets of build environments, an area that we believe has not been explored in these terms before. However, work has been that is based in similar problems arising in large software distributions, and in this section we provide a basic summary of key prior work related to analyzing software distributions and dependencies. For example, González-Barahona *et al.* [7] conducted early studies on Linux distributions, examining metrics such as distribution size, package size in terms of files and lines of code, and programming languages used. Subsequently, Galindo *et al.* [5] used Linux distributions as a basis for studying broader concepts such as variability models for software.

As distributions have grown, the complexity of dependencies and conflicts have proven to be significant challenges for package and distribution maintainers, and modeling these relations has been studied formally. In 2006, Mancinelli *et al.* [10] gave an extended graph model that reflects dependencies and conflicts, and discussed dependency closures in ways similar to our work, but with a focus on binary packages and tasks a maintainer must do to accurately define and visualize package relations. In 2009, de Sousa *et al.* [13] created a similar model and studied the properties of the dependency graph, looking at degree connectivity distribution and modularity, among other measures. While many of these works use the Debian distribution due to its popularity among academics, in 2015 Wang *et al.* [17] perform similar graph modeling to visualize package dependencies in Ubuntu 14.04, although they report only looking at a graph with 2,240 vertices which would be a small subset of the total Ubuntu 14.04 packages.

Researchers have also investigated the impact of package changes on dependency and conflict relationships. In 2013, Di Cosmo, Treinen, and Zacchiroli [4] developed a formal model for analyzing update failures, focusing on end-users updating their systems and maintainers defining appropriate relationships. Their work specifically examined the "co-installability" of binary packages in deployed systems, and did not consider build environments. Another study on end-user installability was conducted by Vouillon and Di Cosmo [16], who linked installability tests to the satisfiability (SAT) problem and raised similar NP-completeness concerns to those we have shown in this paper. They also explored graph simplification and compression techniques similar to those described in Sect. 3.3. In 2015, Claes *et al.* [1] studied package conflicts and broken packages at a fine-grained level, using daily snapshots reflecting ongoing developer work.

Recently, the appearance of language-specific code repositories for developers, such as NPM (for JavaScript), CRAN (for R), and PyPI (for Python), have raised similar dependency challenges, but in a different context [2,3,9]. Of particular interest, Decan, Mens, and Claes [2] show that dependency network topology varies between different language ecosystems, and while they did not use operating system distributions it is reasonable to believe that the range of software included in full operating system distributions will be even more diverse.

The work described above all focused mainly on the challenges end users and developers face in managing dependencies and conflicts for operational systems, and do not address build environments or conflicts between source packages. The only work we're aware of that looks specifically at large-scale software building in open source distributions is the work of Nussbaum [11], which describes re-building an entire Debian distribution from source packages. Nussbaum was interested in whether the minimal build environments, as defined by the "build dependencies," were sufficient for each source package, and used a large grid computing infrastructure to create each individual build environment and attempt the builds. Our work, focused on re-using build environments, installs far more packages than the minimal set for any package, so we would not be able to address Nussbaum's question of whether the defined dependencies were sufficient. We would be able to address another question tested by Nussbaum, however, and that is the question of whether updated tool-chains are still capable of completing a build from the provided source packages.

7   Conclusions and Future Work

In this paper, we explored a problem that arose in applied work analyzing a large collection of open source software through static analysis. Our problems is equivalent to designing environments in which many software packages can be compiled, which we call a "build environment," and minimizing the number of distinct build environments leads directly to performance gains whether interested in the build process or in static analysis. We formalized the problem by examining a graph that we construct from environment conflicts, which we call the "conflict graph," and show that there is a one-to-one correspondence between the problem of minimizing the number of build environments and the problem of minimizing the number of colors required to color the conflict graph.

In our experimental results, we constructed conflict graphs for various Ubuntu Long-Term Support releases, and computed metrics such as graph size and density for these real-world problems. Since coloring is an NP-hard problem, and conflict graphs can be large, we developed ways to simplify the graph and looked at the problem of coloring increasing-size nested subgraphs. After simplifying the graphs, we used an implementation of various graph coloring approximation algorithms to see how few colors we could achieve in practice, and used the colorings to generate sets of build environments for the Ubuntu 20.04 distribution. We were able to construct a set of 11 build environments that were sufficient to build all 30,646 source packages in Ubuntu 20.04, and a set of just 4 environments for building all of the top 1000 "most popular" source packages. We then software for finding max-cliques, since that provides an upper-bound on a graph's chromatic number, and could conclude that in many cases our constructed set of build environments was the smallest possible, while in the remaining cases it was guaranteed to be within one of optimal. Experiments performing builds with the computed build environments showed dramatic decreases in work required, although also exposed some practical difficulties in large-scale batch package building. Referring back to our original motivation, the results here show the value of modeling the problem with graph coloring, providing significant practical improvements over the *ad hoc* approach.

For future directions, we note that our work made some simplifications related to environment conflicts (described in Sect. 2.3) to simplify modeling the problem constraints. A more precise modeling of constraints, particularly of modeling dependency disjunctions ("or-lists") could lead to some improvements. While we used the same or-list prioritization as the standard Debian build tools, resulting in a good approximation of stand-alone build environments, taking a global view and optimizing across or-lists could provide some advantages. For example, the pkgconf package management software is a new re-write of the older pkg-config software, and is designed to be a drop-in replacement for any software that uses pkg-config for building. Since these two packages can't both be installed in the same environment, this introduces a conflict that can be satisfied by either package. Packages generally include an "or-list" that says that either pkgconf or pkg-config can be used, but some older packages prioritize the older pkg-config rather than the newer replacement. Would having a global preference for the newer pkgconf package provide a larger overlap in preferred dependencies, reducing the conflicts and hence the number of build environments required?

A second question that needs more study is the development of a clear objective when dealing with coloring nested subgraphs. Given our success in finding colorings with a small number of colors, we deferred this question by simply optimizing for each nested graph size independently. While this works for our graphs, there may be situations in which this is not sufficient, and beyond the practical issues it is an interesting problem on its own as a general graph theory problem. In our context, we might include some experimental efficiency results to tune our metrics and objectives.

Finally, our experiments showed that in some cases having very large build environments can result in small numbers of build environments, in some situations (such as invoking Python many times with a large number of installed libraries) this resulted in *slower* build time for some packages. Determining if there is a good trade-off between number of build environments and build environment size would be an interesting future direction.

References

1. Claes, M., Mens, T., Di Cosmo, R., Vouillon, J.: A historical analysis of Debian package incompatibilities. In: 2015 IEEE/ACM 12th Working Conference on Mining Software Repositories, pp. 212–223, May 2015
2. Decan, A., Mens, T., Claes, M.: On the topology of package dependency networks: a comparison of three programming language ecosystems. In: Proceedings of the 10th European Conference on Software Architecture Workshops (ECSAW), pp. 1–4, November 2016
3. Decan, A., Mens, T., Grosjean, P.: An empirical comparison of dependency network evolution in seven software packaging ecosystems. Empir. Softw. Eng. **24**(1), 381–416 (2019)
4. Di Cosmo, R., Treinen, R., Zacchiroli, S.: Formal aspects of free and open source software components. In: 11th International Symposium on Formal Methods for Components and Objects (FMCO), pp. 216–239 (2013)
5. Galindo, J., Benavides, D., Segura, S.: Debian packages repositories as software product line models. In: Towards Automated Analysis. In: Proceeding of the First International Workshop on Automated Configuration and Tailoring of Applications (ACOTA) (2010)
6. Garey, M.R., Johnson, D.S.: Computers and Intractability. W.H. Freeman, San Francisco (1979)
7. González-Barahona, J.M., et al.: Analyzing the anatomy of GNU/Linux distributions: methodology and case studies (Red Hat and Debian). In: Free/Open Source Software Development, pp. 27–58 (2003)
8. Jackson, I., Schwarz, C., Morris, D.A.: Debian policy manual (version 4.6.0.1) (2021). https://www.debian.org/doc/debian-policy/

9. Kikas, R., Gousios, G., Dumas, M., Pfahl, D.: Structure and evolution of package dependency networks. In: 2017 IEEE/ACM 14th International Conference on Mining Software Repositories (MSR), pp. 102–112, May 2017
10. Mancinelli, F., et al.: Managing the complexity of large free and open source package-based software distributions. In: 21st IEEE/ACM International Conference on Automated Software Engineering (ASE'06), pp. 199–208, September 2006
11. Nussbaum, L.: Rebuilding Debian using distributed computing. In: Proceedings of the 7th International Workshop on Challenges of Large Applications in Distributed Environments (CLADE), pp. 11–16, June 2009
12. Pattabiraman, B., Patwary, M.M.A., Gebremedhin, A.H., Liao, W.K., Choudhary, A.: Fast algorithms for the maximum clique problem on massive sparse graphs. In: Algorithms and Models for the Web Graph, pp. 156–169 (2013)
13. de Sousa, O.F., de Menezes, M.A., Penna, T.: Analysis of the package dependency on Debian GNU/Linux. J. Comput. Interdisc. Sci. 1(2), 127–133 (2009)
14. Tate, S.R., Yuan, B.: Minimum size build environment sets and graph coloring. In: Proceedings of the 17th International Conference on Software Technologies, ICSOFT 2022, Lisbon, Portugal, 11–13 July 2022, pp. 57–67 (2022)
15. The Ubuntu Web Team: Ubuntu popularity contest (2021). https://popcon.ubuntu.com/
16. Vouillon, J., Cosmo, R.D.: On software component co-installability. ACM Trans. Softw. Eng. Methodol. 22(4), 34:1–34:35 (2013)
17. Wang, J., Wu, Q., Tan, Y., Xu, J., Sun, X.: A graph method of package dependency analysis on Linux Operating system. In: 2015 4th International Conference on Computer Science and Network Technology (ICCSNT), pp. 412–415, December 2015

An AST-Based Code Change Representation and Its Performance in Just-in-Time Vulnerability Prediction

Tamás Aladics[1,2][⊠] [ID], Péter Hegedűs[1,2] [ID], and Rudolf Ferenc[1] [ID]

[1] University of Szeged, Szeged, Hungary
{aladics,hpeter,ferenc}@inf.u-szeged.hu
[2] FrontEndART Ltd., Szeged, Hungary

Abstract. The presence of software vulnerabilities is an ever-growing issue in software development. In most cases, it is desirable to detect vulnerabilities as early as possible, preferably in a just-in-time manner, when the vulnerable piece is added to the code base. The industry has a hard time combating this problem as manual inspection is costly and traditional means, such as rule-based bug detection, are not robust enough to follow the pace of the emergence of new vulnerabilities. The actively researched field of machine learning could help in such situations as models can be trained to detect vulnerable patterns. However, machine learning models work well only if the data is appropriately represented. In our work, we propose a novel way of representing changes in source code (i.e. code commits), the Code Change Tree, a form that is designed to keep only the differences between two abstract syntax trees of Java source code. We compared its effectiveness in predicting if a code change introduces a vulnerability against multiple representation types and evaluated them by a number of machine learning models as a baseline. The evaluation is done on a novel dataset that we published as part of our contributions using a 2-phase dataset generator method. Based on our evaluation we concluded that using Code Change Tree is a valid and effective choice to represent source code changes as it improves performance.

Keywords: Code change representation · Vulnerability prediction · Just-in-time

1 Introduction

Security is an important aspect of software development and as technology progresses it seems to become increasingly hard to handle the rapid increase in vulnerabilities. According to the Mend database which aggregates data from NVD and other vulnerability databases, the number of published open source vulnerabilities is on a steep rise as in 2020 this number has increased by 50% [19].

In software security, finding vulnerabilities as soon as possible is important to minimize the possibility of harm done and to reduce the additional cost of fixing the security holes later. The earliest point when vulnerabilities could be reliably identified in the development pipeline is the time when they are added to the code base, that is, when the changes are added to the version control system (i.e. commit time). Another positive effect of this is that the developers receive immediate feedback regarding possible issues in the software. This practice is called just-in-time vulnerability prediction [20].

H.-G. Fill et al. (Eds.): ICSOFT 2022, CCIS 1859, pp. 169–186, 2023.
https://doi.org/10.1007/978-3-031-37231-5_8

Researchers and interested parties in the industry are actively trying to find ways to become more resilient to software vulnerabilities. The most prominent and sustainable way of this is to use automated techniques to detect if a piece of software is likely to be vulnerable [12,26]. These approaches usually involve extensive static analysis based on rule sets and manually developed pattern matchers, or dynamic analysis based on executing the software. Numerous tools exist for this purpose such as SonarQube[1] and the Clang Sanitizers[2]. Companies have widely adopted these tools to improve the quality of their product and to become less prone to vulnerabilities.

Even though these techniques definitely improve the quality of software, from the point of vulnerability and bug detection they are reported to be mostly ineffective in practice as they can't adapt fast enough to the new vulnerabilities, have scalability issues and/or have high false positive rates [8,18,28].

The trending field of machine learning has proven to successfully solve problems of similar type, when there is an abundance of data yet the problem is hard to formulate or manual, human-powered solutions are too resource-demanding. However, a ML model can only be as good as the data it is trained on. In the case of source code, the form of representation is not trivial: it can be used as raw text, intermediate representations such as abstract syntax trees or control flow graphs can be used or indirect attributes are possible forms too, like software quality metrics [16,42].

Even though there has been substantial research done in just-in-time (JIT) vulnerability prediction, current techniques have little potential in practical usage as their results are usually not localized, have low recall/precision, or are not reproducible [11,29,32]. One of the main challenges that make just-in-time vulnerability prediction hard is that automatization involves finding appropriate ways to represent differences between two states of software: the pre-commit and post-commit states. In a recent analysis of the state of JIT vulnerability prediction, it is shown that using existing metrics and textual features to represent changes in software is not sufficient enough [23]. As our attempt to remedy this situation, we focused on representing this change as differences in source codes as a commit's most vital information is the actual source code it encapsulates.

In our work, we show multiple ways and also propose a novel method for code change representation, the Code Change Tree. To showcase these methods we generate these representations for every entry of a lately released vulnerability introducing commit (VIC) dataset. This generation process is not trivial as VIC databases are scarce in number and can not be directly mapped from existing vulnerability fixing commit (VFC) databases, such as NVD. Therefore, we used our SZZ-based approach [1] which has two phases: in the first phase it generates candidate commits using SZZ, and in the second phase it filters the candidate commits based on scores referenced as relevance scores.

Then, we train multiple machine learning models on these representations and compare their predictive power. Our results are interpreted through the following research questions:

---

[1] https://www.sonarqube.org.

[2] https://github.com/google/sanitizers.

RQ. 1. Can a vulnerability introducing database generated from a vulnerability fixing commit database be used for vulnerability prediction?
RQ. 2. How effective are Code Change Trees in representing source code changes?
RQ. 3. Are source code metrics sufficient to represent code changes?

This work is an extension of our previous conference paper [1] adding the following new contributions:

- A novel way of representing source code changes, Code Change Tree;
- Comparison of multiple code change representation forms;
- Evaluation of the proposed code change representation for just-in-time vulnerability prediction based on the data published in the conference paper [1].

2   Related Work

Heavily motivated by the industry and software security, vulnerability prediction is an actively researched field. The main line of traditional vulnerability prediction models (VPMs) is based on using software metrics - quality indicators derived from the software.

Shin et al. used VPMs using code complexity metrics, code churn, and fault history as predictors on the code base of Mozilla Firefox web browser [38]. They found that fault prediction models can be used for specific cases of vulnerabilities, however, both fault prediction and vulnerability prediction models require significant improvement to reduce false positives while providing high recall. Similarly, other works use LOC metrics supplemented with complexity metrics to train neural networks [41] or mine features based on text mining techniques as input for VPMs [36].

As a vulnerability's severity is directly influenced by how long it remains unexposed, finding vulnerabilities as soon as possible has become a key endeavor for software security research communities. Recently VPMs are actively getting developed to predict vulnerabilities when they are added to the version control system, that is, in commit time. These methods can use different parts of commits as predictors, such as the commit messages and bug reports [43] or the source code's before and after states [27]. A commonly referenced work in this topic is VCCFinder, a tool that combines code metrics with GitHub metadata for features and trains an SVM model on them [32,35].

As reported by Lomio et al. existing metrics are not sufficient enough [23]. In their research, they used several different code metrics and textual features derived from the bag of words representations of the before and after commit states, similarly to VCCFinder. Our work's aim is to contribute to the solution of this problem and provide a way to represent source code changes.

To gain insight it is beneficial to look at related research in source code representation. Apart from metrics, which have already been discussed as a possible form of software state representation, other approaches can use intermediate forms of the source code as input. DeFreez et al. use control flow graphs and perform random walks on inter-procedural paths in the program and use these paths as features [13]. Devlin et al. embed functions by doing a depth-first traversal on the corresponding abstract syntax tree (AST) [14], while Pan et al. used a convolutional neural network architecture to extract features from ASTs [31]. Gaining inspiration from these and other works, we choose to use ASTs to represent code changes.

However, since code changes include a before and after state, each code change has two ASTs corresponding to them: the before and after state's AST. Since we are interested in the difference, or change between the two ASTs, we propose an AST-like structure that we call Code Change Tree, which incorporates the differences between the two ASTs.

After getting the Code Change Tree for a commit, a way of mapping the tree to a vector is needed, so that later it can be fed into machine learning models as inputs. We followed the same approach as we did in our previous work [2], where we performed depth-first traversal on the AST and used Doc2Vec embedding [21] to get fixed size vectors that keep structural information [2]. We choose this method as it is fast to compute and has low resource needs while also having solid theoretical background based on Word2Vec.

Regarding change representation, lately various approaches have been published, one of the most prominent is CC2Vec [17]. CC2Vec uses a hierarchical attention network to extract features from commits. This work is promising, however, it has some differences compared to our method: Code Change Trees represent changes from any two code piece that has corresponding AST, so it is not restricted to commits as CC2Vec (which uses commit-specific metadata, such as commit messages). Also, CC2Vec represents the differences in code changes as the added/removed lines as tokens, while in our work we aim to keep the structural information that ASTs have by representing changes in a tree structure.

Another work in this topic is Commit2Vec [24], which uses a structure derived from Code2Vec that leverages path-contexts: paths in the AST from leaf node to leaf node. We couldn't use this approach as the tools and the code wasn't published. Also, its methodology is different as it learns on the extracted paths, while our approach constructs a tree to keep the structural attributes of the changes.

3   Methodology

3.1   Overview

As mentioned in the previous sections of our work we try to provide a novel way of presenting source code changes: differences between two states of source code. More specifically, let $S = \{t_1, t_2, ..., t_n\}$ be a state of a source code, where t_i are tokens that are present in the source code. Then, a code change is a pair of states that are consequent in time, namely the state before the change $S_{pre} = \{t_1, t_2, ..., t_n\}$, and $S_{post} = \{t_1, t_2, ..., t_m\}$, the state after the change. A simple code change example can be seen in Fig. 1.

Rather than only considering changes in code as raw text (i.e. changes in the token sequences S_{pre} and S_{post}), we try to represent changes happening at a structural level. A good way to reason about the structure is to use an intermediate representation, such as the abstract syntax tree (AST), which can be computed directly from the source code, that is, for each source code state S there exists a corresponding AST (a more formal

```
1  //Before state
2  class HelloWorld {
3      public static void main(String[] args) {
4          System.out.println("Hello, World!");
5      }
6  }
```

```
1  //After state
2  class HelloWorld {
3      public static void main(String[] args) {
4          String msg = "World!";
5          System.out.println("Hello, World!");
6          System.out.println("Hello, " + msg );
7      }
8  }
```

Fig. 1. An example source code change.

introduction to ASTs can be found in Sect. 3.3). One of our main contributions in this work is to represent the differences between AST_{pre} and AST_{post} in a tree.

Also, when reasoning about software representations, another fundamental question is the localization of the prediction, at what granularity is the source code processed. Usually, it happens at statement, method, class, or file level. Since we decided to use the AST as the base structure, any source code element can be represented by our method that has a corresponding AST. In this report, we decided to use function-level predictions as it is more specific than class-level predictions but still has a corresponding AST with meaningful structure -unlike statements, where the corresponding AST is usually too shallow.

To showcase our approach we describe three different approaches to represent changes in source code: a source code metric-based approach (Sect. 3.2), a simple code change approach (Sect. 3.3), which is based on concatenating the flattened ASTs of the before and after states, and the Code Change Tree approach (Sect. 3.4), which is based on concatenating the flattened Code Change Trees of the before and after states.

However, in the case of simple code change and Code Change Tree approaches the flattened before and after states are sequences of tokens which is not a valid input for ML models. To remedy this situation, we employ an embedding from sequences of tokens to vectors using Doc2Vec (Sect. 3.5).

3.2 Metric Based Approach

Many works in source code representation use derived features from the code as predictors, such as source code metrics [30,37]. Source code metrics can be good indicators of many of the software's attributes, such as lines of code (LOC), nesting level (NL) and McCabe's cyclomatic complexity (MCC) [25].

As one of our baselines, we choose to represent changes by aggregating metrics calculated for the before and after state of a code piece. In detail, for a function that is part of a software change's before/after state we measured 37 metrics using the open-source static analysis tool SourceMeter.[3] Then, concatenated the metrics corresponding to the before and after states (S_{pre} and S_{post}) of the function to form a change representation. This way, the source code change in a function consisting of S_{pre} and S_{post} are represented as a vector of 74 elements.

3.3   Simple Code Change Approach

To reflect on the structure of source code, an intermediate representation form (mainly used by compilers), the abstract syntax tree (AST) is considered to be the preferred form in many techniques [7,22,24] as it stores syntactical features on its edges and in the node attributes.

As the AST is an important concept in our approach, we provide a formal definition.

Definition 1 (AST). An abstract syntax tree is a structure of form (N,L,T,r, Ω, Ψ), where:

- N is the set of non-terminals (non-leaf nodes)
- L is the set of terminals (leaf nodes)
- T is a set of tokens
- r is the root node
- Ω is a mapping from nodes to their children: $N \Rightarrow N \cup L$
- Ψ is a mapping from terminals to their corresponding code tokens: $L \Rightarrow T$

An advantage of AST is that it can be directly calculated for source code elements without the need to execute the software, and as such, for each we can generate the corresponding AST_{pre} AST_{post} representations for the source code change states S_{pre} and S_{post}.

Unfortunately, most machine learning models cannot take tree structures as input, so using an AST directly is not suitable. To make an AST usable as input, we need a way to map it to a sequence of tokens. This process is called flattening and there are multiple ways to do it. In our work, we choose to flatten a tree structure by traversing it in a depth-first manner and we represent each node $n \in N \cup L$ in the tree, based on whether it's a terminal or a non-terminal:

- if $n \in N$ return the type of n
- if $n \in L$ return the type and value of n

Note that this way of representing nodes is analogous to many works in the area, where they decided to keep the terminal's value, as it holds important semantic information [4,7].

To provide a baseline for AST-based techniques, we flattened AST_{pre} and AST_{post} using the method we just introduced to get sequences of node representations that can be used in ML models. However, these sequences can be of variable length and content, so we employ an embedding technique based on Doc2Vec to generate fixed-length vectors. For further details regarding the sequence embedding please refer to Sect. 3.5.

---

[3] https://sourcemeter.com/.

3.4   Code Change Tree Approach

The representation method introduced in Sect. 3.3 does inherently capture syntactical information, as it uses the flattened AST for the before and after states. However, it is sub-optimal in representing changes as it contains the whole function (or any other AST structure, depending on granularity as discussed in Sect. 3.1). For example, in Fig. 1, the flattening considers every element of the code, even those that are unchanged, such as the class, function definition, and the line that calls `System.out.println` with the `"Hello, World!"` string as parameter.

As a way to represent only the changes, we designed a novel structure, Code Change Tree, that aims to capture only the differences between two ASTs: it can be calculated for an AST (reference AST) to represent changes to another AST (target AST). To find the changed parts we represent each tree as a set of unique paths from their root to each terminal. Then, the root paths that are identical in both trees are discarded from the reference AST's set of root paths. Finally, a tree constructed from the reference AST's root paths, which we refer to as Code Change Tree. To give more insight into our method, in the following we provide a more precise description of our method and its components.

To reason about specific parts of an AST, a more fine-grained processing is needed than flattening, because as reported by Alon et al. [5], this method creates artificially long distances between the node and ancestor nodes. A solution to this is to consider an AST as a set of unique paths, which is referred to as path-based representation [6]. We decided to use a root-path based representation. Formally:

Definition 2 (AST Path). An AST path p of length k is a sequence $n_1, n_2, \ldots, n_{k+1}, n_i$
$\in N \cup L$, where $n_{i+1} \in \Omega(n_i)$ (that is, each element is a child of the preceding element). For convenience we also define $start(p)$ as n_1 and $end(p)$ as n_{k+1}

Definition 3 (AST root-path). An AST root-path $rpath$ is an AST path, where $start(rpath) = r$ and $end(rpath) \in L$

Using root-paths, we can represent an AST by generating the root-path for each terminal or formally:

Definition 4 (Root-path based AST representation). A root-path based representation can be defined for an AST as a set of unique root-paths $rpath_1, rpath_2, \ldots rpath_n$ where $end(rpath_i) \in L$ and $\forall n \in L$ exists an $rpath_i$ such that $rpath_i = n$.

As each AST can be represented as a set of root-paths, defining a difference between them is needed. To explain the representation of differences between two ASTs, let AST_{ref} be the reference AST (in which we are interested in the changes) and a AST_{target} be the target AST (to which we compare AST_{ref}). To generate the Code Change Tree for AST_{ref} with respect to AST_{target} the root-path based representations must be calculated for both AST_{ref} and AST_{target}, and discard the identical root-paths from the set of root-paths corresponding to AST_{ref}. More specifically:

Definition 5 (Root-path based AST difference). Let $rpaths_{ref}$ and $rpaths_{target}$ be the root-path based AST representations for AST_{ref} and AST_{target} respectively. Note that both $rpaths_{ref}$ and $rpaths_{target}$ are sets.

The root-path based AST difference for AST_{ref} with respect to AST_{target} can be calculated as $rpaths_{ref} \setminus rpaths_{target}$

However, to make $rpaths_{ref} \setminus rpaths_{target}$ a valid operation, the equality of two root-paths must be defined, so that identical root-paths can be removed from $rpaths_{ref}$. Straightforwardly, we define that two root-paths are equal if they have the same length and at every position the nodes are equal.

Definition 6 (Root-path equality). Let $a = a_1, a_2, \ldots a_n$ and $b = b_1, b_2, \ldots b_m$ be root-paths. a represents the same root-path as b, if $n = m$ and $id(a_i) = id(b_i) \, \forall i \in 1, \ldots, n$, where id is a mapping from an AST node to an identifier

Note that root-paths equality depends on the nodes' equality, which is determined by the id mapping that assigns an identifier to a node in an AST. This way, root-path can be compared in a cross-AST manner, as nodes between different ASTs can be compared. This means that the id mapping is a fundamental decision in Code Change Trees. In our work, we propose an id mapping we designed empirically by trial and error, but we don't exclude the possibility that better solutions exist. Our id mapping is a recursive one, that concatenates the ids of every ancestor with the node's child rank (position related to siblings: the leftmost children has child rank 0, etc.) and the node's type. This mapping is more precisely defined through the pseudo-code in 2.

```
1    def id(node):
2    ancestors_id = ""
3    for ancestor in node.ancestors:
4    ancestors_id += id(ancestor)
5
6    identifier = ancestors_id + node.child_rank + node.type
```

Fig. 2. Pseudo code of our proposed id mapping.

This mapping has the advantage that it not only encapsulates local attributes about the node but some contextual information as it concatenates the ancestors' ids too. This way, a node can only be equal to another node if the path leading to it from the root node is the same.

Finally, with the definition of root-path differences, a tree representing the differences between AST_{ref} and AST_{target} can easily be constructed from the root-paths in $rpaths_{ref}$ (after calculating the root-path difference with $rpaths_{target}$), by creating an empty tree and extending it while iterating through each root-path. We provide implementation details with the help of the pseudo-code in Fig. 3.

With Code Change Tree defined, it is possible to describe our method of representing source code changes. As introduced in Sect. 3.1, a code change is a pair of states S_{pre} and S_{post}. Then, the corresponding ASTs to the states (AST_{pre} and AST_{post}) respectively can be generated. In our work, we use the TreeSitter[4] tool to generate the

---

[4] https://tree-sitter.github.io/tree-sitter/.

```
1      def construct_change_tree(root_paths):
2      tree = ChangeTree()
3      for rpath in root_paths:
4      current_change_tree_node = tree.root
5      for node in rpath:
6      extend_tree = True
7      for child in current_change_tree_node.children:
8      if id(child) == id(node):
9      current_change_tree_node = child
10     extend_tree = False
11
12     if extend_tree:
13     current_change_tree_node.children.add(node)
14
```

Fig. 3. Pseudo code of the tree construction from a set of root paths.

ASTs. Employing the steps we introduced before in this section, we generate two Code Change Trees for the before and after states, containing the changes relative to each other. Using the root-path notation, we take AST_{pre} and AST_{post}, generate root-path based representations for them and calculate the root-path differences with AST_{pre} as a reference and AST_{post} as target and vice-versa. Based on the root-path differences, the Code Change Trees for S_{pre} and S_{post} can be calculated.

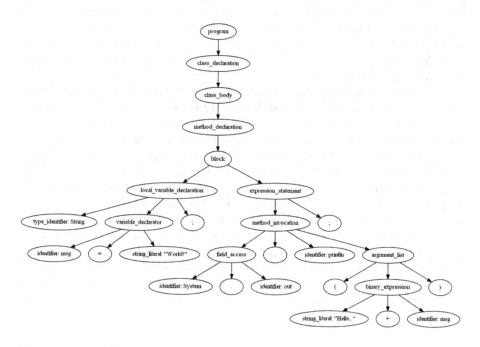

Fig. 4. Code Change Tree for Figure 1.

Example. To demonstrate the usage of Code Change Trees to represent changes, we prepared a simple case study based on Fig. 1. Here, the before state (S_{pre}) consists of a minimal program with a function call, the traditional "Hello World" printout. The change is adding a line before, and after the function call (S_{post}). This change offsets the original method call's position and also adds additional lines so this modification is not trivial to detect. Normally, we would have to calculate the Code Change Trees for both S_{pre} and S_{post}, in this case however the root-path differences for S_{pre} will result in an empty set (every path in S_{pre} is present in S_{post}), so only the root-path differences for S_{post} are relevant. The Code Change Tree generated from the latter can be seen on Fig. 4.

To compare these results with the simple code change representation shown in Sect. 3.3, we generated the ASTs (by using TreeSitter) and flattened them. The before-change state for the simple code change representation contained 31 nodes, the after-change state 55. Using Code Change Tree, the before state has 0 tokens (as it was an empty tree since no paths are unique in it compared to the after state), and the after state has 28 tokens. Overall, representing both states for the simple code change representation would take 86 tokens, while Code Change Tree would take only 28. This is a substantial reduction that keeps relevant data, including contextual information, as whole paths corresponding to a change are stored.

3.5   Doc2Vec Embedding

In Sect. 3.2 we introduced the usage of metrics for code change representation, which generates numerical values as features, thus they can be directly fed into machine learning models as input. Unfortunately, this is not the case for simple code change (Sect. 3.3) and Code Change Tree (Sect. 3.4) based representations, as in both cases the outputs are two trees: ASTs and Code Change Trees corresponding to the before and after change states. These trees are then flattened as described in Sect. 3.3 to sequences of tokens, which are still not numeric values.

To make the tree-based methods applicable to ML models a way to map the sequences to numeric input is needed. We use the technique from our previous work [2] that uses Doc2Vec with some improvements, to embed the token sequences to fixed length vectors. In more detail, to start we selected 2 million methods randomly from the GitHub Java Corpus [3]. We flattened these methods to sequences of tokens, then we preprocessed each of them in line with common NLP practices using the Genism library [34]: replaced whitespaces in strings with underscores and replaced tokens which were not present in at least 1% of the sequences (20.000 methods) with an OOV (out of vocabulary) constant. We trained the Doc2Vec model on this corpus.

Training this model results in a Doc2Vec model that was tailored for Java methods by the design of distributed representations: the learned embedding process generates vectors in a vector space where vectors corresponding to similar methods have ideally small distances. With such a model ready, we used it to embed the variable length sequences to fixed length vectors in Sect. 3.3 and 3.4, as the last steps before evaluation in Sect. 4.

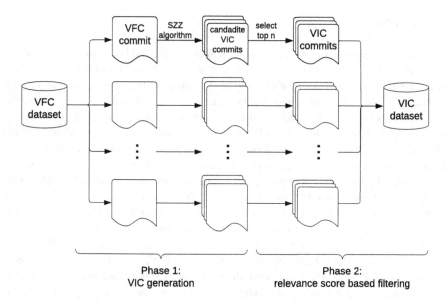

Phase 1:
VIC generation

Phase 2:
relevance score based filtering

Fig. 5. Overview of the VIC dataset generation process.

3.6 Vulnerability DB

This work regarding Code Change Trees is a natural extension to the work we previously published [1] with a vulnerability introducing commit (VIC) database generation process and an actual dataset generated by following our approach. As such, we used this dataset for evaluation purposes. The main idea of this approach is that while there is an abundance of vulnerability fixing commit (VFC) datasets, vulnerability introducing commit (VIC) datasets are in short supply. As a solution, we propose a method that generates VIC datasets from VFC datasets.

The generation process has two phases. The first is the preliminary VIC candidate detection, which takes a VFC database as input, and outputs a set of VIC for each VFC using the SZZ algorithm [39]. However, SZZ is reported to output false positives in many cases and a variable number of results without any order or explanation. The second phase of our algorithm is designed to improve on these weaknesses by performing a filtering based on a score calculated for each candidate commit, referred to as the relevance score. Based on the relevance score we can provide an ordering for the candidate commits and also select the top n best fit. This overview of this process can be observed in Fig. 5

As part of the work in [1], we applied our algorithm with the input VFC dataset being the project-KB [33], a dataset that is manually curated for open source Java projects, with each entry having a reference to the US Nation Vulnerability Database [9]. We used a recent implementation of the SZZ for the first phase, SZZUnleashed [10] and for the second phase, we selected the top 2 best fit VIC for each VFC. The resulting dataset has 564 VFC entries in 198 open-source projects with each of them having at most two VIC commits but on average at least one.

4   Results

To evaluate the approaches we introduced in Sect. 3, we aimed to reason about vulnerability detection at the function level. For that purpose mined a number of vulnerable and non-vulnerable methods by traversing the VIC dataset described in Section 3.6, and for each VIC we looked for functions that were changed in Java files. Similarly, for the VFC entries, we extract the functions that were changed and define the changes' before states with the functions from the VIC and the after states with the functions from the VFC. For non-vulnerability-related function changes, we randomly picked functions from the VIC commit that have no corresponding function in the VFC (this is because we assume that only files changed in the fixing commit were vulnerable). This way, we produced 5934 vulnerable and 29.670 non-vulnerable methods, so that the ratio of vulnerable to non-vulnerable entries is 20% and consequently the dataset mimics the imbalanced nature of the vulnerability detection problem.

Using this dataset of methods, we used the DeepWater Framework (DWF) [15] to facilitate the model running and evaluation tasks. DWF is a server-client architecture written in Python, using the well-known libraries scikit-learn and Tensorflow. It provides multiple pre-configured models, hyper-tuning, and resampling. The various models that we used provided by DWF are the following:

Adaboost: Adaptive Boosting, an ensemble technique typically used for binary classification, which as part of it's learning phase adjusts the weak learners to better work on data points misclassified by previous weak-learners

CDNNC: Custom Deep Neural Network, a feed-forward neural network with early stopping and L2 regularization

Forest: Random Forest, an ensemble technique that uses (ideally not too deep) decision trees as weak learners

KNN: K-nearest neighbors, a non-parametric method that predicts a data point's class by observing and aggregating the n closest (defined by a previously decided distance metric) datapoints

Logistic: Logistic Regression, a traditional method for classification that fits the sigmoid function on the given data

SDNNC: Standard Deep Neural Network, a simple feed-forward neural network that is trained for a number of epochs

Tree: Decision Tree, a non-parametric technique that predicts a datapoint's class by learning decision rules

As our choice of evaluation metric, we used the F1-score, a widely accepted metric in situations where accuracy does not suffice because of the imbalanced nature of the dataset. It is calculated as the harmonic mean of precision $(TP/((TP + FP)))$ and recall $(TP/(TP + FN))$, where TP stand for true positive, FP for false positive and FN for false negative.

All of these methods were hyper-tuned by generating 100 instances of each model with different parameters, where the parameters were explored using grid-search. The evaluation was done in a 10-fold cross-validation manner, with some special modifications to battle the imbalance problem that occurs both in the train set and in real-life scenarios: we used up-sampling to get 50% vulnerable and non-vulnerable entries for each fold. The results can be seen in Table 1, where the Random Guesser stands for the bare minimum baseline that for any input predicts true with 20% probability (equal to the ratio of positive-negative samples). The F1-score is calculated with its formula by considering the positive-negative ratio (0.2) and the probability of predicting true (0.2). In the following two RQs, we aim to interpret our results and also provide some more insight into our approach.

Table 1. Results (F1-score).

Random Guesser	20							
	Adaboost	CDNNC	Forest	KNN	Logistic	SDNNC	Tree	Average
Metrics	36.99	31.84	37.96	38.32	19.25	29.31	36.80	32.92
Simple	40.62	40.33	41.73	**47.46**	29.82	**44.33**	40.20	40.64
Change Tree	**41.37**	**44.38**	**43.38**	43.28	**38.06**	44.28	**41.69**	**42.34**

4.1 RQ1: Can a Vulnerability Introducing Database Generated from a Vulnerability Fixing Commit Database Be Used for Vulnerability Prediction?

In this RQ, we reason about the usefulness of an automatically generated, vulnerability-related dataset. In more detail, it is important for such a dataset to be structured in a way that it can be easily used for downstream machine learning tasks. In our work, we focus on the problem of just-in-time vulnerability prediction, that is, given an instance of source code change by the before and after states, we predict its likeliness to be a change that leads to a vulnerable state of the software. We found that the dataset described in Sect. 3.6 is suitable for such tasks, as it contains pairs of fixing and introducing commits and as such, it is straightforward to extract the before and after states. The database has a reasonable size and is filtered out of many false positives as a result of the filtering phase in our VIC dataset generator algorithm.

After training multiple ML models and simulating their prediction power on unseen examples through 10-fold cross-validation we could achieve an F1-score averaging 45% (see Table 1), which even though is far from optimal, it is substantially better than random guessing, and could be a good indicator for vulnerability prediction in a just-in-time manner. As a conclusion, we can say that we can generate accurate vulnerability introducing commit datasets from existing vulnerability fixing datasets in an automated way, that can be effectively used for training just-in-time vulnerability prediction ML models.

4.2 RQ2: How Effective are Code Change Trees in Representing Source Code Changes?

Answering this RQ is based on the results shown in Table 1 and the observation of average tree size changes between the simple change representation and Code Change Tree representation.

Firstly, the advantage of AST based representation forms over metrics based is evident as there is at least 8% increase in average F1-score. This finding further supports that AST based representations capture (most likely structural) information uncaught by metrics. A not that substantial, but still noticeable difference can be seen between the two AST based approaches, as Code Change Tree performs better by nearly 2%.

Another advantage that Code Change Tree has over the simple change representation is the tree size. We recorded the number of nodes in the trees for both representation forms for all the 59.340 functions that were considered as part of the change representations. In the case of the Code Change Tree, the average node number count was 51, while using the AST's in the simple code change representation it was 174. This is a reduction in size by more than 70%, which means that Code Change Tree effectively reduces the size of representing change between source code states while still improving on the predictive power. To our understanding this is possible because Code Change Tree discards paths that are unchanged between the two states and consequently are irrelevant to the change.

To summarize we can conclude that Code Change Trees perform substantially better than the metrics-based approach and marginally better than simply embedding and concatenating before and after states while reducing the tree size considerably.

5 Threats to Validity

There are several issues that pose threats to the validity of the presented work. We use an automatically generated dataset for training just-in-time vulnerability prediction models and to evaluate the proposed Code Change Tree representation. Even if the original dataset of vulnerability fixing commits is fully validated, our method might introduce false entries to the generated dataset (i.e., code changes that are not introducing vulnerabilities). As this would hinder the conclusions of our study, we tried to mitigate the issue by performing a manual evaluation of the generated vulnerability introducing dataset on a random sample. We found that all the commits marked by our extraction method are linked to code changes introducing vulnerable functionality, therefore, the risk of relying on noisy data for evaluation is low.

We compared our Code Change Tree based representation with naive approaches only (i.e., static source code metrics, token-based embedding). Therefore, we cannot state anything about its performance compared to other code change representations, like Commit2Vec [24]. Even though it was out of the scope of this paper, we tried to use Commit2Vec but we were not able to find a publicly available implementation. However, an extensive comparative study of the just-in-time vulnerability detection capabilities of the various code change representations is in our future plans.

We presented empirical results on vulnerability detection in Java systems, therefore our method to represent code changes and the prediction models might not generalize. However, as the method relies on the AST representation of the code in the before and after change states, it is easy to implement to other languages. If one could acquire a good quality vulnerability fixing dataset for a certain language, our method can be adapted. Nonetheless, a replication of the presented study might be desirable for other languages as well to increase the confidence of the generalizability of the approach.

6 Future Work

As our work is a preliminary research on the usage of Code Change Trees related to just-in-time vulnerability detection and our results are promising, there are many possibilities for improvement. Mainly, we use a tree structure but lose a lot of its representative power by flattening. We plan on trying different ways of leveraging the information inherent to the AST derived tree structure in Code Change Tree, such as using graph neural networks [40].

Also, it would be beneficial to compare our method to other similar ones, we also plan to extend the baselines with more complicated works than the ones we explored in this work.

Acknowledgement. The research was supported by the European Union project RRF-2.3.1-21-2022-00004 within the framework of the Artificial Intelligence National Laboratory and by project TKP2021-NVA-09. Project no. TKP2021-NVA-09 has been implemented with the support provided by the Ministry of Innovation and Technology of Hungary from the National Research, Development and Innovation Fund, financed under the TKP2021-NVA funding scheme. Furthermore, the research was partly financed by the EU-funded project AssureMOSS (Grant no. 952647).

References

1. Aladics., T., Hegedűs., P., Ferenc., R.: A vulnerability introducing commit dataset for Java: an improved SZZ based approach. In: Proceedings of the 17th International Conference on Software Technologies - ICSOFT, pp. 68–78. INSTICC, SciTePress (2022). https://doi.org/10.5220/0011275200003266

2. Aladics, T., Jász, J., Ferenc, R.: Bug prediction using source code embedding based on doc2vec (2021). https://doi.org/10.48550/ARXIV.2110.04951, https://arxiv.org/abs/2110.04951

3. Allamanis, M., Sutton, C.: Mining source code repositories at massive scale using language modeling. In: The 10th Working Conference on Mining Software Repositories, pp. 207–216. IEEE (2013)

4. Alon, U., Brody, S., Levy, O., Yahav, E.: code2seq: generating sequences from structured representations of code. In: International Conference on Learning Representations (2019). https://openreview.net/forum?id=H1gKYo09tX

5. Alon, U., Sadaka, R., Levy, O., Yahav, E.: Structural language models of code. In: III, H.D., Singh, A. (eds.) Proceedings of the 37th International Conference on Machine Learning. Proceedings of Machine Learning Research, vol. 119, pp. 245–256. PMLR, 13–18 July 2020. https://proceedings.mlr.press/v119/alon20a.html

6. Alon, U., Zilberstein, M., Levy, O., Yahav, E.: A general path-based representation for predicting program properties (2018). https://doi.org/10.48550/ARXIV.1803.09544, https://arxiv.org/abs/1803.09544

7. Alon, U., Zilberstein, M., Levy, O., Yahav, E.: Code2vec: learning distributed representations of code. Proc. ACM Program. Lang. 3(POPL), 40:1–40:29 (2019). https://doi.org/10.1145/3290353, https://doi.acm.org/10.1145/3290353

8. Antunes, N., Vieira, M.: Benchmarking vulnerability detection tools for web services. In: 2010 IEEE International Conference on Web Services, pp. 203–210 (2010). https://doi.org/10.1109/ICWS.2010.76

9. Booth, H., Rike, D., Witte, G.: The national vulnerability database (NVD): Overview (2013-12-18 2013). https://tsapps.nist.gov/publication/get_pdf.cfm?pub_id=915172

10. Borg, M., Svensson, O., Berg, K., Hansson, D.: SZZ unleashed: an open implementation of the SZZ algorithm - featuring example usage in a study of just-in-time bug prediction for the Jenkins project. In: Proceedings of the 3rd ACM SIGSOFT International Workshop on Machine Learning Techniques for Software Quality Evaluation - MaLTeSQuE 2019. ACM Press (2019). https://doi.org/10.1145/3340482.3342742

11. Cadar, C., Sen, K.: Symbolic execution for software testing: three decades later. Commun. ACM 56(2), 82–90 (2013). https://doi.org/10.1145/2408776.2408795

12. Conti, M., Dehghantanha, A., Franke, K., Watson, S.: Internet of things security and forensics: challenges and opportunities. Future Gener. Comput. Syst. 78, 544–546 (2018)

13. DeFreez, D., Thakur, A.V., Rubio-González, C.: Path-based function embedding and its application to error-handling specification mining. In: Proceedings of the 2018 26th ACM Joint Meeting on European Software Engineering Conference and Symposium on the Foundations of Software Engineering, pp. 423–433. ESEC/FSE 2018. Association for Computing Machinery, New York, NY, USA (2018). https://doi.org/10.1145/3236024.3236059

14. Devlin, J., Uesato, J., Singh, R., Kohli, P.: Semantic code repair using neuro-symbolic transformation networks (2017). https://doi.org/10.48550/ARXIV.1710.11054, https://arxiv.org/abs/1710.11054

15. Ferenc, R., Viszkok, T., Aladics, T., Jász, J., Hegedűs, P.: Deep-water framework: The swiss army knife of humans working with machine learning models. SoftwareX 12, 100551 (2020)

16. Harer, J.A., et al.:: Automated software vulnerability detection with machine learning. CoRR abs/1803.04497 (2018). https://arxiv.org/abs/1803.04497

17. Hoang, T., Kang, H.J., Lo, D., Lawall, J.: CC2vec. In: Proceedings of the ACM/IEEE 42nd International Conference on Software Engineering. ACM, June 2020. https://doi.org/10.1145/3377811.3380361

18. Johnson, B., Song, Y., Murphy-Hill, E., Bowdidge, R.: Why don't software developers use static analysis tools to find bugs? In: 2013 35th International Conference on Software Engineering (ICSE), pp. 672–681 (2013). https://doi.org/10.1109/ICSE.2013.6606613

19. Johnson, P.: The state of open source vulnerabilities 2021 - whitesource, June 2022. https://www.mend.io/resources/research-reports/the-state-of-open-source-vulnerabilities/

20. Kamei, Y., et al.: A large-scale empirical study of just-in-time quality assurance. IEEE Trans. Softw. Eng. 39(6), 757–773 (2013). https://doi.org/10.1109/TSE.2012.70

21. Le, Q.V., Mikolov, T.: Distributed representations of sentences and documents (2014). https://doi.org/10.48550/ARXIV.1405.4053, https://arxiv.org/abs/1405.4053

22. Lin, B., Wang, S., Wen, M., Mao, X.: Context-aware code change embedding for better patch correctness assessment. ACM Trans. Softw. Eng. Methodol. 1 (2021). https://doi.org/10.1145/3505247

23. Lomio, F., Iannone, E., De Lucia, A., Palomba, F., Lenarduzzi, V.: Just-in-time software vulnerability detection: are we there yet? J. Syst. Softw. 188, 111283 (2022)

24. Lozoya, R.C., Baumann, A., Sabetta, A., Bezzi, M.: Commit2vec: learning distributed representations of code changes. SN Comput. Sci. 2(3) (2021). https://doi.org/10.1007/s42979-021-00566-z

25. McCabe, T.: A complexity measure. IEEE Trans. Softw. Eng. SE-2(4), 308–320 (1976). https://doi.org/10.1109/TSE.1976.233837

26. McKinnel, D.R., Dargahi, T., Dehghantanha, A., Choo, K.K.R.: A systematic literature review and meta-analysis on artificial intelligence in penetration testing and vulnerability assessment. Comput. Electr. Eng. 75, 175–188 (2019)

27. Minh Le, T.H., Hin, D., Croft, R., Ali Babar, M.: DeepCVA: automated commit-level vulnerability assessment with deep multi-task learning. In: 2021 36th IEEE/ACM International

Conference on Automated Software Engineering (ASE), pp. 717–729 (2021). https://doi.org/10.1109/ASE51524.2021.9678622

28. Morrison, P., Herzig, K., Murphy, B., Williams, L.: Challenges with applying vulnerability prediction models. In: Proceedings of the 2015 Symposium and Bootcamp on the Science of Security. HotSoS '15. Association for Computing Machinery, New York, NY, USA (2015). https://doi.org/10.1145/2746194.2746198

29. Neuhaus, S., Zimmermann, T., Holler, C., Zeller, A.: Predicting vulnerable software components. In: Proceedings of the 14th ACM Conference on Computer and Communications Security. CCS '07, pp. 529–540. Association for Computing Machinery, New York, NY, USA (2007). https://doi.org/10.1145/1315245.1315311

30. Nguyen, V.H., Tran, L.M.S.: Predicting vulnerable software components with dependency graphs. In: Proceedings of the 6th International Workshop on Security Measurements and Metrics. MetriSec '10. Association for Computing Machinery, New York, NY, USA (2010). https://doi.org/10.1145/1853919.1853923

31. Pan, C., Lu, M., Xu, B., Gao, H.: An improved CNN model for within-project software defect prediction. Appl. Sci. 9(10) (2019). https://doi.org/10.3390/app9102138

32. Perl, H., et al.: VCCfinder: finding potential vulnerabilities in open-source projects to assist code audits. In: Proceedings of the 22nd ACM SIGSAC Conference on Computer and Communications Security. CCS '15, pp. 426–437. Association for Computing Machinery, New York, NY, USA (2015). https://doi.org/10.1145/2810103.2813604

33. Ponta, S.E., Plate, H., Sabetta, A., Bezzi, M., Dangremont, C.: A manually-curated dataset of fixes to vulnerabilities of open-source software. In: Proceedings of the 16th International Conference on Mining Software Repositories, May 2019

34. Rehurek, R., Sojka, P.: GenSim-Python framework for vector space modelling. NLP Centre, Faculty of Informatics, Masaryk University, Brno, Czech Republic, vol. 3, no. 2 (2011)

35. Riom, T., Sawadogo, A.D., Allix, K., Bissyandé, T.F., Moha, N., Klein, J.: Revisiting the VCCfinder approach for the identification of vulnerability-contributing commits. Empir. Softw. Eng. 26, 46 (2021)

36. Scandariato, R., Walden, J., Hovsepyan, A., Joosen, W.: Predicting vulnerable software components via text mining. IEEE Trans. Softw. Eng. 40, 993–1006 (2014)

37. Shin, Y., Meneely, A., Williams, L., Osborne, J.A.: Evaluating complexity, code churn, and developer activity metrics as indicators of software vulnerabilities. IEEE Trans. Softw. Eng. 37(6), 772–787 (2011). https://doi.org/10.1109/TSE.2010.81

38. Shin, Y., Williams, L.: Can traditional fault prediction models be used for vulnerability prediction? Empir. Softw. Eng. 18 (2011). https://doi.org/10.1007/s10664-011-9190-8

39. undefinedliwerski, J., Zimmermann, T., Zeller, A.: When do changes induce fixes? In: Proceedings of the 2005 International Workshop on Mining Software Repositories. MSR '05, pp. 1–5. Association for Computing Machinery, New York, NY, USA (2005). https://doi.org/10.1145/1083142.1083147

40. Wu, Z., Pan, S., Chen, F., Long, G., Zhang, C., Yu, P.S.: A comprehensive survey on graph neural networks. IEEE Trans. Neural Netw. Learn. Syst. 32(1), 4–24 (2021). https://doi.org/10.1109/tnnls.2020.2978386

41. Zagane, M., Abdi, M.K., Alenezi, M.: Deep learning for software vulnerabilities detection using code metrics. IEEE Access 8, 74562–74570 (2020). https://doi.org/10.1109/ACCESS.2020.2988557

42. Zhang, J., Wang, X., Zhang, H., Sun, H., Wang, K., Liu, X.: A novel neural source code representation based on abstract syntax tree. In: 2019 IEEE/ACM 41st International Conference on Software Engineering (ICSE), pp. 783–794 (2019). https://doi.org/10.1109/ICSE.2019.00086

43. Zhou, Y., Sharma, A.: Automated identification of security issues from commit messages and bug reports. In: Proceedings of the 2017 11th Joint Meeting on Foundations of Software Engineering, p. 914–919. ESEC/FSE 2017. Association for Computing Machinery, New York, NY, USA (2017). https://doi.org/10.1145/3106237.3117771

Towards Extracting Reusable and Maintainable Code Snippets

Thomas Karanikiotis$^{(\boxtimes)}$ⓘ and Andreas L. Symeonidisⓘ

Department of Electrical and Computer Engineering, Aristotle University of Thessaloniki,
Thessaloniki, Greece
{karanikio,symeonid}@ece.auth.gr

Abstract. Given the wide adoption of the agile software development paradigm, where efficient collaboration as well as effective maintenance are of utmost importance, and the (re)use of software residing in code hosting platforms, the need to produce qualitative code is evident. A condition for acceptable software reusability and maintainability is the use of idiomatic code, based on syntactic fragments that recur frequently across software projects and are characterized by high quality. In this work, we propose a methodology that can harness data from the most popular GitHub repositories in order to automatically identify reusable and maintainable code idioms, by grouping code blocks that have similar structural and semantic information. We also apply the same methodology on a single-project level, in an attempt to identify frequently recurring blocks of code across the files of a team. Preliminary evaluation of our methodology indicates that our approach can identify commonly used, reusable and maintainable code idioms and code blocks that can be effectively given as actionable recommendations to the developers.

Keywords: Code idioms · Syntactic fragment · Software reusability · Software maintainability · Software engineering · Software repositories

1 Introduction

Given the increasing demand to reduce the time-to-market, while coping with continuously changing user requirements, agile development methodologies have become state-of-practice. In this context, software development is an iterative process of introducing new and updating existing features while narrowing down the release schedules. In the "speed vs. quality" dilemma, faster release cycles appear more beneficial in a short term perspective. However, in a mid- to long-term perspective, maintaining software at good quality ensures that risks are mitigated more easily, while technical debt does not "explode", this way leading to failure or challenged (in cost and time) software projects.

In order to reduce the effort given in a software project, minimize the risks of defective software and reach the goal of narrow time-to-market, developers have turned towards software reusability, in an attempt to exploit the already implemented, released and tested software components/libraries/code snippets, which reside in some code

© The Author(s), under exclusive license to Springer Nature Switzerland AG 2023
H.-G. Fill et al. (Eds.): ICSOFT 2022, CCIS 1859, pp. 187–206, 2023.
https://doi.org/10.1007/978-3-031-37231-5_9

hosting facility. However, due to the fact that the quality of the (re)used components is not a given, suboptimal searches may lead to code snippets of poor quality that are tough to integrate and could possibly introduce bugs. So, there is a high need for software components that the developers can easily reuse and integrate into their software and that can guarantee acceptable quality.

This requirement can be satisfied by two different perspectives. The first one exploits the use of idiomatic code or code idioms. Code idioms are small syntactic fragments that recur frequently across various software projects, with simple tasks to execute. According to Allamanis et al. [3], code idioms appear to be significantly different from "previous notions of textual patterns in software", as they involve syntactic constructs (decision-making statements, loops and exception-handling blocks). Code idioms can make the code significantly easier to maintain [11], since they are characterized by high reusability and can improve the overall quality of the software they are used into. However, there are only few approaches that aspire to mine code idioms automatically [3]. The few existing ones are mostly based on statistical methods and are not able to capture idioms based also on their increased usage among top-level and popular repositories.

The need for reusable software components, which will be easily integrated into a given software project, can be viewed also from a different perspective. Given a number of different projects and/or code files, a set of code blocks can be extracted that represent the main code snippets the developers make use of and, thus, define the main styling used within the project(s). The identification of such code blocks can speed up the development of the team (using a set of a priori familiar code blocks), help the developers easily maintain and reuse specific code snippets, while keeping a common formatting across the whole project. This perspective exploits the idiom mining procedure at project(s) level, since it is based on the identification of small syntactic fragments that recur frequently.

In this work, we aspire to create a mechanism that can harness data from the top-level, most popular repositories, from the well-known code hosting platform GitHub, in order to identify and extract a set of reusable and maintainable code idioms, in a completely unsupervised manner. This mechanism extracts the most-used code blocks found across different projects, compares both their structural and their semantic information and groups code snippets with similar architecture and functionality. After automatically processing the generated clusters and discarding the ones that do not meet specific requirements, our system produces a set of code idioms that have been used considerably across top-level projects. At the same time, we make use of the constructed mechanism in order to identify a set of code snippets or code blocks that are widely used across the files of one or more software projects of the same team of developers, that way extracting a set of code styling that should be adopted across all the files of the project. In order to accomplish that, we extend our previous work [16], where we proposed a methodology for comparing code snippets, in order to evaluate the level of semantic and structural similarity between them. In the current work, we make use of this similarity algorithm in order to identify and extract patterns of code blocks that are widely used across the code files of a software project.

Summarizing, the advances of this work with respect to our previous paper [16] are the following:

- The application of the previously proposed methodology in identifying frequently recurring code blocks within one or more software projects.
- The use of a GPU oriented implementation, in order to speed up the distance matrix calculations.
- The integration of more repositories, not only for the idioms mining step, but also for the evaluation stage.
- The generalization of the parameter thresholds that need to be met in order for a generated cluster to be considered an idiom.

The rest of this paper is organized as follows. Section 2 reviews the current approaches in the literature that aspire to extract small fragments of code that recur frequently across projects and are characterized by high quality. Our methodology, along with the dataset we have created, the processing steps and the models we have employed are depicted in Sect. 3, while in Sect. 4 we evaluate the code idioms and code blocks that were extracted by our approach. In Sect. 5, we analyze potential threats to the internal and external validity of our approach and, finally in Sect. 6 we provide insight for further research and conclude the paper.

2 Related Work

The constantly changing features of software projects, along with the high maintenance costs and the narrow time-to-market schedules, have turned the interest of the recent approaches towards software maintainability and reusability, pillar aspects of software quality. Towards that direction, a lot of methodologies have been proposed in the context of component-based software, which, since it is mostly based on independent code blocks, is easy to debug, maintain and reuse. These independent code blocks, i.e. software components and functions, are well-defined self-standing fragments of code, which execute specific programming tasks and can be easily understood by the developers. By definition, idiomatic code or code idioms are such small syntactic blocks that recur frequently across different projects and execute simple tasks. Idioms can significantly improve the software maintainability of a project, while they provide small, compact and highly reusable code blocks, which the developers can effortlessly comprehend and (re)use.

There are a lot of approaches in the literature that aspire to extract useful information from semi-structured data and identify frequently encountered snippets. Even though mining frequent patterns is an important task, it is not directly correlated to the idioms mining challenge. A problem that is highly connected to idioms mining is the identification of code clones, the main target of which is the detection of code blocks that spread across different projects and exhibit similar structural behavior. Ji et al. [12] exploit the hierarchical structure of the Abstract Syntax Tree (AST), in order to apply an attention mechanism to examine the importance of different tree nodes. Their methodology achieves superior results compared to the baseline methods, based on the evaluation results. At the same time, Zhang and Wang [23] created CCEyes, which makes use of the semantic vector representations of big repositories in order to identify similar code fragments. The tool they proposed outperforms state-of-the-art approaches in code cloning detection.

A lot of research methodologies have been also proposed that are targeted towards the API mining problem. The primary goal of these approaches is the extraction of sequences or graphs of API method calls. Wang et al. [20] evaluated the approaches proposed at that time and concluded that they lack appropriate metrics to evaluate the quality of their results. In order to cope with this limitation, the authors proposed two metrics that can measure the quality of the mined usage patterns of API methods, called succinctness and coverage. The authors proposed also a system, called UP-Miner, that can mine API usage patterns from source code based on the similarity of the sequence and a clustering algorithm. From the evaluation experiments conducted, it is concluded that the proposed system outperforms the existing approaches. Towards that direction, Fowkes and Sutton [10] identified the problems of the expensive parameter tuning and the large and difficult to understand set of API calls returned. In order to cope with these limitations, the authors proposed the Probabilistic API Miner (PAM), a probabilistic algorithm that evades the large parameter-tuning constraint, which achieved better results than the existing approaches.

The aforementioned approaches aspire to mitigate the problems of API mining, code search and code cloning detection. Even though these approaches are closely related to idioms mining, there are also significant variations. The API mining problem is mainly targeted towards sequences or graphs mining and not on the code itself. At the same direction, code search is not usually focused on code quality and maintainability, but only on the identification of the code snippet that best matches the request. Similarly, code clones are solely based on detecting similar code from the functionality perspective, resulting in code snippets that may not be identical.

When it comes to idiom mining, research approaches try to model the problem from a statistical point of view. One of the first approaches in that area was proposed by Allamanis and Sutton [3], who created a system, called HAGGIS, that can extract idioms used in a variety of different software projects based on non-parametric probabilistic tree substitution grammars. Despite the large variety of idioms extracted by HAGGIS, the majority of them perform only simple tasks, such as object creation, which provide little benefit to the developers. In an attempt to cope with this limitation, Allamanis et al. [2] made also use of the probabilistic tree substitution grammars, improving the previously proposed architecture with important semantics. The authors were solely based on loop idioms, aspiring to identify loop blocks that recur frequently and meet the basic requirements of code idioms. The code idioms extracted seem to appear frequently across multiple projects. However, Tanaka et al. conducted a study [19], which concluded that the majority of the code idioms identified by the related approaches have not appeared to be useful for the developers, since they are rarely used in practice. At the same time, the lack of complete idioms or examples leads to bad idioms usage. Finally, Sivaraman et al. [17] proposed Jezero, a system that uses nonparametric Bayesian methods, in order to extract canonicalized dataflow trees. Even though Jezero performs better than other baseline approaches, it appears to significantly depend on the extent and the nature of the code it is applied to.

In order to cope with the aforementioned limitations, in this work we propose a methodology that can be used to identify similar snippets of code that are used across different projects, in order to extract code idioms from the most popular and reused projects from GitHub. Since these projects are characterized by high maintainability and reusability [15], the identified code blocks satisfy the main requirements posed by the mining idioms problem. Towards that direction, we split the software into small meaningful code snippets and group commonly used code blocks across different projects that have similar structural and semantic information. We then discard any code snippet that contradicts the basic requirements of the idiomatic code. We argue that code idioms can effectively help the developers during both the development phase, where components that accomplish simple tasks are selected to be reused, and the maintenance phase. At the same time, we argue that the extraction of the code idioms from repositories that have a big number of stars (users that can comprehend the main content and functionality of the project) and forks (users that use the whole project or project components), along with their long lifespan, is a good indicator of idiomatic code. At the same time, we employ the snippet similarity algorithm in order to identify and extract code blocks that recur frequently across the files of one or more software projects of a given team of developers. That way, we aspire to point out patterns of code that are widely used by the same team or company of developers, which would help the developers keep a common formatting across the whole project, maintain or reuse certain pieces of code and even help new members adopt a uniform way of developing software.

3   Methodology

In this section we present the architecture of our similarity scheme algorithm and the code idioms mining system, along with the methodology of identifying common blocks of code recurring across the code files of a software project (shown in Fig. 1). The figure has been altered from the one originally presented in [16], in order to include the recurring code blocks identification case.

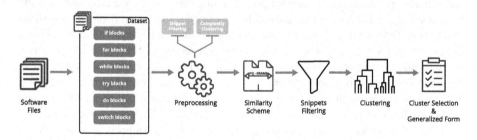

Fig. 1. Overview of the Code Idioms and Recurring Code Blocks Mining System.

3.1   Dataset Construction

In the first step of our approach and towards identifying code idioms that are used across multiple projects of high quality, we need to create the dataset consisting of code snippets from the most popular software projects. The programming language selected for creating our corpus is Java, as it is a well-structured language and is considered ideal for mining code patterns.

Towards that direction, we selected the 3,000 most popular repositories residing in GitHub[1], which are written in Java. Further extending our previous work [16], we employed 1,500 more repositories, in order to further examine the appearance and the usefulness of our extracted idioms in practice. The selection of the most popular ones was based on the number of stars and forks they contain, along with their lifespan, i.e. their lifetime since their first official release. The initial dataset used in our system needs to include idiomatic code, i.e. qualitative code that is popular among the developers. Basic conditions for reusable and maintainable code are the reputation metrics of each project, since a large number of forks, i.e. the number of times a software repository has been cloned, indicates great reusability, while a large number of stars reflects the attractiveness of the project with a large lifespan and, thus, maintainable software. Moreover, apart from the qualitative criteria, some additional requirements should be met by the projects that constitute the dataset, which are posed by the idioms mining problem. Each project needs to exhibit a large number of different contributors as well as steady and short release cycles (i.e. new features constantly added). These requirements typically ensure maintainability and reusability.

From the initial set of 3,000 software repositories, we split the projects and create two subgroups of a) 2,000 repositories that are used to identify the code idioms and b) the remaining 1,000 repositories to evaluate the extracted idioms. The source code of these projects needs to be converted into a form suitable for our models. For this purpose, we employ the Abstract Syntax Tree (AST) representation, which maintains both the structural and the semantic information of the source code. Specifically, the execution order of the code statements is encoded in the structure of the AST, while the semantic information is stored in the leaves of the tree, where the names of variables, methods and objects are found. The transformation of the source code files to ASTs is performed with the use of the ASTExtractor[2] tool.

Code idioms, by definition, are small syntactic fragments with a single semantic role that execute specific and well-defined programming tasks. Thus, we can easily assume that code idioms usually concern a small block of code, such as an if-block or a while-block. Therefore, we mainly focus on fragments of code that belong to the Control Flow Statements (CFSs), which break up the sequential execution of the code with looping, decision-making or exception-handling statements. The most usual CFSs that exist in almost any programming language are the *If, For, Try, While, Do* and *Switch* statements. Thus, we first traverse the generated AST for each code file, in which we identify and extract all the code blocks that belong to the aforementioned categories. Since the code idioms mining problem considers only almost identical code snippets and code blocks that belong to different CFS categories present no such similarity between them (that could lead to the identification of a code idiom), we can handle each CFS category independently. Table 1 depicts the number of snippets that each category of the CFS contains, where the Enhanced For statements refer to the iteration on the elements of an array or collection. It should be noted that Table 1 has been altered from the respective

---

[1] https://github.com.

[2] https://github.com/thdiaman/ASTExtractor.

one presented in [16], in order to include also the additional blocks contained in the extra repositories used in the current work. In total, our current work employs about 4.3 million snippets of code more than our previous one.

Table 1. Number of Snippets per Category.

Type of CFS Blocks	# Snippets
If	7,934,152
For	712,013
Enhanced For	852,123
Try	1,251,004
While	312,057
Switch	197,741
Do	16,732

3.2 Preprocessing

Before proceeding to the similarity matrix calculation, a set of preprocessing steps have to be applied, in order to reduce the computational cost that emerges from the inclusion of a large number of repositories and, at the same time, discard data that may lead to deficient results, while maintaining the basic principles of the mining idioms problem. Therefore, we apply some preprocessing steps, which make the implementation of the main clustering procedure feasible.

As it has been already mentioned, the idiomatic code consists of small blocks of code, i.e. small syntactic fragments, with specific functionality and well-defined tasks to execute. Taking this definition into account, it is obvious that a large code snippet would not be part of a code idiom, as it contradicts with the main principles of code idioms. Therefore, and in an attempt to reduce the computational cost, we exclude code snippets that exceed a predefined threshold regarding the lines of code, i.e. executable lines of code, as idioms need to be significantly small and execute simple tasks and they usually do not exceed the above threshold[3, 4]. In our previous work [16], we had defined this threshold to be seven logical lines of code, eliminating any code snippet larger than this value. In the current work we decided to expand this threshold to twelve logical lines of code, in order to evaluate our initial assumption and evade a potential threat to the validity of our approach. It should be mentioned, however, that this is just a tunable parameter in our methodology and can easily be changed for further experimentation. Table 2 depicts the number of code snippets each category contains, after removing the large snippets of code. It should be noted that this table has been altered from the respective Table 2 of our previous work [16], in order to include also the new repositories added into the current approach, as well as the expanded threshold described above, which lead to using about twice as many snippets per category.

As we can conclude from the statistics depicted in Table 2, the first four CFS categories, i.e. the If, For, Enhanced For and Try statements, contain a large number of code snippets, which greatly impedes the effective clustering analysis of the next steps,

---

[3] https://programming-idioms.org/.

[4] https://www.nayuki.io/page/good-java-idioms.

Table 2. Number of Snippets per Category after Filtering.

Type of CFS blocks	# Snippets
If	2,312,147
For	364,782
Enhanced For	348,122
Try	453,961
While	101,250
Switch	88,741
Do	7,523

especially during the calculation of the similarity matrices. To that end, we decided to further preprocess the selected categories, in order to split them into smaller parts, in an attempt to perform only targeted comparisons, during the main clustering stage, avoiding the comparisons between code blocks that are considerably different.

In order to split the respective categories into smaller groups of code snippets, we firstly calculated the code complexity of the snippets. Code blocks that appear to have quite large difference in their complexity probably perform different tasks, while, even if they serve the same programming task, they are based on different approaches. Therefore, we perform an initial pre-clustering approach based on two complexity metrics; the McCabe's Cyclomatic Complexity [14], which counts the independent execution paths of the source code, as well as the total number of variables, methods and objects that the code contains. These two metrics are used as features for the clustering algorithm, in order to create groups that contain snippets with the same characteristics. Using the aforementioned pre-clustering step, we create several subsets of the initial CFS categories, which contain significantly fewer snippets. The main point of this modelling step is that each of our sets contains only fragments of code that appear to have similar code complexity and hence they could lead to the identification of a code idiom. Table 3 depicts a summary of the pre-clustering results, i.e. the number of groups created for each CFS category, along with the average number of code snippets each group contains.

Table 3. Initial Clustering Results.

Type of CFS Blocks	# Groups	Average # Snippets
If	43	54,587
For	15	23,854
Enhanced For	18	19,547
Try	20	25,613

3.3 Similarity Scheme

In order to perform the main clustering algorithm, we first need to calculate a distance matrix between all the code snippets that belong to each subset in our corpus, which reflects the similarity degree between the two code blocks. For the comparison of the snippets, we use their AST representations and calculate the Tree Edit Distance (TED). TED is defined as the minimum cost sequence of edit operations (node insertion, node deletion and label change) that can transform one tree into another [18]. There have been a lot of research approaches that have been proposed over the years in order to perform the calculations needed for the TED and that aspire to improve the runtime algorithm's complexity [13,22]. It is remarkable, though, that the complexity in all these implementations is greater or equal to $O(n^2)$. In order to avoid using such a computationally expensive method, we approximate the TED by using the pq-Grams algorithm [5].

The ASTs that are generated from the ASTExtractor first need to be transformed into an ordered label tree T, in order for the pq-Grams algorithm to be applied, using the type of AST statements as labels and connecting the nodes so that the tree is traversed in a preorder manner. Then a pq-Extended-Tree T^{pq} is constructed by adding null nodes on the tree T. Precisely, $p - 1$ ancestors are added to the root of the tree, $q - 1$ children are added before the first and after the last child of each non-leaf node and q children are inserted to each leaf of T. In our methodology, we define $p = 2$ and $q = 3$, as these values have been used significantly in tree matching approaches with great results. Figure 2 illustrates the extended tree transformation of a simple labelled tree, where $p = 2$ and $q = 3$, as it was originally presented in [16].

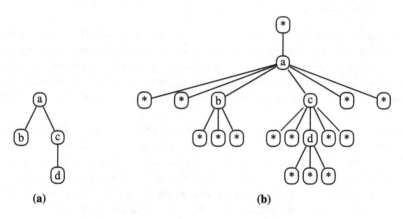

Fig. 2. (a) Example tree T. (b) $T^{2,3}$ Extended-Tree.

For each one of these Extended-Trees we need to calculate the complete list of pq-Gram patterns it contains, which is defined as a subtree with $p - 1$ ancestors and q children. The set of pq-Gram patterns define the *Profiles* $P(T)$ of the Extended-Tree and can be then used in order to evaluate the similarity between two trees. For the Extended-Tree illustrated in Fig. 2, the profile is defined as the list $[*a * *b, *a * bc, *abc*, *ac * *, ab * **, ac * *d, ac * d*, acd * *, cd * **]$. Using the generated profiles for two trees T_1 and T_2, we can easily calculate the pq-Gram distance, using the Eq. 1, which was first presented in [16]:

$$distance(T_1, T_2) = 1 - 2 * \frac{|P^{p,q}(T_1) \cap P^{p,q}(T_2)|}{|P^{p,q}(T_1) \cup P^{p,q}(T_2)|} \quad (1)$$

The distance between two trees T_1 and T_2 is calculated based on the number of mutual pq-Grams patterns that are included in the profiles of the two trees, divided by the total number of pq-Grams patterns that appear on either profile. The lowest possible number for the distance score is 0, when the union contains double the instances of the intersection [4] and the highest is 1, when there is no common pq-Grams pattern between the two profiles. It is obvious that the similarity between two trees can be easily calculated using the formula $1 - distance(T_1, T_2)$. The final similarity value ranges from 0 to 1.

The process of calculating the distance matrices for all the code snippets that belong to the same CFS category and pre-clustering group is significantly slow and computationally expensive, which has already been noted in our previous work [16], where we proposed the exploration of various methods towards speeding up this procedure. In our current work, we make use of various GPU implementations that can exploit the GPU unit in order to accelerate the distance matrix computation. At the same time, we employ a batch parallelization procedure, in which the similarity between the code snippets is performed in a set of parallel parcels, in an attempt to fully take advantage of the GPU capabilities.

3.4 Snippets Filtering

The pq-Gram algorithm discussed in the previous section outputs the distance matrices calculated between code snippets in the same subsets presented above. Before proceeding with the main clustering algorithm, we have also identified two cases of duplicate instances, which need to be removed in order to ensure that the resulting clusters will contain patterns used by many different software projects and, therefore, many different developers.

The first occasion refers to snippets with zero pq-Gram distance that belong to the same code repository, as it is quite common for a fragment of code to be used numerous times in the same repository, while the second one to snippets with zero pq-Gram distance that are derived from different code repositories but, however, originate from the same package or library. It is a usual case, when developers need to make a change to an existing library or package and, thus, they include it into their project.

3.5 Clustering

In the main clustering step, we make use of the Agglomerative Hierarchical Clustering in order to split the code snippets of each CFS category and pre-clustering group into collections of code blocks that appear to look alike. The Agglomerative Hierarchical Clustering is a bottom-up approach that initially considers each snippet as a separate cluster and iteratively merges the groups with the lesser distance. The average linkage algorithm is selected for the distance between the clusters, which denotes the average distance between all the snippets of one cluster. The selection of the optimal number of clusters for each occasion is performed based on the average silhouette score, which ranges from -1 to 1, indicating whether the point is assigned to the correct cluster (positive value) or not (negative value). Equation 4 depicts the calculation of the silhouette metric, using the mean intracluster distance (variable a) and the min nearest cluster distance (variable b) as shown in Eqs. 2 and 3 respectively.

$$a(i) = \frac{1}{|c_i| - 1} \sum_{\substack{j \in C_i \\ j \neq i}} d(i, j) \tag{2}$$

$$b(i) = \min_{k \neq i} \frac{1}{|c_k|} \sum_{j \in C_k} d(i, j) \tag{3}$$

$$s(i) = \frac{b(i) - a(i)}{\max\left(a(i), b(i)\right)} \tag{4}$$

Figure 3 illustrates a histogram of the cohesion achieved on a set of different clusters for the If statements, while Table 4 depicts the average number of snippets per cluster, along with the average cohesion of the clusters and the average number of repositories found within the cluster. Both the Fig. 3 and the Table 4 has been altered from the respective ones that were originally presented in [16], in order to include all the new experiments and repositories.

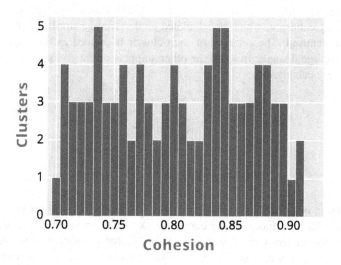

Fig. 3. A histogram of the cohesion achieved in a set of different clusters.

Table 4. Clustering Results.

Type of CFS Blocks	Cluster Size	Cohesion	# Repos
If	713.3	0.79	86.7
For	281.1	0.78	73.0
Enhanced For	541.7	0.80	98.1
Try	341.7	0.84	114.2
While	218.9	0.86	111.7
Switch	104.4	0.77	57.4
Do	32.7	0.84	7.2

3.6   Cluster Selection and Generalized Form

In the last step of our methodology and after having performed the clustering analysis and split the snippets into the appropriate clusters, the final step of the idioms mining procedure examines the generated clusters, in order to select only the ones that meet the requirements posed by the idioms mining problem. There are two important criteria that need to be met from the extracted idioms and the generated clusters. First of all, the idioms have to be widely used by a lot of different developers and, thus, it is important to examine the number of different code repositories that contain snippets within a cluster. Additionally, the clusters derived from a clustering algorithm have to be cohesive, so that the code snippets they carry are quite similar both structurally and semantically.

Based on the aforementioned remarks, we define the three necessary parameters that designate an optimal cluster, which have been already identified in our previous work [16]:

- The number of code snippets it contains
- The number of different repositories that contain at least one snippet in the cluster
- The cluster cohesion, which is calculated as the average similarity of the snippets from the centroid. The centroid of each cluster is defined as the snippet with the lowest average distance from all the other snippets of the group. Equations 5 and 6 depict these calculations:

$$\bar{m} = \min_{i} \left(\frac{1}{|C| - 1} \sum_{\substack{j \in C \\ j \neq i}} d(i, j) \right) \tag{5}$$

$$cohesion = 1 - \frac{1}{|C| - 1} \sum_{x \in C} d(x, \bar{m}) \tag{6}$$

Contrary to our previous work [16], where we defined different parameter thresholds for each CFS category, in the current work and in an attempt to emend the use of different parameters per category, we define global parameter thresholds. Table 5 depicts these values, which have been carefully selected, taking into account the number of the available snippets and the clustering results. Discarding the generated clusters that do not meet these thresholds, a total of 142 optimal clusters have been produced. From each of these optimal clusters, we extract the centroid of the cluster as the representative one, i.e. the code idiom of the respective cluster.

Table 5. Threshold Parameters.

# Snippets	# Repos	Cohesion
100	100	0.7

The last step in our approach is to transform the generated idioms into a generalized form, that can be easily recognized and used by any developer. The main task of this step is the identification of variables, functions and objects that are commonly used within the idiom, which remain as is. On the other hand, all the other names, that change according to the domain the idiom is used on, are replaced with an abstract naming convention. For this purpose, we compute the frequency of each token of the centroid in the snippets of the corresponding cluster. All the tokens of the centroid, with a frequency lower than a specific threshold, which in our case is set to 0.5 (i.e. less than half of the snippets in the cluster contain the examined token), are replaced by an abstract token. Figure 4 depicts an example idiom extracted by our approach, as well as the generalized form it is transformed to. This figure has been originally presented in [16].

```java
try {
    writer.close();
}
catch (IOException e) {
    throw new RuntimeException(e);
}
```

(a)

```java
try {
    $(object).close();
}
catch (IOException e) {
    throw new $(method)(e);
}
```

(b)

Fig. 4. (a) An example idiom extracted by our system. (b) Generalized form of the pattern adding metavariables.

Figure 5, originally presented in [16], depicts some examples of the top idioms that were extracted using our methodology, according to the number of different repositories they are found in. These abstract code snippets meet the basic requirements set for the code idioms, as they are small syntactic fragments that perform well-defined programming tasks and that are used widely by a number of different developers.

3.7   Recurring Code Blocks

In the last step of our proposed methodology, we aspire to exploit the algorithm described in the previous subsections in order to identify blocks of code that are met frequently within the code files of one or more projects/repositories of the same team of developers. By doing so, our system can extract a set of code snippets that are frequently used by the developers, which will speed up the development of the team, while maintaining a common way of using these code blocks and ensuring high readability and maintainability degree.

Towards that direction, we first collect all the Java files met within the project(s) selected by the developers. Then, the code included in these files is transformed into an AST and the code blocks that belong to the CFS categories are extracted, as it is described in the Subsect. 3.1. The similarity scheme based on the TED and pq-Grams

```
try {
  Thread.sleep($(variable1));
}
catch (InterruptedException e) {
}
```

(a)

```
if (value == null) {
  $(method1)();
}
else {
  $(method2)(( String ) value);
}
```

(b)

```
for (Thread thread : threads) {
  thread.$(method1)();
}
```

(c)

```
while ($(object1).hasNext()){
  $(object2).add($(object1)
    .next());
}
```

(d)

Fig. 5. Examples of idioms extracted using our approach (a) Suspends a thread for a period of time. (b) Checks if a value is equal to null and calls the appropriate method. (c) Iterates over a sequence of threads calling a method (e) Adds the values of iterator to an object.

is also used in order to calculate the similarities between all the code snippets in the corpus. Moreover, the clustering step of Subsect. 3.5 is once again applied in order to group code blocks that appear to be both semantically and structurally similar. Finally, the clusters created by the Agglomerative Clustering are examined, based on the number of code snippets they contain and their cohesion (the condition regarding the number of different repositories cannot be applied in this case), while also the generalized form that represents the centroid of each cluster is created.

Using the 2,000 most popular repositories from GitHub that were employed also in the previous steps and examining each repository independently, we were able to identify 23 frequently recurring code blocks on average at each repository.

4 Evaluation

In this section, we employ a set of different scenarios in order to evaluate our methodology, both for extracting code idioms from the most popular GitHub repositories and for identifying frequently recurring code blocks across the files of a software project. The evaluation is performed in three diverse axes. At first, we examine the extracted idioms based on a set of repositories used for testing and assess their association with top repositories. Additionally, towards the evaluation of the effectiveness of our approach in practice, we investigate the applicability of our extracted idioms, by employing the most popular questions and answers from *StackOverflow*. Finally, in an attempt to evaluate the usefulness of the extracted code blocks from a set of given repositories, we examine the presence of the extracted snippets within the repository from which they originated.

4.1   Evaluation of Extracted Idioms

In the first step towards the evaluation of the proposed methodology, we examine the usefulness and the applicability of the extracted idioms in practice and, in particular, in the most popular and (re)used repositories. Specifically, we examine the code blocks of the generalized code idioms against code snippets coming from a set of testing repositories, in order to identify blocks of code in these projects that are identical to the extracted idioms.

From the initial dataset (which has been expanded since our previous work [16]) of the 3,000 most popular GitHub repositories, we made use of only the 2,000 of them and the remaining ones were left apart, in order to be used for evaluation. We use the projects of these repositories as our main testing set, in which we examine whether they make use of our extracted idioms or not. Table 6 depicts some statistics on these repositories, which presents different statistics compared to the respective one in [16].

Table 6. Testing Repositories Statistics.

Metric	Value	Value in [16]
Mean Stars	1,211	1,385.8
Mean Forks	452	499.2
Mean Commits	5,234	3,344.7
Mean Watches	614	620.7

In order to compare the extracted code idioms with the code blocks coming from the testing set, we need to perform three steps. First of all, the code blocks need to be transformed into ASTs and the nodes that belong to CFSs are identified and extracted. Next, the AST coming from a code idiom and the respective one from the code block are edited and the leaves, which contain the names of the variables, methods and objects, are removed, so that we can compare only the syntactical similarity of the two snippets, using the pq-Grams algorithm as it is defined in the previous section. If the resulting distance is zero, the snippets are syntactically similar and the next step can be executed. In the final step of the comparison, we examine the original variables included in the two code snippets and, specifically, we check if all the variables, excluding the ones that were replaced by meta-variables in the generalized form of the tested snippet are also contained in the generalized idiom. In this case, the two code snippets are both structurally and semantically similar and the idiom is considered to be used by the project.

Comparing the code idioms extracted by our approach with the code blocks included in the testing repositories, it appears that only 9 of our extracted idioms are not used at all by any repository of the testing set. In fact, each code idiom can be found at least once in 127 different repositories on average. Figure 6a illustrates the number of different code repositories where the extracted idioms are used at least once.

Additionally, we evaluate the usefulness of the extracted idioms by measuring the extent to which these idioms participate in the software development procedure. Thus, we calculated a histogram of the number of idioms from our extracted data that are used in practice and are employed within the repositories of the testing set. The results

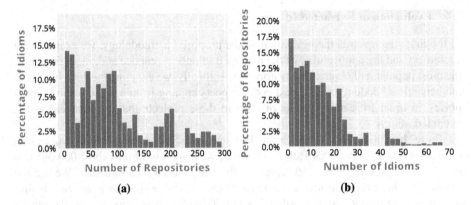

(a)   (b)

Fig. 6. (a) Number of different repositories in which our extracted idioms can be found in. (b) Number of our extracted idioms used by the repositories of the testing set.

depicted that only 63 projects from the testing set do not use any of our code idioms at all, which can be justified by the fact that the selected projects span along a wide variety of domains and functionalities. Moreover, each testing repository appears to include about 18 code idioms at least once. Figure 6b illustrates the number of idioms extracted by our methodology that are used at least once in the testing repositories.

4.2 Applicability Evaluation in Practice

In the next step of our evaluation and towards assessing the usefulness and the applicability of our methodology in providing actual and useful recommendations to the developers, we made use of the *StackOverflow* questions dataset [6]. As it is known in the related community, StackOverflow usually contains short code snippets that need to cover the requested functionality, so they are traditionally concise, cover only the essential code statements and represent the best programming practices. Thus, StackOverflow is considered to incorporate highly idiomatic code snippets.

From the initial dataset provided by StackOverflow, we created two subgroups of answers on Java-tagged questions; the first contains all the code blocks found within the answers, while the second one includes only the snippets that belong to the answers marked as correct.

In order to compare the code idioms generated by our approach with the code blocks coming from the StackOverflow dataset, we employ the comparison algorithm that was described in the Subsect. 4.1. For the evaluation, we make use of two different metrics, the precision of the extracted idioms, which refers to the percentage of code idioms found within the StackOverflow answers, and the average number of times a code idiom is being used in these snippets. Table 7 depicts the results, in which the precision metric for the whole StackOverflow dataset is 68% and for the accepted answers 65%, while our idioms were found in 286 different posts and 33 correct answers on average. The reduced metrics on the accepted answers dataset were expected, as this set contains significantly fewer code snippets. It should be noted that Allamanis and Sutton [3] achieved a precision of 67% on the StackOverflow answers dataset.

Table 7. Evaluation results on StackOverflow dataset.

Dataset	Precision	Average # Occurrences
Answers	68%	286
Accepted Answers	65%	33

4.3 Recurring Code Blocks

Finally, in an attempt to evaluate the usefulness of the extracted code blocks that are met frequently within one or more given project(s), we examine the number of times these code blocks appear (either identical or with small changes) within the repository they originate from. A code block that recurs very frequently, even with small changes, could be a useful recommendation to the developers.

In order to compare the extracted frequently recurring code blocks with the code snippets coming from the source code, we once again make use of the comparison algorithm described in the Subsect. 4.1, with some modifications. At first, we do not demand the resulting pq-Grams distance between two code snippets to be zero, which means that these snippets are syntactically identical, but only lower than a predefined threshold, which was set to 0.2. That way, an extracted code block is considered to be used in practice even when the actual code snippet is slightly modified syntactically. Additionally, in the last step of the comparison, where the variables are examined, and in cases that only few variables appear to be different between the two code snippets, we investigate whether these variables could be transformed into meta-variables, in order for the code blocks to fully match.

Comparing the frequently recurring code blocks extracted by our approach and the code snippets of the repositories they came from, we conclude that each recurring code block appears at least 8 times within its repository, even with slight modifications. Figure 7 illustrates the number of times each recurring code block appears within the repository it originated from.

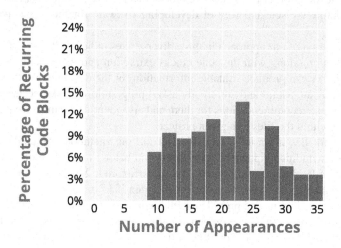

Fig. 7. Number of times a recurring code block appears within its repository.

5   Threats to Validity

In this work, we proposed a methodology towards extracting maintainable and reusable code idioms from the most popular code hosting platforms, as well as identifying the most common code blocks that are used across different files of one or more software projects of the same team of developers. Based on the evaluation performed, the only limitation that applies to the internal validity of our system is the selection of the repositories based on their number of stars and forks, as a reflection of their reusability. In the first step of our methodology, the most popular GitHub repositories were employed, in order to mine and extract our code idioms. Even though this fact could be considered as a threat to the external validity of our system, the maintainability and reusability degree of these repositories have been proven in practice, since they are widely used by a large number of different developers that evinces the qualitative code. Moreover, many researchers have argued that projects that exhibit large numbers of stars and forks, also exhibit high quality [8,9,15], involve frequent maintenance releases [7] and have sufficient documentation [1,21].

As far as the external validity of our approach is concerned, the design choice of identifying code idioms only within CFSs can be considered as a potential threat. Even though this fact can be considered as a limitation of our approach, in fact it is proven in our evaluation section that code idioms extracted from CFS are really useful.

6   Conclusions and Future Work

In this work, we proposed an automated mechanism for identifying and extracting a set of code idioms from the most popular repositories, which are characterized by high reusability and can be easily used by developers, in order to accelerate the software development procedure, while improving the quality of the project and ensuring an acceptable level of maintainability. At the same time, we applied our methodology on a repository level, in order to detect code blocks that recur frequently across the project and, thus, define the selected way of developing software for the respective team of developers.

The evaluation of our approach in three diverse axes indicates that the snippet comparison algorithm, along with the code blocks extraction and the generalization of the identified idioms can produce valuable information for the developers, extracting code idioms that execute useful and commonly asked programming tasks, seem natural and can be actionable recommendations for them and also identify the most frequent blocks of code used within the files of a given project.

Future work lies in various axes. First of all, our methodology could be further expanded by including snippets of code that do no belong to CFS, in order to identify also general code idioms. Additionally, the recurring code blocks methodology could be further expanded, in order to compare the identified code blocks with a set of a priori known code idioms and provide useful recommendations to the developers about adopting a different qualitative approach. Finally, the usefulness of the generated idioms and the recurring code blocks could be further evaluated on the basis of a developer survey.

References

1. Aggarwal, K., Hindle, A., Stroulia, E.: Co-evolution of project documentation and popularity within github. In: Proceedings of the 11th Working Conference on Mining Software Repositories. MSR 2014, New York, NY, USA, pp. 360–363. Association for Computing Machinery (2014). https://doi.org/10.1145/2597073.2597120
2. Allamanis, M., Barr, E.T., Bird, C., Devanbu, P., Marron, M., Sutton, C.: Mining semantic loop idioms. IEEE Trans. Software Eng. **44**(7), 651–668 (2018). https://doi.org/10.1109/TSE.2018.2832048
3. Allamanis, M., Sutton, C.: Mining idioms from source code. CoRR abs/1404.0417 (2014). http://arxiv.org/abs/1404.0417
4. Augsten, N., Böhlen, M., Gamper, J.: The PQ-gram distance between ordered labeled trees **35**(1) (2008). https://doi.org/10.1145/1670243.1670247
5. Augsten, N., Böhlen, M., Gamper, J.: Approximate matching of hierarchical data using PQ-grams - slides **1**, 301–312 (2005). https://doi.org/10.5167/uzh-56101
6. Baltes, S., Dumani, L., Treude, C., Diehl, S.: Sotorrent: Reconstructing and analyzing the evolution of stack overflow posts. CoRR abs/1803.07311 (2018). http://arxiv.org/abs/1803.07311
7. Borges, H., Hora, A., Valente, M.T.: Understanding the factors that impact the popularity of github repositories. In: 2016 IEEE International Conference on Software Maintenance and Evolution (ICSME), pp. 334–344 (2016). https://doi.org/10.1109/ICSME.2016.31
8. Dimaridou, V., Kyprianidis, A.C., Papamichail, M., Diamantopoulos, T., Symeonidis, A.: Towards modeling the user-perceived quality of source code using static analysis metrics, pp. 73–84, July 2017. https://doi.org/10.5220/0006420000730084
9. Dimaridou, V., Kyprianidis, A.-C., Papamichail, M., Diamantopoulos, T., Symeonidis, A.: Assessing the user-perceived quality of source code components using static analysis metrics. In: Cabello, E., Cardoso, J., Maciaszek, L.A., van Sinderen, M. (eds.) ICSOFT 2017. CCIS, vol. 868, pp. 3–27. Springer, Cham (2018). https://doi.org/10.1007/978-3-319-93641-3_1
10. Fowkes, J., Sutton, C.: Parameter-free probabilistic API mining across github. In: Proceedings of the 2016 24th ACM SIGSOFT International Symposium on Foundations of Software Engineering. FSE 2016, New York, NY, USA, pp. 254–265. Association for Computing Machinery (2016). https://doi.org/10.1145/2950290.2950319
11. Hnatkowska, B., Jaszczak, A.: Impact of selected java idioms on source code maintainability – empirical study. In: Zamojski, W., Mazurkiewicz, J., Sugier, J., Walkowiak, T., Kacprzyk, J. (eds.) Proceedings of the Ninth International Conference on Dependability and Complex Systems DepCoS-RELCOMEX. June 30 – July 4, 2014, Brunów, Poland. AISC, vol. 286, pp. 243–254. Springer, Cham (2014). https://doi.org/10.1007/978-3-319-07013-1_23
12. Ji, X., Liu, L., Zhu, J.: Code clone detection with hierarchical attentive graph embedding. Int. J. Software Eng. Knowl. Eng. **31**(06), 837–861 (2021). https://doi.org/10.1142/S021819402150025X
13. Klein, P.N.: Computing the edit-distance between unrooted ordered trees. In: Bilardi, G., Italiano, G.F., Pietracaprina, A., Pucci, G. (eds.) ESA 1998. LNCS, vol. 1461, pp. 91–102. Springer, Heidelberg (1998). https://doi.org/10.1007/3-540-68530-8_8
14. McCabe, T.: A complexity measure. IEEE Trans. Software Eng. **SE-2**(4), 308–320 (1976). https://doi.org/10.1109/TSE.1976.233837
15. Papamichail, M., Diamantopoulos, T., Symeonidis, A.: User-perceived source code quality estimation based on static analysis metrics. In: 2016 IEEE International Conference on Software Quality, Reliability and Security (QRS), pp. 100–107 (2016). https://doi.org/10.1109/QRS.2016.22

16. Papoudakis, A., Karanikiotis, T., Symeonidis, A.: A mechanism for automatically extracting reusable and maintainable code idioms from software repositories. In: Proceedings of the 17th International Conference on Software Technologies - Volume 1: ICSOFT, pp. 79–90. INSTICC, SciTePress (2022). https://doi.org/10.5220/0011279300003266

17. Sivaraman, A., Abreu, R., Scott, A., Akomolede, T., Chandra, S.: Mining idioms in the wild. CoRR abs/2107.06402 (2021). https://arxiv.org/abs/2107.06402

18. Tai, K.C.: The tree-to-tree correction problem. J. ACM **26**(3), 422–433 (1979). https://doi. org/10.1145/322139.322143

19. Tanaka, H., Matsumoto, S., Kusumoto, S.: A study on the current status of functional idioms in Java. IEICE Trans. Inf. Syst. **E102.D**, 2414–2422 (2019). https://doi.org/10.1587/transinf. 2019MPP0002

20. Wang, J., Dang, Y., Zhang, H., Chen, K., Xie, T., Zhang, D.: Mining succinct and high-coverage api usage patterns from source code. In: 2013 10th Working Conference on Mining Software Repositories (MSR), pp. 319–328 (2013). https://doi.org/10.1109/MSR.2013. 6624045

21. Weber, S., Luo, J.: What makes an open source code popular on git hub? In: 2014 IEEE International Conference on Data Mining Workshop, pp. 851–855 (2014). https://doi.org/10. 1109/ICDMW.2014.55

22. Zhang, K., Shasha, D.: Simple fast algorithms for the editing distance between trees and related problems. SIAM J. Comput. **18**(6), 1245–1262 (1989). https://doi.org/10.1137/ 0218082

23. Zhang, Y., Wang, T.: CCEYES: an effective tool for code clone detection on large-scale open source repositories. In: 2021 IEEE International Conference on Information Communication and Software Engineering (ICICSE), pp. 61–70 (2021). https://doi.org/10.1109/ ICICSE52190.2021.9404141

A Deep Learning Architecture Based on Advanced Textual Language Models for Detecting Disease Through Its Symptoms Associated with a Reinforcement Learning Algorithm

Mourad Ellouze[(✉)] and Lamia Hadrich Belguith

ANLP Group MIRACL Laboratory, FSEGS, University of Sfax, Sfax, Tunisia
ellouzemourad@yahoo.fr

Abstract. In this paper, we propose a deep architecture, taking advantage of different methods of artificial intelligence (AI) and advanced textual language models to identify users with a personality disorder disease. This is achieved by measuring the degree of existence of each personality disorder symptom expressed in the text production of social media users. Our proposed approach addresses various issues related to the natural language processing research axis (NLP) based on the advanced machine learning techniques by: (i) combining different model languages to transform text data into numeric data, (ii) using CNN layers to extract only the relevant part of the entry form, (iii) preserving long-term dependencies through the BiLSTM layer which can assist in measuring the degree of symptoms, (iv) using an SVM classifier to identify a disease based on previously identified symptoms, which guarantees that our method employs the human logic by first detecting symptoms, then the disease, (v) applying a relearning method to relearn for every period the new lexicon appering. We obtain an F-measure rate of 72% for measuring symptoms and 68% for detecting paranoid people using this method. The obtained results are motivating and encouraging researchers to improve them given the interest and the importance of this research axis.

Keywords: Personality disorder detection · Language models · Deep neural networks · Reinforcement learning · Social media

1 Introduction

A mental disorder is defined as a significant impairment in cognitive state, emotional regulation, or manifest behaviour, which indicates a dysfunction in psychological, biological, or developmental processes (DSM-5[1]). According to DSM, a person becomes disordered when he extends his particular inadequacy to many of these inner and social life situations which can limit his abilities and cause discomfort with his surroundings. This may cause the sick person to exhibit signs that have a negative impact on himself as well as on the environment, such as behaving impulsively, expressing suicidal

---

[1] DSM-5 is the standard classification of mental disorders used by mental health professionals in the United States.

© The Author(s), under exclusive license to Springer Nature Switzerland AG 2023
H.-G. Fill et al. (Eds.): ICSOFT 2022, CCIS 1859, pp. 207–229, 2023.
https://doi.org/10.1007/978-3-031-37231-5_10

thoughts, driving dangerously, consuming alcohol or drugs excessively, etc. Despite the risk posed by these illnesses, there is an increase in the population of persons suffering from psychological disorders, especially in impoverished countries [23]. In this context, according to [20] Nicaragua has a homicide rate of 8.7 per 100,000 people. In this context, the Nicaragua Women's Network Against Violence reports that 87 women were slain by men in Nicaragua in 2010 and 76 in 2011, whose 37 of these women were murdered by their spouses in 2010 and 34 in 2011. In the same context, the World Health Organization (WHO) has reported that one among four people around the world suffers from mental illness[2]. In spite of those shocking stats, until today the world's nations do not devote enough financial and material resources to address psychological issues and counteract their effects. In this regard, the WHO states that in half of the world's countries, there is only one psychiatrist for every 100,000 people. In addition, 40% of the nations have fewer than one mental health bed for every 10,000 people. For that, the WHO, as the main organization that deals with global health in the word, has included in its "Mental Health Gap Action Programme (mhGAP)" numerous measures for the management of mental disorders. This is accomplished through enhancing the research on mental health and putting forth promotion and preventative techniques to fulfill patients' demands and offer social support services[3].

In the area of scientific research, several researchers have also focused on monitoring patients with a personality disorder by taking advantage of leading-edge technologies like the Internet of Things (IOT) and signal processing. In this context, we can refer to the work of [42], who presented a review of existing research works in the literature address the interest in implementing IoT services and applications in the field of Mental Health diseases. This task was done by linking various physical and virtual components including electronic elements, actuators, sensors, and software allowing to collect and exchange data. Morover, [5] propose an open multi-modal dataset composed of spoken language and EEG data related to depressed people that were carefully selected and diagnosed in hospitals by professional psychiatrists for the study of mental disorders. Despite the importance of these works and the WHO's efforts in terms of social impact, this remains very limited since it requires a lot of resources to analyze a small group of people. For example, over the next ten years, the Canadian federal government plans to invest $5 billion into the mental health care system [29]. It should mentioned that one city as Quebec has allocated $85 million for crisis prevention and response services for mental disorder[4].

Nowadays, social network is one of the most conducive environments in which users can interact and express themselves freely about everything that's going on in the world without fear of censure or punishment. Therefore, social media may provide an appropriate environment for people with personality disorders to exhibit their inappropriate behavior such as violence, aggression, and so on. For this reason, we have seen a significant increase in the level of violence and harassment on social media in recent years. In this context, [32] has affirmed that 20% of users of social media in Venuzwella

---

[2] https://solidarites-sante.gouv.fr/IMG/pdf/projet_territorial_sante_mentale_93.pdf.

[3] https://www.who.int/fr/news-room/fact-sheets/detail/mental-disorders.

[4] https://ici.radio-canada.ca/nouvelle/1857007/sante-mentale-plan-action-interministeriel-carmant-quebec.

has posted Crime-related tweets including murder, violence and sexual crime. All these reactions are due to the symptoms of the different types of personality disorder disease illness such as aggressiveness, grudge, feelings of superiority, expectation of attacks from others, and so on. These effects may represent a dangerous source that affect people morally and physically which makes the navigational environment awkward. In this context, [Statista] affirmed that 64% of women have blocked someone for not being bothered by his messages[5].

As a result, several social media platforms, as Twitter, attempt to block malicious content such as terrorism and violent extremism, child sexual exploitation (CSE), hateful conduct, non-consensual nudity and so on. This was achieved by leveraging the benefits of sharing information collaboratively with industry peers and trusted partners, as well as by using reported tweets[6].

Despite the significance of the work done to date, it should be noted that it is still limited, since according to [Statista], roughly 350 000 tweets are posted every minute (500 million per day)[7]. Aside from the volume criterion, there is the criterion of non-structuring and variety (text, multimedia content, etc.). Nowadays, there is a remarkable evolution of new computer science technologies such as big data tools, artificial intelligence (AI), and natural language processing (NLP). These technologies have been used by several researchers to address the latest mentioned issues. As a result, there are approximately 17 400 results about these three axes in Google scholar, just for the year 2022.

For that, we intend in this work to benefit from these techniques to propose an automatic and intelligent approach as a service for experts and scientists involved in social media data analysis. That may allow them to monitor the health status of people around the world while addressing the ethical issue by anonymizing our data and only using our results in a positive sense. For that, we divided our work in this paper into three objectives:

1. Measure the appearance degree of each symptom of paranoid disease for each user profile from their textual data. That will ensure the reliability of our final results by providing an explanation and justification for our decision. This task was achieved by combining a deep learning CNN-LSTM model with an advanced language model architecture.
2. Detect people with paranoid personality disorder disease by applying a machine learning method to the results of the previous step devoted to the detection of symptoms degrees.
3. Ensure re-learning to take into account the variation of the lexicon over time based on an approach that incorporates the concept of reinforcement learning and a semi-supervised learning method. While using various NLP-related resources.

As demonstrated beyond the social impact ensured by our approach to ensure the well-being of many people around the world. Our approach integrates a significant

---

[5] https://fr.statista.com/statistiques/944602/part-femmes-ayant-deja-bloque-utilisateur-harceleur-sur-site-de-rencontre/.

[6] https://help.twitter.com/en/safety-and-security/phishing-spam-and-malware-links.

[7] https://www.blogdumoderateur.com/chiffres-twitter/.

number of technologies in order to take their benefits into account and address their drawbacks. In our previous work [14], we have worked on the first and the second items. However, in this work, we intend to conduct more experiments on these two items compared to the last cited work. We aim also to incorporate a third item to address other issues related to NLP technique.

We organized our paper as follows. We present in the following section some studies done in this field and their limitations. Next, we describe our methodology in depth, including each step and the various tools used depending on our needs. Then, we present our corpus used and we make a discussion about the results achieved. Finally, we conclude our work with a conclusion and some perspectives.

2   Related Works

Despite the fact that social networks are regarded as a valuable resource for conducting numerous analytical studies due to the large and diverse amount of data that contain. Practically everyone in the world has an account on at least one of their platforms which encourages researchers to invest in these platforms for their research study. However, it should be noted that processing data related to this source is specific in comparison to the processing of data that was obtained from other sources such as clinical reports, corpora derived from academic journals, or social daily journal. This specification is due to the intervention of certain criteria that may influence the generated data. These criteria can be related to the age of the person, the level of his education, the country where he lives etc., or it can group a person's reaction to the published content. Especially as social media is not a formal setting for this reason many users used in their writing style irony, sarcasm, etc. Furthermore, social media platforms disregard grammatical conventions like capitalization, punctuation and so on. Even sometimes their users use words that do not belong to the lexicon of a particular language, and in several cases, they form a single sentence in more than one language, etc. Therefore, all of these side effects can disrupt treatment afterward, but they have not discouraged researchers to choose social media data as their primary source. In this section, we have divided the various papers analyzed as part of the analysis of personality disorders into two parts.

2.1   Explicit Treatment of Personality Disorders

Detecting psychological problems explicitly involves detecting personality disorders or symptoms of those disorders. In this context, several researchers have proposed different methods using different approaches such as approaches based on classic machine learning techniques, neuronal techniques, or statistics techniques.

The work [41] is one among the works that employed methods that are part of classic machine learning techniques. The authors of this work proposed an approach for identifying whether a person is depressed based on the analysis of their textual production on the Vkontakte[8] application. Next, they used SVM to perform the classification step, exploring several morphological criteria such as *the number of verbs, pronouns,*

---

[8] The most used social network in Russia.

infinitive form, etc.. In the same context [31] presented an approach for mental disorders detection on social networks using machine learning techniques. The collection of data was done manually from Facebook. The different features used in this work include firstly social interactions between individuals and secondly personal characteristics such as *honesty* and *sincerity*. The objective of this work was to classify the profiles of people using Naïve Bayes into three classes: 1. Dependence on the cybernetic relationship (CR), 2. Net compulsion (NC), 3. Information overload (IO). Moreover, [40] were working in the same area by proposing an approach based on NLP[9] and machine learning techniques to detect antisocial people from their behaviors on Twitter. After the step of data collection that has been done using keywords. A step of transforming the textual data into a matrix was done by taking advantage of TF-IDF measure. Then, by using the "Random Forest" algorithm which gave a high F-measure rate, each tweet is classified as antisocial or not antisocial.

Other works have focused on detecting users with a psychological problem using an approach based on neuronal techniques. We can cite in this context, [26] among the works that used methods that are part of this approach to detect automatically the stress of individuals via social networks. Starting with the step of extracting features which includes: (i) features related to a single tweet such as *text, social interactions*, (ii) statistical features related to a user such as *time, types, and writing styles of a tweet*. Then, using a convolutional neural network (CNN) with auto-encoders to combine weekly low-level content features and generate user-scope features. Finally, taking advantage of a neural network model (DNN) to learn higher-level features and detect the psychological stress of users. In the same context, [15] sought to detect people with paranoid disorder from a set of their posts on Twitter, the set of features used in this work includes text, meta-data, timeline and linguistic types. While using the principal component analysis technique (PCA) in order to reduce the size of the different features to not influence the performance of the combination of the two algorithms (LSTM+SVM) in the classification task. This work repeat the task of classification but in the second case to classify each tweet talking about Covid-19 topic into two classes (appropriate behavior or inappropriate behavior) in order to detect the behavior of people with paranoid disease towards the epidemic. The purpose of this task is to monitor the mental health of sick persons.

2.2 Implicit Treatment of Personality Disorders

The detection of personality disorder with implicit way, meaning the possibility to detect the consequences of psychological disorders such as *violence and suicide*. In this context [36] took advantage of data mining and NLP techniques to detect violent tweets based on the calculation of n-gram weights. To perform that, an expert selected profiles of people who are extremist and profiles of people who are not extremist. Then, they built using the profiles selected 2 types of lexicon. Each lexicon is composed of simple and compound words in the form of n-gram While indicating the weight (degree) of belonging of a word to this lexicon. Finally, they used statistical measurement to calculate the degree of belonging of a tweet to each class. Thus, [1] has as objective the

---

[9] Natural Language Processing.

detection of weird tweets by classifying them into four classes: *compliance, dominance, submission, and influence*. The result of this work is a visualization in different forms of output *(graph,..)* to show the distinction of simple and compound words between classes. In general, this visualization can facilitate the dissemination of knowledge.

Detection of suicide on social media is an evolutionary axis of research. For that [27] proposed an approach to detect profiles of people with suicidal ideation from Twitter using a classification algorithm. Several features related to several information have been used to perform the classification step such as: (1) linguistic features like *POS*[10], *frequent word, n-gram, etc.*, (2) emotional features such as *emojis, depression terms, etc.*, (3) facial features such as *age, hair, mustache, etc,* which are extracted from the profile photo of the user, (4) chronology features such as *the number of publications per day, per month, etc.*, (5) public information such as *country, etc.*.

In [13], the authors have proposed other way to detect the PD implicitly, this by taking advantage of the annotation of the corpus @PanClef2015 for author profiling task [34]. This corpus is annotated to detect the degree of each personality trait of people in social networks. For this reason, it presents for each text of a specific user five values between [−0.5, +0.5], indicating the presence degree of each personality trait. In the last cited work, the authors consider that if the value predicted for a specific personality trait is between [−0.5, −0.1] therefore the person has an unstable situation. To do that, They present an idea that combine: (i) lexico-semantic approach using word embedding and WordNet knowledge base resources, (ii) statistical measurement to calculate the similarity between the results of the proposed approach and the annotation performed. The statistical measure is used in this context to take advantage of the notion of fuzzy logic to handle the limitations of machine learning techniques that are based on a deterministic approach.

2.3   Limits Analysis

After the analysis of the different mentioned papers, we note that most of authors have focused on the detection of the consequences of psychological diseases such as violence, terrorism or suicide [1,27,36]. However, only a few researchers who worked on the detection of personality disorders types cited by DSM-5. Even those who worked on disease detection did not follow a specific treatment based on human logic, which makes their results not explainable and interpretable. Moreover, we note an excessive use of the English language, despite the existence of other languages with the same importance. Besides, several authors do not take into account the different issues related to the natural language processing. In this context, several papers are based on the lexical approach [36] which is articultaed on the research of keywords from the corpus (lexicons related to each class). Among problems related to this technique is the difficulty of finding a training corpus which includes all lexicons related to a specific class. Moreover, there are many problems related to this approach such as the variation in the lexicon over time also this approach allow to detect explicit information but not implicit information. In addition, they do not treat linguistic phenomena such as relation between words. We

---

[10] Part of speech.

note also an excessive use of machine learning algorithms in classic way [26,41] which makes the obtained results very abstracts, lack of explanation and difficult to interpret.

3 Proposed Approach

In this study, we propose an approach illustrated in Fig. 1 allowing Twitter to analyse in real time the textual production of their users in order to apply the whole process of diagnosis committed by the psychiatrist. This process involves listening to the patient's cries, identifying the various symptoms and the disease while taking into account the evolution of the world's lexicon.

This was accomplished using a novel deep learning model that included a set of convolution layers (CNN) for the task of automatic features extraction from textual data. This is due that, in the context of detecting implicit information we do not precisely know the criteria needed to recognize the class. Next, we used a BiLSTM layer to highlight the long-distance dependencies between the different lexical units in order to classify the degree of each paranoid disease symptom from the textual part. Then, we employed SVM algorithm in order to detect paranoid disease based on the degree of each symptom because SVM is one of the most adaptable learning algorithms (see Fig. 2 extracted from our previous work [14]). Finally, we included a relearning phase in our approach that allows to take into account the evolution of the lexicon over time using the reinforcement technique.

In addition, our approach addresses other issues at the same time such as: (1) the imbalanced corpus by using the synthetic data generation step, (2) the lexical approach, using the sentence embedding technique allowing to determine the meaning of a word in the sentence.

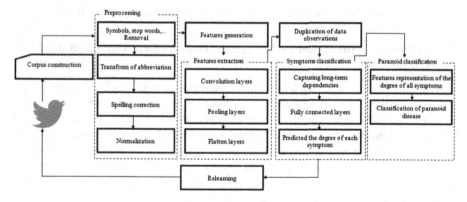

Fig. 1. Diagram of the proposed approach for the detection of paranoid disease through the detection of its symptoms associated with a relearning phase.

3.1 Pretreatment of Twitter's Text Portion

In this step, we focused on preparing our corpus by removing unnecessary elements that do not differentiate between classes. This is to avoid negatively affecting the subsequent

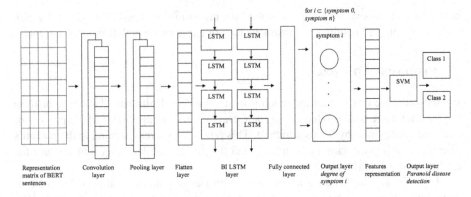

Fig. 2. Deep CNN-LSTM-SVM proposed model for detecting paranoid disease based on the detection of the degree of its symptoms [14].

processing, especially that our work is based on data obtained from Web 2.0 [30]. This task was done by following these steps: For the first time, we removed all stop words including articulatory words such as *and, also, therefore, etc.*. These words are used by any anyone, therefore they do not help in distinguishing between different classes. Following that, we removed from our data-set the various symbols used to express money, time, number, and so on. Then, in order to standardize our corpus, we changed capital letters to lowercase letters and acronyms to their full forms using the resource Google Graph Knowledge like *AI* to *Artificial Intelligence*. Finally, we converted the inflectional shapes of words into a common root to make our approach behaves in the same way for words having the same common root as *transform, transformation, transforming, etc.*. This step was done using the library NLTK (Natural Language Toolkit).

3.2 Extraction of the High-Level of Textual Features from Our Pre-trained Corpus

This step consists of converting textual data into numerical vectors which can be manipulated by machine learning algorithms. According to our assessment of multiple works, there are numerous techniques to accomplish this transformation, we cite the Word Embedding technique [4] as the most frequently utilized. However, The main issue with this technique is that it does not retain the whole meaning of the sentence. That makes a difficulty for the algorithm to assess the text's nuance and intention. For this reason, we decide to perform the transformation using the sentence embedding technique. We describe some models of this technique below:

- Universal Sentence Encoder (USE) [6] is a language model for encoding textual data into high-dimensional vectors. These vectors are a digital representation of text data. This model is trained on various data sources such as Wikipedia, web news, web question-answer pages, and discussion forums to learn for a wide range of NLP tasks, as text semantic similarity, classification, and clustering. The USE model has demonstrated an excellent performance on the semantic textual similarity benchmark (STS).

- InferSent [35] is a sentence embeddings method that is presented by Facebook AI Research in 2018, it provides a semantic representation of sentences. It is trained using data obtained from Natural Language Inference (NLI) resource, more especially, the Stanford Natural Language Inference dataset (SNLI). It is composed of 570k pairs of human-generated English sentences, that have been manually labeled with one of the three categories: contradiction, entailment, or neutral. It is well generalized to a wide range of NLP-related tasks.
- Language-Agnostic SEntence Representations (Laser) [3] is a set of scripts and models developed by Facebook research group to compute multi-lingual sentence embedding for cross-lingual transfer with zero-shot. Therefore, LASER has the ability to convert into language-independent vectors, which means regardless of the input language, similar words are mapped to close vectors. This technique help for example Facebook and others NLP-related tasks, for classifying movie reviews as favorable or unfavorable. This task is ensured by implementing a model in one language and then expanding it to more than 100 additional languages.
- SImple SenTence EmbeddeR (SISTER) [9]: This model is composed of 300 dimensions of pretrained word embedding. It try to build the sentence embedding based on FastText model. This model supports the following languages: English, Japanese, French.
- Paragraph Vector (Doc2Vec) [25]: It is an unsupervised algorithm based on extension of Word2Vec technique. This model was introduced in 2014 and it can be considered as one of the most popular techniques of sentence embedding. When compared to Word2Vec, Word2Vec learns to project words into a latent d dimension space, whereas Doc2Vec seeks to learn how to project a text into a latent d dimension space.
- Bidirectional Encoder Representations of Transformers (Bert) [10]: it is a pretrained language representation model. This model has demonstrated a good performance due to its architecture, which combines a multi-layer bidirectional Transformer encoder with multiple attention heads. The cited model was trained using a corpus that included books and english Wikipedia resource through the Masked Language Modeling (MLM), also the Next Sentence Prediction (NSP) which enables it to solve the classification problem in small corpora.
- RoBERTa [28]: Compared to BERT, RoBERTa's training methodology integrates an extended MLM technique rather than an NSP. In addition, the RoBERTa model is trained on a larger corpus, and it includes more informal text data in the training phase such as a Reddit corpus.
- DistilBERT [38]: The objective of DistilBERT is to reduce the size of the core BERT model, making it less computationally costly alternative and more attractive. However, the DistilBERT model preserves the majority of BERT's language understanding and general-purpose training.
- XLM BERT Base [43]: The XLM model is a multilingual version of distilroberta-v1, which was trained on parallel data obtained from more than 50 languages and composed of millions of sentence fragments.
- XLNET [8]: This model is a generalized autoregressive language model (AR) that enables permutation language modeling (PLM) for learning in bidirectional contexts. XLNet employs the functioning principle of the autoencoder language model

and the autoregressive language model while avoiding their limits. In addition, XLNet surpasses BERT, on twenty challenges, including, natural language inference, sentiment analysis, question answering and document ranking.

Following an empirical study, we decided to focus more on the languages models based on BERT and their combination since these models are trained on a large amount of data. Moreover, they have a specific architecture that enables them to learn in a deep bi-directional representations also they accept a large number of parameters, making them more adaptable [11]. Generally, these techniques are based on calculating the similarity between sentences by using pooling layers in order to retain only important descriptors. In addition, these techniques produce a set of standardized vectors while resolving many well-known issues related to the size of the data set and the diversity of vocabularies in the corpus. In our study, we have only relied on textual data and we do not use other kinds of information such as the number of retweets per tweet or the number of retweets per user. This is because we have used data that was collected in a streaming way, therefore at the beginning, the value of these properties is null. In addition, our approach is based on a deep learning approach so its particular architecture offers assistance to separate automatically the relevant features from the raw data.

3.3   Selection of the Most Relevant Features Extracted

After automatically extracting the various features from our corpus. We ended up with a huge number of features that could have a negative impact on the execution time of our approach. Besides, the classifier may later be deceived because they may contain parasites. There are numerous methods for filtering these features, including correlation measures, which express the degree to which each feature has a linear relationship with the class. Thus, the principal component analysis (PCA) [21] is a data reduction technique that converts a large number of correlated variables into a smaller set of correlated variables known as principal components. As stated above, we intend to apply deep learning techniques to each step of our work, given the recent interest of these techniques for various tasks, including those related to NLP.

For this reason, we used in our work the Convolutional Neural Network (CNN) architecture [2] since it performed well on different tasks of natural language processing, given its ability to capture both syntactic and semantic aspects [12]. The architecture of the Convolutional Neural Network differs from the classic architecture of the Multi Layers Perceptron model (MLP) [39], this difference mainly revolves around the convolutional part. The execution of this task was done by flowing the input (tweets) through a succession of filters, the output of these filters is called convolution maps. The resulting convolution maps are concatenated into a feature vector called CNN code.

3.4   Synthetic Generation of Data Observations for Obtaining a Balanced Corpus

In this step, we aim to maximize the number of instances given the difficulty of annotating the collected data in order to obtain balanced data. For this purpose, there are various methods like Exploratory Data Analysis (EDA) for handling duplicate records, Multi-objective Genetic Sampling for Imbalanced Classification (E-MOSAIC) [18], Synthetic Minority Over-sampling Technique (SMOTE) [7], etc. Following an empirical study, we decided to use the SMOTE technique, since it has demonstrated great success in a variety applications and fields [22, 33], especially that our corpus is not tied to a specific field. This technique aims to addressing imbalanced datasets by oversampling the minority class. The simplest technique of SMOTE involves duplicating examples in the minority class, but these examples do not provide any new insights into the model. In order to generate new synthetic data, SMOTE uses the closest neighbours' algorithm.

3.5 Capturing Long-Term Dependencies for Symptoms Classification Task

LSTM is an extension of RNN architecture that was created to address RNN's problem of explosion and vanishing gradient since we may encounter unknown-duration lags between the various events of a time series [19]. Therefore, using LSTM the information can be efficiently controlled since it try to detect the long-term correlations in arbitrary length sequences while avoiding vanishing gradient. As illustrated in Fig. 3, the LSTM architecture includes a newly added memory cell that selectively retains information for a longer period of time without degeneration. Thus, for processing the input vectors, LSTM implements recursive execution of the current cell block using the former hidden state (ht1) and the current input C_t, where (t) and (t-1) denote, respectively, the present time and the previous time. Therefore, the LSTM network is dedicated to the classification, processing and the realization of predictions based on time series data. In our work, we chose to use BiLSTM in order to maintain the dependency links between the lexicon extracted and selected in previous steps [44]. For that, we concatenated the output of the convolutional layer to two LSTM layers in order to measure the interdependence of terms. The last layer is composed of 6 neurons (numbered 0 to 5) that assess the severity of each disease symptom such as negative interpretation of the gestures of others, exaggerated mistrust, incessant doubt, etc. The low occurrences of certain degrees are the reason for considering the challenge as a classification rather than a regression. The classification process was repeated nine times (the most appeared

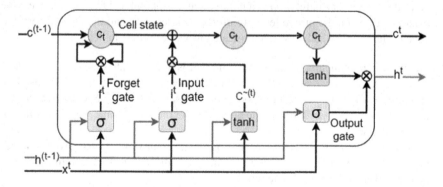

Fig. 3. Long-term memory structure including memory cell.

number of symptoms of paranoid disease). In fact in each case, we focus on detecting the degree of a specific symptom. This is due that in our case it is a multi-label issue, a person can suffer from more than one symptom at the same time.

3.6   Classical Binary Classification for Paranoid Detection Task

The task of disease detection is extremely sensitive due to the lack of specific rules that allow for decision-making. For example, it is not necessary for a person to exhibit all symptoms in order to be identified as having the illness. Moreover, it is difficult to find someone who has simultaneously these symptoms constant doubt and self-confidence. In addition, there are numerous combinations of symptom degrees to detect precisely the disease. For that, in this step, we used the degree of all symptoms detected in the previous step related to a specific person in order to generate a vector that enumerate the list of symptoms. After that, we handed this vector to the SVM layer for making the detection of the disease. In this sub-section, the number of features is reduced for that we limited ourselves by using the classical classification algorithms such as SVM, Naive Bayes, decision tree, etc.

In our case, we choose to use the SVM algorithm since we have an important number of features with varying importance also we seek to make a binary classification. The SVM classifier concept aims to place the best hyperplane in such a way that it separates all the data points related to a class from those in the other class. The hyperplane with the biggest margin between the two classes is the optimum hyperplane for the algorithm. Margin refers to the maximum width of the slab parallel to the hyperplan which does not have internal data points.

3.7   Re-learning

Every language's lexicon evolves over time, with new words appearing and disappearing depending on the circumstances of life. This evolution cannot be treated by supervised learning algorithms because the learning stage is only performed once. This may have a negative impact on the result over time (the learning phase's lexicon is associated with a specific time period). In order to create an approach that can track the evolution of the vocabulary in relation to a temporal and geographical framework, we were motivated to draw on the principles of reinforcement learning and the semi-supervised approach. The steps listed below demonstrate our work process in detail:

1. We categorize both simple and compound words that indicate the presence of each symptom into two categories (high indication $>= 3$, low indication <3) based on common words between different symptom classes. This is done while treating the notion of negation (see Table 1, the choice of the threshold value was done after an empirical study).
2. We enriched our lexical base (for each group) with context words using word embedding [24] and WordNet [16] resources since it is difficult to find a training corpus that includes all the appropriate words.

Table 1. An example of some raw forms of words (translated to English) belonging to each category.

Symptoms	Categories	Words
feeling the superiority	high indication	if I trust you, I'm the only one, I despise you, I want not to scare them, I abused them,
	low indication	To be frank, I'm the one who was supposed to, he had marked me, I'm my only priority,
aggressiveness	high indication	I'm so pissed off, I'll stop you right there, I want to kill myself, Overthrow this power,
	low indication	I swore, We demand the cancellation, I wanted to react anyway, It's time to talk loud,

3. We compared the degree of belonging of the new instance (a set of 20 tweets) to each category of words using the score returned by Google Knowledge Graph [17] for each combination of two words. Then, we apply the different rules obtained using Jhonson algorithm [37]. For example, if we discovered that among a person's 20 tweets, more than 10 words fall into the category of low indication of the symptom *aggressiveness*. Thus, this person uses more than 5 terms that fall into the category of highly indicative aggressiveness symptoms, we can infer that this person exhibit high levels of aggression ($>= 3$).
4. We compared the results of our rules with the predicted value by the relearning algorithm. If our criteria suggest that the new instance contains a high level of aggressiveness and the relearning algorithm anticipated that the degree of aggressiveness is 3, 4, or 5. In this case, we believe the algorithm's response is correct (due to the challenge of developing exact standards for determining the severity of each symptom). In this case, the algorithm will use this instance later to do the relearning process once more, otherwise, it will abound this case.

Note 1: It is possible that the abandoned case is correct and that our algorithm did not make a mistake, but we decided to drop it because we want to do the relearning part with data that is highly accurate.

Note 2: This work is dedicated just for the detection of symptoms task since our input is a lexicon that varies over time. For the task of disease detection we have been limited by the data set obtained.

4 Experiments and Results

This section presents the different details about our data-set, LSTM settings for "negative interpretation of others' actions" symptom classification and an extract of our results. This work has been implemented using the python programming language which integrates the Tensorflow framework.

4.1 Dataset

We applied our method to a set of tweets containing a vocabulary related to the disease's negative effects of personality disorders such as *I congratulate myself, I am in the confusion of, I am wary, etc.* This data was obtained in real time using Apache Spark Streaming tool for tweets written in French language from 01-03-2020 to 30-05-2020.

Two psychiatrists were asked to double annotate this corpus based on their knowledge and experience. In order to construct a manual of annotation and to better understand the intricacies associated with the language of social networks. The annotation process started with an empirical investigation of a 10% portion of the corpus. The remaining 90% of the corpus was then annotated separately by each annotator. Both forms of classification's annotations are done independently, therefore for each user profile's (20 tweets), each annotator provides the following information: (i) the degree of each symptom (a number between 0 and 5 where 0 indicates the absence of the symptom and 5 indicates the high degree of the presence of a symptom), (ii) their decision about the state of the person *normal person* or *paranoid person*. We consider someone with a paranoid personality disorder if in their last 20 tweets there is a redundancy of language indicators that show the symptoms of this disease. In this context, we can take as an example the semantic information indicating terrible disturbance and fear. The Table 2 shows some expressions for the two symptoms overestimation of self and underestimation of others.

Table 2. Example of tweets (translated to English) indicating the presence of the two symptoms overestimation of self and underestimation of others.

Underestimation of others	Overestimation of self
The police unions' communication is aimed at attacking journalists and lawyers to attract a base	If I confide in you, tell you that you are not just anyone
The government and #LREM refuse. A quick recap of government transparency on the subject #Neveragain	I need people to get to know me, how I work and to adapt to support me
This guy is not afraid of anything, he is a stupid incompetent but he comes back to teach us the absolute truth	I am really only good with myself and I have always been "self-sufficient"
This government smells like shit because it is shit.	In any case, anyone who wants to harm me in any network, ...is useless and without effect because I belong to Christ
Pfff...too bad, too close to reality...	sometimes you can have a feeling of superiority over them

We set a limit of 20 tweets per user because we aim to develop an approach that is able to recognize people with PD through the fewest number of tweets possible. That to guarantee early prevention while ensuring the credibility of the results obtained.

The choice of paranoid symptoms are based on the most well-known symptoms of paranoid disorder. We have chosen to present each of them at levels 1–5 to be more precise. Following the annotation phase in which the two experts annotated the degree of presence of symptoms as well as the presence of the disease, we proceed to calculate the rate of agreement between these two experts using Cohen's Kappa. In this context, a value of 0.9 was obtained for disease detection and 0.73 for symptom level detection. Conflicting cases are mainly related to the misinterpretation of cases (misinterpretation in measuring the degree of the intensity of symptoms as well as between missing information or diligence). We describe below some examples showing cases of disagreement:

1. The overlap in the interpretation for example *It is the strongest woman that I know* (exaggeration which indicates a strong dependence or gratitude).
2. The redundancy of reduced messages which contain expressions such as *no, it is not possible, it's not logical* (frequent refusals or we should know the reason why he said "no", they are not vulgar words like an insult).
3. The measure of the intensity of expression and the combination between them to judge the case.

For that, We asked our experts to reconvene and choose between (agreement or removal) conflicting cases. Tables 3 and 4 show in more detail the distribution of tweets used per class.

Note 1: In our work, we have used the same corpus used in our previous work [14], since in the literature we have not found any corpus that annotated by degree of symptoms and disease at same. However, we have annotated new data composed of 600 tweets related to 30 users for the relearning part.

Note 2: Table 4 shows the number of paranoid symptoms displayed by each user in Table 3, implying that one person in Table 3 can appear up to nine times in Table 4.

Note 3: It should be noted that, in certain cases, we have encountered difficulties in collecting data. For example, for people who think they are always right or they are always isolated, they do not have to talk to other people in order to try to persuade them. Especially for the first case, that tend to be self-absorbed. While in the case of "reading hidden meanings in the innocent remarks" and "recurrent suspicions", everything can be a trigger and an inducement for these people to write and show which is not expressed (hidden ideas).

Table 3. The distribution of instances for paranoid classification [14].

Paranoid	YES	NO
Number of instances	280 users (5600 tweets)	450 users (9000 tweets)

Table 4. The distribution of instances for symptoms classification [14].

Symptoms	Number of instances
aggressiveness	121 users (2420 tweets)
perceives attacks	163 users (3260 tweets)
recurrent suspicions	282 users (5640 tweets)
isolation	46 users (920 tweets)
believing they are always right	76 users (1520 tweets)
read hidden meanings in the innocent remarks	227 users (4540 tweets)
poor relationships with others	273 users (5460 tweets)
doubt the commitment	193 users (3860 tweets)
unforgiving and hold grudges	187 users (3740 tweets)

4.2   Results

In our work, we used three convolution layers, 320 feature maps, and an activation function called "Relu" for the various settings that were applied to each layer in our model. Moreover, three pooling layers with a pool size of (1,9). Then, we used two LSTM layers, the first of which had 250 neurons and the second had 150 neurons, along with a hidden layer that had "softmax" as its activation function. Finally, we used an output layer, which had six neurons (representing the degree of each symptom). We carried out this work nine times (number of symptoms), and in each instance, we predicted a value that corresponds to the degree of each symptom. We used the same parameters of our model of CNN input and output presented in our previous work [14] as it shown in the Table 5.

Table 5. Model parameter structure [14].

Layer type	Output shape	Param#
Input Layer	(768,1)	
conv1d (Conv1D)	(768, 320)	3200
max_pooling1d	(233, 320)	0
dropout (Dropout)	(233, 320)	0
conv1d_1 (Conv1D)	(233, 320)	921920
max_pooling1d_1	(85, 320)	0
dropout_1 (Dropout)	(85, 320)	0
conv1d_2 (Conv1D)	(85, 320)	921920
max_pooling1d_2	(9, 320)	0
dropout_2 (Dropout)	(9, 320)	0
time_distributed	(1, 8000)	0
lstm (LSTM)	(250)	1211000
lstm_1 (LSTM)	(100)	240600
classification layer	6	906

The vector composed of the degree of the nine symptoms obtained in the previous step was then passed to an SVM layer for classification of paranoid disease. We used the SVM layer with a linear kernel and gamma scale because our instances are linearly separable. For the purpose of managing these numerous layers and their settings, we use the Python programming language. The following Table 6 shows an excerpt of our results for paranoid's symptoms degrees detection.

4.3   Evaluation

We evaluated the performance of our various tasks by applying the classical criteria recall, precision, and F-measure to each type of classification (symptoms, disease). We calculated the mentioned criteria for the results of our model's first output layer for the classification of symptom degrees (degree of symptom i) which means for each symptom of paranoid disease. For the assessment of the classification of paranoid disease results, we applied the last cited criteria to the results of the last layer of our model.

Note 1: The error rate calculated for the detection of symptom degrees is included in the evaluation of the classification of paranoid disorder.

Table 6. Extract of results (translate to English) of paranoid's symptoms degrees detection.

user's tweets	underestimation of others	overestimation of self
1. on a regarder naruto mais vu que ta compris que t'etais en tors tu veut essayer de mettre fin au débat conclusion. (we watched naruto but since you understood that you were wrong you want to try to end the debate conclusion.) 2. Mais sal merde t'es con ou tu fait exprès. (But damn it, are you stupid or are you doing it on purpose) 3. Sa sert a rien il veut pas ce rendre compte qu'il est dans le floue. (It's useless, he doesn't want to realize that he's in the dark.) 4. Be rikoudo il donne son chakra a naruto et sasuke mais il en avait deja que je sache (be rikoudo he gives his chakra to naruto and sasuke but he already had some as far as I know.) 5. Tes con c le site officiel du manga sal merde. (Your stupid c the official site of the manga damn it.) 6. Trop de fierté pour avoué que ta tords t'ira pas loins mon gars. (Too proud to admit that your wrong won't go far my guye.) 7. C'est un truc avéré par le createur du manga lui même alors chut stp. (it's a thing proven by the creator of the manga himself so shh please.) 8. Putain t'a lu l'article ou pas. (Damn did you read the article or not.) 9. Bientot y vas nous dire que rock lee et gai sensei ils ont pas de chakra. (Soon you will tell us that rock lee and gay sensei they have no chakra.) 10. Ya bien écrit a TOUS LES HUMAINS alors un humain sans chakra sa n'existe pas.(Well written to ALL HUMANS then a human without chakra does not exist.) 11. Lit le truc que j'ai mit et ferme bien ta gueule. (Read the thing that I put and shut your mouth.) 12. Be il marche pas, c trop vieux car au temps de naruto dans sa génération vivre sans chakra c impossible. (Well it doesn't work, it's too old because at the time of naruto in his generation living without chakra it's impossible.) 13. Bref t'a pas un exemple qui marche ? (Anyway, do you have an example that works?)	3	2

The evaluation of our method for symptoms detection using the various languages models is shown in greater detail in the various Tables 7, 8, 9 and 10. The Table 11 shows the improvement due to the use of the re-learning step compared to our baseline and our previous work [14]. The Table 12 shows the results of our approach for Paranoid disease detection. The Table 13 shows the results of our approach for Paranoid disease detection in comparison to the two baselines. The variation between baselines 1 [12] and 2 [14] demonstrates the impact of the layer allowing the detection of symptoms

Table 7. Comparison of F-score for each language model of sentence embedding for symptoms classification.

Symptoms	Doc2Vect	Laser	USE	BERT
aggressiveness	64	71	69	79
perceives attacks	55	68	64	66
recurrent suspicions	49	60	63	61
isolation	68	80	81	81
believing they are always right	66	83	78	81
read hidden meanings in the innocent remarks	53	64	65	69
poor relationships with others	48	54	57	53
doubt the commitment	59	69	66	71
unforgiving and hold grudges	67	78	79	80

Table 8. Comparison of F-score for each language model of sentence embedding based on BERT model for symptoms classification.

Symptoms	BERT	XLNET	RoBerta	Distlbert	XLM
aggressiveness	76	79	79	76	76
perceives attacks	68	66	68	66	65
recurrent suspicions	60	60	63	61	61
isolation	81	80	81	79	78
believing they are always right	81	81	83	81	82
read hidden meanings in the innocent remarks	67	65	72	68	70
poor relationships with others	57	54	57	51	48
doubt the commitment	69	69	66	69	70
unforgiving and hold grudges	77	78	79	79	78

before the disease on the results. The comparison of the baseline 2 and our approach is intended to demonstrate the effect of the relearning step on the final results.

Note 2: We used the cross-validation technique for our approach's evaluation task. It should be noted that each time we switch between the training folds and the test fold. We apply only the SMOTE technique to the training folds to avoid influencing the evaluation results of our approach.

Note 3: We were tolerated in assessing symptoms levels classification results, this is at the acceptance level of (+1) difference between the real and the predicted value (the opposite direction is not acceptable). However, this remains true except in cases where the value is between 1 and 5, indicating that our system made an error in the degree selection rather than the presence of the symptom.

Table 9. F-score comparison for the combination of various sentence embedding models based on BERT model for symptom classification.

Symptoms	Bert+Roberta	BERT+Distil.	Roberta+Distil.	BERT+Roberta+Distil.
aggressiveness	79	71	73	78
perceives attacks	70	65	64	65
recurrent suspicions	59	50	56	58
isolation	80	65	65	76
believing they are always right	81	72	74	74
read hidden meanings in the innocent remarks	70	64	65	67
poor relationships with others	55	47	50	55
doubt the commitment	68	58	61	65
unforgiving and hold grudges	80	69	74	81

Table 10. Variation of the RoBerta model's recall, precision, and F-measure according to the LSTM classifier.

Symptoms	Recall	Precision	F-measure
aggressiveness	81	77	79
perceives attacks	68	68	68
recurrent suspicions	64	63	63
isolation	84	78	81
believing they are always right	83	83	83
read hidden meanings in the innocent remarks	75	69	72
poor relationships with others	57	57	57
doubt the commitment	71	61	66
unforgiving and hold grudges	81	77	79

Table 11. F-score comparison of our results with the baseline results for symptom classification.

Symptoms	[14]	Our approach
aggressiveness	76	79
perceives attacks	68	68
recurrent suspicions	60	63
isolation	81	81
believing they are always right	81	83
read hidden meanings in the innocent remarks	67	72
poor relationships with others	53	57
doubt the commitment	69	66
unforgiving and hold grudges	77	79

Table 12. Variation of Recall, Precision and F-measure according to the selected classifier.

	Gradient Boosting	KNN	AdaBoost	Random Forest	SVM
Recall	61	65	67	63	69
Precision	59	63	65	62	67
F-measure	60	64	66	62	**68**

Table 13. Comparison of our results with the baseline results for the classification of paranoid using recall, precision, and F-measure.

	Recall (%)	Precision (%)	F-measure (%)
Baseline 1 [12]	59	53	56
Baseline 2 [14]	66	64	65
Our architecture	**70**	**66**	**68**

5   Discussion

This paper introduced an intelligent approach based on machine learning and natural language processing techniques. Our objective using this approach is to assess the rate of the presence degrees of symptoms in order to identify in a next step paranoid disease among people using Twitter. This work takes into account the limitations listed in the related works section by respecting the logical progression for diagnosing the disease (detect the disease through its symptoms) which makes our results precise, interpretable and reliable. Moreover, detecting symptoms may help Twitter in the task of filtering inappropriate content with different way. For example if a tweet is posted by a person with a high rate of aggressiveness there is a high probability that this tweet contains inappropriate content and in this case Twitter can hide his content. In addition, we used the entire deep learning approach in our work (features extraction and classification techniques) since we do not know exactly which are the relevant characteristics that help to distinguish the various classes. Moreover, we addressed issues associated with the size and the unbalanced corpus using the technique of data generation. Thus, issues with the lexical method that can be resolved using BERT-based sentence embedding technique, which deals with the meaning of the words in sentences. Besides, our approach take into account the evolution of the lexicon over time, using the relearning step. Our classification process takes into account the notion of detecting hidden information such as personality disorder. For that, it consults a history of a person's publications and not just working on one tweet as well as to carry out a deep analysis which has been done by using deep learning algorithms. We got the most satisfactory results for the following symptoms classification degrees: *believing they are always right* and *isolation* for all language models used. We obtained the poorest results (F-measure equal to 51%) for the classification of *poor relationships with others symptom*. This distinction results from the language specificity associated with each symptom class and the way of reacting of the algorithm to various circumstances. In the same context, get the most accurate result for the classification of symptom *believing they are always right* even the lack of data compared to the symptom *poor relationships with others*. This is supported by the fact that the second symptom is measured by four degrees with a high error rate, but in the first case the symptom is measured using just two degrees since we do not find a wide range of data in this context. Moreover, we may conclude that the task of data generation has assisted us in solving the issue of data reduction. For the task of disease classification, we achieved the best results with SVM algorithm because the various instances of our corpus are linearly separated. As regards the mean results achieved for the detection of certain symptoms in relation to the results of the detection of the disease, this is due to the: (i) linguistic phenomena such as negations, irony, and so on, (ii) high level of symptoms not similar to the binary classification of the disease, (iii) issues related to the use of features with lexicon format (an idea can be written in more than one way, general lexicon, and so on). Finally, this work offers Twitter the opportunity to monitor the health state of its users (if the degree of symptom evolution is greater than x time or if any new symptom that appear over time).

6   Conclusion

In this paper, we proposed a method for detecting people with paranoid personality disorder by detecting their symptoms. This method has an advantage over other works in that it provides explanatory results by displaying the reasons (symptoms) for each final result of disease detection. Furthermore, it uses a deep learning approach that combines feature extraction and classification tasks at the same time. In addition, through the task of generating data it addresses problems of unbalanced data and reduced size of the corpus. Our proposed method was implemented and evaluated, and the achieved results are encouraging, indeed, the F-measure rate for symptoms classification is equal to 72% and the F-measure for paranoid classification is equal to 68%. As perspectives, we envisage testing our approach on several other types of personality disorders with other particular application fields.

References

1. Ahmad, N., Siddique, J.: Personality assessment using twitter tweets. Procedia Comput. Sci. **112**, 1964–1973 (2017)
2. Albawi, S., Mohammed, T.A., Al-Zawi, S.: Understanding of a convolutional neural network. In: 2017 International Conference on Engineering and Technology (ICET), pp. 1–6. IEEE (2017)
3. Artetxe, M., Schwenk, H.: Massively multilingual sentence embeddings for zero-shot cross-lingual transfer and beyond. corr abs/1812.10464 (2018). arXiv preprint arXiv:1812.10464 (2018)
4. Bakarov, A.: A survey of word embeddings evaluation methods. arXiv preprint arXiv:1801.09536 (2018)
5. Cai, H., et al.: A multi-modal open dataset for mental-disorder analysis. Sci. Data **9**(1), 1–10 (2022)
6. Cer, D., et al.: Universal sentence encoder. arXiv preprint arXiv:1803.11175 (2018)
7. Chawla, N.V., Bowyer, K.W., Hall, L.O., Kegelmeyer, W.P.: Smote: synthetic minority over-sampling technique. J. Artif. Intell. Res. **16**, 321–357 (2002)

8. Das, S., Deb, N., Cortesi, A., Chaki, N.: Sentence embedding models for similarity detection of software requirements. SN Comput. Sci. **2**(2), 1–11 (2021)

9. Delianidi, M., Diamantaras, K., Chrysogonidis, G., Nikiforidis, V.: Student performance prediction using dynamic neural models. arXiv preprint arXiv:2106.00524 (2021)

10. Devlin, J., Chang, M.W., Lee, K., Toutanova, K.: Bert: pre-training of deep bidirectional transformers for language understanding. arXiv preprint arXiv:1810.04805 (2018)

11. Eke, C.I., Norman, A.A., Shuib, L.: Context-based feature technique for sarcasm identification in benchmark datasets using deep learning and Bert model. IEEE Access **9**, 48501–48518 (2021)

12. Ellouze, M., Hadrich Belguith, L.: A hybrid approach for the detection and monitoring of people having personality disorders on social networks. Soc. Netw. Anal. Min. **12**(1), 1–17 (2022)

13. Ellouze, M., Mechti, S., Belguith, L.H.: Automatic profile recognition of authors on social media based on hybrid approach. Procedia Comput. Sci. **176**, 1111–1120 (2020)

14. Ellouze, M., Mechti, S., Belguith, L.H.: Deep learning CNN-LSTM approach for identifying twitter users suffering from paranoid personality disorder. In: Proceedings of the 17th International Conference on Software Technologies, pp. 612–621. SCITEPRESS (2022)

15. Ellouze, M., Mechti, S., Krichen, M., Ravi, V., Belguith, L.H.: A deep learning approach for detecting the behaviour of people having personality disorders towards COVID-19 from twitter. Int. J. Comput. Sci. Eng. **25**(4), 353–366 (2022)

16. Fellbaum, C.: Wordnet. In: Poli, R., Healy, M., Kameas, A. (eds.) Theory and Applications of Ontology: Computer Applications, pp. 231–243. Springer, Dordrecht (2010). https://doi.org/10.1007/978-90-481-8847-5_10

17. Fensel, D., et al.: Introduction: what is a knowledge graph? In: Knowledge Graphs, pp. 1–10. Springer, Cham (2020). https://doi.org/10.1007/978-3-030-37439-6_1

18. Fernandes, E.R., de Carvalho, A.C., Yao, X.: Ensemble of classifiers based on multiobjective genetic sampling for imbalanced data. IEEE Trans. Knowl. Data Eng. **32**(6), 1104–1115 (2019)

19. Graves, A.: Long short-term memory. In: Supervised Sequence Labelling with Recurrent Neural Networks, pp. 37–45 (2012)

20. Guillén, A.I., Panadero, S., Rivas, E., Vázquez, J.J.: Suicide attempts and stressful life events among female victims of intimate partner violence living in poverty in Nicaragua. Scand. J. Psychol. **56**(3), 349–356 (2015)

21. Hoffmann, H.: Kernel PCA for novelty detection. Pattern Recogn. **40**(3), 863–874 (2007)

22. Ishaq, A., et al.: Improving the prediction of heart failure patients' survival using smote and effective data mining techniques. IEEE Access **9**, 39707–39716 (2021)

23. Kõlves, K., Värnik, A., Schneider, B., Fritze, J., Allik, J.: Recent life events and suicide: a case-control study in Tallinn and Frankfurt. Soc. Sci. Med. **62**(11), 2887–2896 (2006)

24. Lai, S., Liu, K., He, S., Zhao, J.: How to generate a good word embedding. IEEE Intell. Syst. **31**(6), 5–14 (2016)

25. Lau, J.H., Baldwin, T.: An empirical evaluation of doc2vec with practical insights into document embedding generation. arXiv preprint arXiv:1607.05368 (2016)

26. Lin, H., et al.: Detecting stress based on social interactions in social networks. IEEE Trans. Knowl. Data Eng. **29**(9), 1820–1833 (2017)

27. Mbarek, A., Jamoussi, S., Charfi, A., Hamadou, A.B.: Suicidal profiles detection in twitter. In: WEBIST, pp. 289–296 (2019)

28. Murarka, A., Radhakrishnan, B., Ravichandran, S.: Classification of mental illnesses on social media using Roberta. In: Proceedings of the 12th International Workshop on Health Text Mining and Information Analysis, pp. 59–68 (2021)

29. Palay, J., et al.: Prevalence of mental disorders and suicidality in Canadian provinces. Can. J. Psychiatry **64**(11), 761–769 (2019)

30. Petz, G., Karpowicz, M., Fürschuß, H., Auinger, A., Stříteský, V., Holzinger, A.: Reprint of: computational approaches for mining user's opinions on the web 2.0. Inf. Process. Manage. **51**(4), 510–519 (2015)

31. Philomina, J., Jayaraman, M., Yuvasri, S.: Idisorder detection using machine learning. Int. J. Res. Sci. Eng. Technol. **6**(3), 12–18 (2019)

32. Prieto Curiel, R., Cresci, S., Muntean, C.I., Bishop, S.R.: Crime and its fear in social media. Palgrave Commun. **6**(1), 1–12 (2020)

33. Quan, Y., Zhong, X., Feng, W., Chan, J.C.W., Li, Q., Xing, M.: Smote-based weighted deep rotation forest for the imbalanced hyperspectral data classification. Remote Sens. **13**(3), 464 (2021)

34. Rangel, F., Rosso, P., Potthast, M., Stein, B., Daelemans, W.: Overview of the 3rd author profiling task at pan 2015. In: CLEF, p. 2015. sn (2015)

35. Reimers, N., Gurevych, I.: Sentence-Bert: sentence embeddings using SIAMESE Bert-networks. arXiv preprint arXiv:1908.10084 (2019)

36. Rekik, A., Jamoussi, S., Hamadou, A.B.: Violent vocabulary extraction methodology: application to the radicalism detection on social media. In: Nguyen, N.T., Chbeir, R., Exposito, E., Aniorté, P., Trawiński, B. (eds.) ICCCI 2019. LNCS (LNAI), vol. 11684, pp. 97–109. Springer, Cham (2019). https://doi.org/10.1007/978-3-030-28374-2_9

37. Ruiz, R., Maroto, C.: A comprehensive review and evaluation of permutation flowshop heuristics. Eur. J. Oper. Res. **165**(2), 479–494 (2005)

38. Sanh, V., Debut, L., Chaumond, J., Wolf, T.: Distilbert, a distilled version of Bert: smaller, faster, cheaper and lighter. arXiv preprint arXiv:1910.01108 (2019)

39. Singh, J., Banerjee, R.: A study on single and multi-layer perceptron neural network. In: 2019 3rd International Conference on Computing Methodologies and Communication (ICCMC), pp. 35–40. IEEE (2019)

40. Singh, R., et al.: A framework for early detection of antisocial behavior on twitter using natural language processing. In: Barolli, L., Hussain, F.K., Ikeda, M. (eds.) CISIS 2019. AISC, vol. 993, pp. 484–495. Springer, Cham (2020). https://doi.org/10.1007/978-3-030-22354-0_43

41. Stankevich, M., Smirnov, I., Kiselnikova, N., Ushakova, A.: Depression detection from social media profiles. In: Elizarov, A., Novikov, B., Stupnikov, S. (eds.) DAMDID/RCDL 2019. CCIS, vol. 1223, pp. 181–194. Springer, Cham (2020). https://doi.org/10.1007/978-3-030-51913-1_12

42. de la Torre Díez, I., Alonso, S.G., Hamrioui, S., Cruz, E.M., Nozaleda, L.M., Franco, M.A.: IoT-based services and applications for mental health in the literature. J. Med. Syst. **43**(1), 1–6 (2019)

43. Velankar, A., Patil, H., Joshi, R.: Mono vs multilingual Bert for hate speech detection and text classification: a case study in Marathi. arXiv preprint arXiv:2204.08669 (2022)

44. Zhang, Y., Rao, Z.: n-BiLSTM: BiLSTM with n-gram features for text classification. In: 2020 IEEE 5th Information Technology and Mechatronics Engineering Conference (ITOEC), pp. 1056–1059. IEEE (2020)

Author Index

H.-G. Fill et al. (Eds.): ICSOFT 2022, CCIS 1859, p. 231, 2023.
https://doi.org/10.1007/978-3-031-37231-5

Printed in the United States
by Baker & Taylor Publisher Services